MARKETS AN[...]
forces for chang[...]
media of Western Europe

Anthony Weymouth and Bernard Lamizet

Longman
London and New York

Pearson Education Limited
Edinburgh Gate, Harlow
Essex CM20 2JE, England
and Associated Companies throughout the world.

*Published in the United States of America
by Longman Publishing, New York*

First published 1996
Second impression 1999

ISBN 0 582 27565-2 PPR

British Library Cataloguing-in-Publication Data
A catalogue record for this book is
available from the British Library

Library of Congress Cataloging-in-Publication Data
Markets and myths : forces for change in the media of Western Europe /
    [edited by] Tony Weymouth
        p.   cm.
    Discusses media in Britain, France, Germany, Italy, and Spain.
    Includes bibliographical references and index.
    ISBN 0–582-27565-2
    1. Mass media—Europe, Western—History—20th century.
I. Weymouth, Tony, 1938–
P92.E9M37   1996
302.23'094—dc20   95–47529
                                                                  CIP

Set by 5 in 10/11pt Palatino

Transferred to digital print on demand, 2002

Printed and bound by Antony Rowe Ltd, Eastbourne

Contents

List of figures

List of tables

Preface

The volume of analysis and comment undertaken in Media Studies in the second half of this century has been, by any standard, formidable. This is hardly surprising. In a century marked by the clash of ideologies and the cataclysmic tragedy of the Second World War, the battle of words, and through them for hearts and minds, has never been more intense, and the power of the media never more appreciated.

Universal access to information is one of the keystones of all stable and mature democracies. If language is the social phenomenon by which information is carried, then the media (the written press, radio, television and telecommunications) are the gates through which it flows. Small wonder, then, that the integrity, motivation and behaviour of the gatekeepers (the media conglomerates, the broadcasters and others) should be the objects of the close attention of all those for whom the maintenance of democratic values is a passionate imperative. By the act of bringing information to the people, and through the attitudes which they bring to this task, the media often claim to be acting in the public interest, and by so doing, upholding the most basic principles which underpin democracy in Western Europe. However, the socio-economic changes which have taken place since 1945, not just in Western Europe but on a more global scale, have given rise to concerns relating to the function as well as to the quality of media performance, and no more so than in the last two decades of the twentieth century.

The general aim of this book is to make a highly complex process of media development accessible to readers from a range of disciplinary backgrounds who are approaching the study of the media in Western Europe for the first time. This task is not without its problems. Such is the volume and complexity of current research in this area that students risk becoming so lost in the detail that they fail to see the significance of the picture overall. We overcome this danger in Chapter 1 by offering a short account of media development from 1945 to the present on a 'new reader start here' basis. In particular we seek to identify the principal factors which explain the radical changes which are taking place in the Western European media at the end of this century and which will continue into the next. Our account is written from a perspective of history, economics, politics and communication science, thus underlining the importance of a multi-disciplinary approach to the examination of media issues. Chapter 1 is essentially the story of transition from one phase of media development to another, characterised, above all, by the emergence of market forces as significant new players in the public sphere.

Against this explanatory backdrop of Chapter 1, the individual contributors then identify, in Chapters 2–6, the principal landmarks of media development for their own particular country. They also analyse these trends and assess their significance for the future direction that their own national media will take. Their accounts are of interest not just from the point of view of the *different* national perspectives, particular problems and attitudes which they bring to the task, but also because of the emerging picture wherein certain *common* and, to some extent, disquieting and controversial features can be perceived.

One of the specific aims of this book is to examine both the implications of the changes occurring in the media, as well as the concerns which accompany them, in order to ascertain the direction in which the Western European media in general is heading. An interesting question, in this respect, relates to the present and future role of the media in representing (or mediating) a new concept of a more unified Western Europe to the citizens of the European Union. This issue is addressed principally in Chapter 7. In this final chapter we also examine the related questions of the future of public service broadcasting in Europe, as well as the direction that future policy-making may take.

Our investigation is on a limited scale. We confine ourselves to examining the media of five countries – Britain, France, Germany, Italy and Spain – and thus our references to 'Western Europe' and sometimes to 'Europe', even, draw heavily upon the media development in those countries alone. We believe, however, that the trends revealed from this study have a more universal significance which extends beyond the frontiers of the countries examined. This book is an essential starting-point for students in Media Studies, Politics, History, Cultural Studies and Modern Languages (the list is not exhaustive) who wish to understand the role of the media in its current state of transition. Indeed, it goes further than that, and points to the likely significance of these changes, not just for the media but also for the people whom they serve, and for the future of the wider concept of European Union to which a large part of the old Continent is committed.

We wish to express our gratitude to the many people who have assisted in the preparation of this book. We are particularly indebted to Granville Williams, Michael Bromley, Gordon Parsons and Christopher Williams for their comments and helpful suggestions for improving the text. Naturally, we accept responsibility for any of its shortcomings.

The University of Central Lancashire,
Preston, England.
The University of Avignon,
France.
14 August 1995

Acknowledgements

We are grateful to the following for permission to reproduce copyright material:

Il Sole – 24 Ore for the figure "Berlusconi's Fininvest empire"; Radio Advertising Handbook for the figures "Current share of radio listening", "Radio advertising revenue 1980–93 (£ million)", "The Development of commercial radio in the UK" and "The audience share in the UK"; *The Independent* for the figure "The ITV Franchises 1991"; *Le Monde* for the figure "TV Audience Share (1995)"; Fundesco and OJD for the figures, "The development of the daily written press in Spain" and "Index of press distribution in the European Community" from *Comunicacion Social, 1993*; Nielsen Repress for the figure "Advertising investment in the Media in 1993" from the *Anuario de Publicidad, 1994*; The European Institute for the Media for the tables, "Process of media concentration and diversification" and "Daily newspaper circulation in Europe" in Sánchez-Tabernero's *Media Concentration in Europe, 1992*; Documentation Française for the tables "Ten leading dailies in France, 1992", "Decline of national and regional titles and trends towards press concentration 1914-1990" and "French audience share(%) in 1994"; *Cable and Satellite Europe* for "Cable and satellite penetration in Western Europe in 1995"; *Media Perspektiven* for the use of the table "Overview of the written daily press in Germany" by Walter J. Schultz, the tables "Popular Magazines: developments in the circulation of major publishers", "Bertelsmann/Gruner + Jahr: popular magazines published abroad", "Burda: popular magazines published abroad", "Springer: popular magazines published abroad" and "Bauer: popular magazines published abroad" by Horst Roper, the tables "TV advertising turnover 1980–93", "Overall % share in the TV advertising market 1989–93", "Shares in national TV companies 1994 as %" and "The 50 most important daily newspapers in the EC (1991–2)" by Jurgen Heinrich; *Media Key* for the tables "Advertising share of principal agencies for magazine market (%)", "Total media share of publicity revenue (%)", "Total share of television advertising market (%)", "Radio: market share of principal broadcasters (%)" and "Revenue derived from advertising, licence fees and direct sales (written press only) of the principal media organisations (in billion lira) 1993"; Blackwell publishers for the use of a quote from *The Transformation of the Public Sphere* by Jurgan Habermas; John Libbey and Company for a quote from *Broadcasting and Policy in the European Single Market* by R. Collins; Routledge for quotes from *Freedom without Responsibility* by J Curran and A Seaton, and from *Life and Times of Post-modernity* by K Tester. All rights reserved.

Glossary

This glossary is confined to the explanation of a selection of the terms and abbreviations most frequently used in this book and is intended as a guide for an international readership.

Access   The receiving of information via any media form.

Advertiser   (Usually) a commercial company which promotes its services or products via the media.

Advertising   The commercial promotion of goods or services in the media.

Advertising agency   Private company, acting on behalf of commercial clients, specialising in the conception and placement of publicity in the media.

AFN   American Forces Network, radio station serving the American army in Germany in the post-war period.

AFP   Agence France-Presse, the biggest French news agency.

AM   Amplitude Modulation. What is commonly known as 'medium wave': an improved radio transmission frequency introduced to broadcasting in the post-war period.

Anti-monopoly legislation   Laws existing in all countries of the European Union designed to curb trends towards concentration of ownership when the latter is considered to be against the public interest.

ARD   The public corporation responsible for the broadcasting of public service television in Germany.

ARTE   The jointly operated Franco-German television channel specialising in cultural programming and the use of bilingual broadcasting techniques.

Associative Radio   Private-sector radio operated by an association of interested members (France).

Audience   The total number of people who view or listen to a particular broadcasting medium, hence **Audience Share,** a specific media calculation of the number of persons using a particular medium at a given time. (See 'readership' for written press, below.)

Audio-visual The mass media which use a combination of sound and pictures for the transmission of messages (film, television, videotext).

BBC British Broadcasting Corporation, the principal public service radio and television broadcaster in the United Kingdom.

BCC Broadcasting Complaints Commission, the body with responsibility to ensure the fair and just treatment of information as well as of individuals by the media in the United Kingdom.

BR Bayerischer Rundfunk, one of the eight regional radio stations set up by the American administration in Germany after the Second World War and based in Munich.

BSC Broadcasting Standards Council, the body with responsibility for monitoring the portrayal of sex and violence and other matters relating to public decency in the British media.

BSkyB Satellite and cable channel belonging to the media empire of Rupert Murdoch and transmitting to the United Kingdom under licence from Luxembourg.

CDU German Christian Democrat Party usually associated with the CSU (see below).

Censorship Intervention from an external source which restricts, modifies or removes media information originally destined for the public sphere.

CLT The German press group owned by Bertelsmann.

CNN Cable News Network, the American-owned international news satellite channel.

Code of practice Rules, agreements and guidelines establishing good or acceptable standards of journalistic conduct.

Communication The exchange of meaning/messages between individuals (intersubjective communication) or the mass circulation of information/messages within a social space (mediated communication).

Computerised copy-making The use of computers, especially by the written press for the setting out of journalists' text (or copy) directly on to the newspaper page.

Concentration The grouping of several, formally independent, media companies under one single group or conglomerate by the process of merger or takeover.

Coverage The quality, style and volume of information which typifies a particular medium, i.e. press coverage, television coverage.

CSA Conseil supérieur de l'audiovisuel, the current French regulatory body for public service and commercial radio and television broadcasting in France.

CDU/CSU The frequently associated right-of-centre alliance of the German Christian Democrat and the Christian Social parties. CDU, Christlich Demokratische Union, may be compared to the Conservative Party in the United Kingdom (it is the party of Chancellor Kohl); the CSU, Christlich–Soziale Union, is the sister party of the CDU, based only in Bavaria. It has a strong Catholic bias and politically is more to the right than the CDU.

Cultural colonisation The alleged risk of one culture being unduly influenced by another through excessive media exposure. This concept is particularly strong in France with regard to alleged Anglo-Saxon (English/American) influences.

Culture Common national or ethnic denominators realised in thought, language and social activities, the essence of mediated information.

DAB Digital Audio Broadcasting, the latest technological advance in the transmission of radio sound, as yet in its early stages of operation in Europe.

DBS Direct Broadcasting by Satellite, television broadcasting by satellite which is received by the viewer using a dish aerial.

Deregulation The global trend which began in the 1980s, aimed at the opening up of national markets to greater competition. Given the sensitive socio-cultural implications this activity holds for the media, deregulation is a controversial activity in this sector.

DGT The original name of the French public telecommunications government office: Direction Générale des Télécommunications, now known as France Télécom.

Dirigisme The French term designating the exercising of strong national or institutional influence in the running of national (or supranational) affairs.

DLM Direktorenkonferenz der Landmedienanstalten, German regulatory body for commercial television comprising members of all the Land corporations.

DOM/TOM Départments d'Outre Mer/Territoires d'Outre Mer, former French colonies currently administered by the French Republic.

Duopoly The name given to the shared responsibility for television broadcasting held jointly by the BBC and ITV from 1954 to 1990 in the United Kingdom.

EBU European Broadcasting Union, the association of (mostly) public service broadcasting corporations in Europe, responsible for the production and networking of programmes to all its members (Eurovision). Particularly strong in sport coverage.

ETA Euskadi Ta Askatasuna (Basque Homeland and Liberty), the nationalist and separatist movement of the Spanish Basque region.

EU European Union, the post-Maastricht title of the former European Community (although the latter is still used in certain contexts).

Eutelsat European Telecommunications satellite.

Fascism Political regime of the extreme Right originally created by the Italian nationalists under Mussolini from 1922–43. Used too to characterise German Naziism as well as the Spanish regime under Franco.

FDP Frei Demokratische Partei, the German Liberal Party.

Fininvest The Italian conglomerate owned by Silvio Berlusconi.

FM Frequency Modulation, the technological advance in radio transmission which revolutionised popular radio broadcasting in the mid-1960s.

Fragmentation (social) The perceived breakdown in the post-war period in the traditional social groupings such as social class, religion, political parties, trade unions. In the media this fragmentation is reflected in current trends of targeted, thematic, 'narrowcasting' rather than mass 'broadcasting' which characterised the earlier part of the century.

Franchise Legal right of a commercial broadcaster to operate under licence in either radio or television in a defined geographical location in a particular role designated by a government or its delegated authority, i.e the ITV franchises in the United Kingdom.

Free press Newspapers 'given away' free to the public and paid for entirely out of advertising revenue.

GDR German Democratic Republic (Deutsche Demokratische Republik), the former communist state of East Germany.

GEZ Body responsible for the collection of the television licence fee in Germany.

Globalisation The penetration of national markets by international capital and production strategies which were encouraged by the deregulatory policies of the 1980s. In the media the phenomenon of globalisation is particularly apparent in the strategies of the American corporations such as Disney and Time Warner, the Japanese company Sony, and in Rupert Murdoch's News International.

Hispasat Spanish television satellite.

HR Hessischer Rundfunk, one of the eight regional radio stations created by the American administration in West Germany and based in Frankfurt.

IBA Independent Broadcasting Authority, the second regulatory body to be created for commercial television in the United Kingdom. The **IBA** was succeeded by the **ITC** in 1990 (see below).

ILR Independent Local Radio (United Kingdom). See also **INR** below.

Information (prioritisation of) The representation of events by the media, and the order in which this representation of events is made (from which its importance may be imputed).

INR Independent National Radio (United Kingdom), currently comprising Classic FM, Virgin and Talk Radio.

Integration Characteristic of the kind of structural organisation of a media group or conglomerate, i.e. vertical integration (including all phases of production), horizontal integration (including several media outlets from a single sector such as magazines or regional newspapers, etc).

ITA Independent Television Authority, the first regulatory body established for commercial television in the United Kingdom in 1955, succeeded by the **IBA** (see above) in 1973 which in turn was replaced by the **ITC** in 1990 (see below).

ITC Independent Television Commission, the latest regulatory body for commercial television in the United Kingdom, established by the Broadcasting Act of 1990.

ITV Independent Television, the original administrative company set up to operate commercial television in the United Kingdom in 1955.

LWTV London Weekend Television, one of the successful bidders for the post-1991 ITV franchises in the United Kingdom, now taken over by Granada.

Media (mass) Communication/information outlets comprising the written press, the radio and the audio-visual (now beginning to include the new forms of the latter using computer, line and satellite links for interactive user services).

Mediated communication The representation of events by the mass media within the public sphere.

Mediation The symbolic representation by the mass media of socio-cultural matters which explain them as well as create social links between individuals and the society to which they belong.

Minitel The public computerised data system operated by France Télécom (accessed by telephone).

Monopoly Generally designates the domination of a single company in a particular market operating against the public interest. However, it is also used in a less pejorative sense to describe the state-sponsored public service broadcasting systems (i.e. state monopoly), particularly in France, Spain and Italy.

MP Member of Parliament in the United Kingdom.

Multi-media 1. (commercial) A phenomenon resulting simultaneously from technological advances and deregulation in the field of communications, wherein formerly distinct sectors of the media are increasingly perceived as complementary, and grouped commercially under a single owner or group: 2. (technological) The convergence of hitherto separate technological fields of activity – computing, telephone, cable, and satellite – to form an integrated and interactive communications system.

MVDS Multivideo distribution system.

NATO North Atlantic Treaty Organisation, the military alliance between the principal countries of Western Europe and the USA established in the late 1940s as a consequence of the Cold War.

NBC National Broadcasting Corporation, one of the principal national commercial networks in the United States.

Network Group of television or radio stations organised for the simultaneous broadcasting of certain programmes throughout a region or country.

NWDR Nordwestdeutscher Rundfunk, one of the eight regional radio stations created by the Americans in post-war Germany, based in Hamburg.

OFT Office of Fair Trading; British body with responsibility, among others, for investigating alleged monopolistic activity in industry.

ORTF Office de Radiodiffusion–Télévision Française, former name of the French public service broadcasting organisation (changed in 1974).

Pay-TV Designates television programmes which are transmitted in encrypted form and received only by subscribers equipped with special 'keys'. Canal Plus in France is a good example of pay-TV.

PCC Press Complaints Commission, voluntary regulatory body which monitors the conduct of the written press in the United Kingdom.

Pluralism Designates the desirable (if not real) condition in which several independent media outlets provide the ideal context for communication, debate and decision-making in the public sphere.

PME *Petites et moyennes entreprises*, designating in France companies which employ fewer than fifty employees.

Prime time The period of the day (i.e. the mid-evening 8.30–10.30 slot) when television audiences are available in the greatest number.

Privatisation The sale of former state-owned utilities, including radio and television, to the private sector.

Product Increasingly this term is used to designate what may have formerly been termed a programme or series. Its use reflects the encroachment into the communication field of market (economic) concepts.

Programmer Person or department responsible for the devising of radio and television schedules.

Programming Another name for the television or radio schedule (or 'line up' of programmes).

PSB Public Service Broadcasting designates the (mainly) state-sponsored broadcasting sector, particularly in the United Kingdom, although the public service responsibilities in Britain were traditionally shared between the BBC and the ITV.

PSOE The Spanish Socialist Workers' Party, the principal socialist party in Spain.

Public sphere The shared social space in which goods, ideas and services are exchanged in a manner which promotes social coherence and cultural identity.

RAI Radio Audizioni Italiane. The Italian state-sponsored public service radio and television corporation.

Rating The evaluation of programme popularity through a calculation of audience size.

RB Radio Bremen. One of the eight radio stations created by the Americans in post-war Germany.

Readership The total number of persons who read a given newspaper or periodical on a daily or periodic basis. Because more than one person may have access to a single copy, the readership of a paper may exceed sales.

Regulation Mandatory rules relating to the organisation of a media sector and the professional conduct of journalists or broadcasters. Codes of practice relating to the latter which, as in the case of the British written press, are voluntary.

Regulator The person or office responsible for the post-privatisation monitoring of former public utilities, including sectors of the media.

RTF Radiodiffusion–Télévision Française (1945), the former name of the state-run public radio and television services superseded by the ORTF (see above) in 1974.

RTL Private German television channel partly owned by Bertelsmann.

RTVE Radio Televison Española, the Spanish public service radio and television corporation.

SDR Suddeutscher Rundfunk, one of the eight regional radio stations originally created by the allies in post-war Germany and based in Stuttgart.

SED Sozialistiche Einheitpartei Deutschlands, the Communist Party of the former GDR.

SER Sociedád Española de Radiodiffusion, the original and leading private radio network in Spain.

Sponsorship An indirect form of advertising where the advertiser is promoted in return for financially supporting the content of a radio or television programme.

Supranational Designating activities, i.e. legislation, regulation, policy-making, which transcend national boundaries.

SWF Sudwestfunk, one of the eight regional radio stations created by France in post-war Germany in the Saar region.

Tabloid (1) (pejorative) – designates the particular section of the British written press dedicated more to sensationalist, human interest material than to information of a more serious nature. (2) (literal) vertically folded paper, approximately half the size of the more traditional horizontally folded 'broadsheet' (sometimes found as insertions to broadsheets). 'Serious' tabloid format newspapers are common in France i.e. *Libération, La Croix*.

TDF Télédiffusion de France, French public company charged with the technical aspects of programme broadcasting, set up in 1974.

TF1 Name of the first and principal public service television channel in France, privatised in 1986 by the Chirac government.

Transparency Idealised quality of 'total information' to be made available by the media relating to identity of ownership and sources of investment.

ZDF Zweite Deutsche Fernsehen, the name of the second Germany public service channel created in 1963.

CHAPTER 1

Introduction: the role of the media in Western Europe

Anthony Weymouth

I Introduction

The relationship between the European media and the late twentieth-century society is complex and currently undergoing significant change. Such is the nature and scale of this change that perhaps the only certainties to be drawn from it are that the media in the next millennium will be more varied, more economically powerful and more used by the citizenry of Europe than ever before. However, the answers to important questions concerning the effects of these new kinds of media upon the society of the new century can only remain a matter for speculation.

In this chapter we shall examine the changing nature of the relationship between the media and Western European society from the immediate post-war period until the present. We are, as we have said, spanning fifty years of extraordinary change for which the explanations are complicated and, since we are dealing with controversial issues, they are sometimes contested. We have therefore set out to answer (or perhaps 'throw light upon' would be a better way of putting it) certain key questions relating to the past, present and future role of the media in Western Europe. These questions can be summarised as follows:

- What are the most commonly accepted views of the function of the media in contemporary European society?
- Has this function been modified since 1945 and, if so, what is the nature of this modification and how is it explained?
- What are the future implications for Western Europe of the current media revolution?

In order to begin to answer these questions it is first necessary to examine a process associated with the role of the media at its most general level of social interaction. This process is described conceptually as mediation.

1

The concept of mediation

Until comparatively recently the so-called public sphere of western democracies was founded upon a more concrete and perceivable reality than it is today. In the eighteenth and nineteenth centuries the very concept of the public sphere was less widespread and developed. There were, among other factors, lower levels of literacy on one hand, and an inequality of suffrage on the other, and both left the public sphere, if it can be so called at this time, in the hands of a small number of elite social and political classes. The public sphere was the meeting point, passing place and debating forum for a small group of 'real' players – politicians, lawyers, soldiers and clerics (and a relatively undeveloped press) – who represented the wider national community and dominated public life. In so far, then, as the public sphere existed at all in these precursors of modern democracies, it did so either in the minds of theorists or as the result of the activities of a small number of practitioners.

It could be argued that the growing complexity of modern society which has accompanied improved living standards, better education and universal suffrage has been matched by (perhaps given rise to) a commensurate growth in its systems of communication and the consequent enlargement of the public sphere. The increased buying power of the masses in the nineteenth century, coupled with the industrialisation of printing methods, made access to a newspaper the right of every citizen. One political consequence of the growth of the newspaper industry in the nineteenth century was the consolidation of the concept of the nation-state. Technological progress this century has resulted in the further extension of the communication system into the domains of sound and vision and has further refined this process of nationalism. By reaching more of the people, themselves better educated than before, with information relating not only to local interest and obligations, but to persons, debates

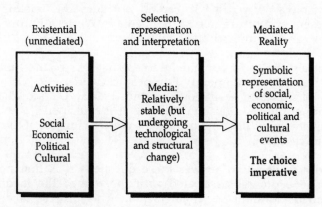

Figure 1.1   The process of mediation

and events of national import, the media have played a key role in the promotion of social order and identity within the nation-state.

This process can be seen upon reflection as being selective by nature. In its effort to offer the national community a cogent, perceivable image of itself, the media selected from the existential mass of everyday events firstly, a symbolic representation of the nation, and secondly, an account (or 'discourse') which rendered these events intelligible within a framework of culturally shared knowledge. This process can be referred to conceptually as mediation and as such will play a major role in later discussions in this book. The process of mediation can be summarised as shown in Figure 1.1.

The process of mediation

It is commonplace to describe the media as a force for the promotion of social cohesion and order. In a recent, more contemporary review of this media function, McQuail points to the functional ambivalence of communication, which he claims can in fact either serve to weaken or to strengthen social cohesion. However, whilst the media can be viewed – particularly by authority – as a disruptive force, for the most part they are seen as 'indispensable to the maintenance of order' (McQuail, 1992:74). But even this positive view of the role of the media as one of promoting social cohesion may also be interpreted ambivalently. For some they are considered unequivocally as a force for the maintenance of the essential democratic values which underpin western society (see Scannell, 1989), whilst for others the media constitute a more sinister force for the political and economic control and exploitation of the masses (see Habermas, 1989; Chomsky, 1989). For reasons which will become clear later, we take as our starting-point the former, more positive view of media function rather than the latter.

McQuail distinguishes between two kinds of cohesive function generated by the mediation process. The first relates to the symbolic representation of national events, people and institutions, and the second to the creation of social-relational meanings or, as he puts it, 'to a sense of belonging to a significant social group and to the capacity to enjoy an authentic and personally valued culture' (McQuail, 1992: 75). These distinctions coincide with our own account of the mediation process offered earlier in this chapter.

The political role of the mediating function

Part of the socio-cultural meaning referred to by McQuail is undoubtedly of a political nature. Mediated communication, operating within the wider context of socio-cultural events, is the starting-point of the process, vital to a democracy, of group formation and political affiliation. Not surprisingly, perhaps, important questions are raised here relating to the manner by which the media achieve this particular goal. In particular, attention is often focused on the ethical aspects of media 'performance', and aimed at identifying the meaning of such concepts as neutrality, objectivity and truth in the media context.

Opinions vary considerably on the manner in which such principles are or should be observed by the media in western democracies. Lichtenberg points out that the nineteenth-century written press was highly partisan, politicised and biased in its presentation of news and made no claims to neutrality or objectivity. Such attitudes on the part of the media are presumably tolerable provided that they are declared and operate within a pluralistic media context. However, Lichtenberg argues that the development of the mass media in the twentieth century and their claims to describe the world 'as it is' imposes upon them the obligation to distinguish themselves from their historical precursors and perform in an objective and neutral way in the processing and relaying of information (Lichtenberg, 1990:124).

Arguing from a theoretical perspective, Habermas claims that the services historically performed by the printed media in promoting what he calls the 'rational critical debate' in the public sphere have been largely undermined by two significant factors this century. The first is the accelerated progress towards commercialisation of the media industry itself, and the second is the sharp increase in and influence of the advertisers. The effect of these developments has been the reduction in the quality of information (and discourse) in the public sphere.

According to Habermas the western media (he mostly refers to the printed press) has undergone a major structural transformation this century which has been imposed by the movement of the market towards economic concentration. The consequences are, among others, the emergence of large media groups and equally large and monolithically organised press agencies such as Reuters and Agence France Presse which serve them. The result of this concentration in the industry has been the 'homogenisation' of information. In particular this process is reinforced by the common business practice of multi-title ownership which tends to promote editorial homogenisation within a newspaper group (see below for further discussion).

Superimposed upon this first process of commercial concentration is the second, that of the upsurge of the importance of the advertisers. In parallel with the growth of the news agencies, this century has seen a dramatic increase in the activities of the advertisers, advertising agencies, and the importance of advertising revenue to the financial viability of the press.

For Habermas the power of the advertisers is of such force that the legitimate space in the public sphere for rational-critical debate has been usurped and replaced by a 'fake' agenda confected by powerful private players (big business and press owners) who have a privileged access to the media. In other words, the media lead and shape public opinion along lines determined by a powerful élite rather than represent and promote it by rational-critical debate.

This manipulation of the public sphere has been further refined this century by the development of the corporate art of public relations. According to Habermas public relations, whilst it is an indirect form of advertising, also has political ambitions. Its practice is a deception whose objectives are the exploitation of public opinion for political ends or, as Habermas puts it: 'It mobilises for the firm an entire system of quasi-political credit, a respect that one displays towards a public authority' (Habermas, 1989:194).

This view of the mass media as the fraudulent agenda-setter in a world of 'virtual politics' is not uncommon and it has plausible variations in the writings of other contemporary observers, such as Foucault (1971), Fairclough (1989) and Hall (1980). However, these negative readings of the influence of the media as a socio-cultural force for control should be treated with care. Whilst it is true that powerful players such as the press barons, the advertisers and the public relations agencies play a significant role in attitude formation (more in some areas than in others), it is equally demonstrable that this influence is not as all-pervasive as some theories suggest. Despite the underlying force of the arguments there still exists sufficient evidence in the European radio, television and print media of a separation of interests between owners and advertisers, on one hand, and journalists, on the other, to put pressure upon Habermas's theory of the transformation of the public sphere from one of 'real' to one of 'virtual' politics. Nevertheless, the arguments which support this negative reading of the media are powerful and cannot be ignored. This would seem to be an appropriate moment to modify our original diagram representing the mediation process to take them into account (see Figure 1.2).

We have tempered Habermas's extreme view of a wholly manipulative media with one which claims that a separation of interests between powerful influences and interpretation of infor-

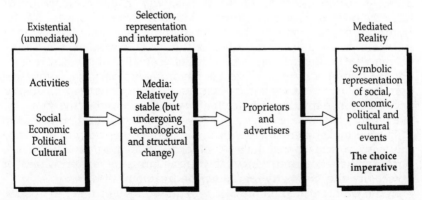

Existential (unmediated)	Selection, representation and interpretation		Mediated Reality
Activities Social Economic Political Cultural	Media: Relatively stable (but undergoing technological and structural change)	Proprietors and advertisers	Symbolic representation of social, economic, political and cultural events **The choice imperative**

Figure 1.2   The process of mediation modified to include external influences

mation still exists in sufficient strength to sustain the 'rational critical debate' in the public sphere. Nevertheless, we accept that a substantial part of the European printed press and certain private, commercial broadcasters are still either overtly biased, or (more sinisterly) covertly biased in the way Habermas suggests.

A more pragmatic and less ideological approach to the question of media bias is to pose the issue in terms of the need or otherwise of neutrality and objectivity in the interpretation of information. In a study of journalists' attitudes towards the issue of media objectivity, Boyer (1981) identifies the following six constituent elements:

- balance and even-handedness in presenting different sides of an issue;
- accuracy and realism in reporting;
- presenting of all main relevant points;
- separation of facts from opinion, but treating opinion as relevant;
- minimising the influence of the writer's own attitude, opinion or involvement;
- avoiding slant, rancour or devious purpose (in McQuail, 1992: 184).

Empirical evidence suggests that the application of the principles implied here is somewhat uneven in the European context. Despite a reduction in its pluralistic structure, the printed press is still partisan in nature[1] (provided this bias is overt, we would argue that it constitutes a legitimate part of the discourse of the public sphere). The political affiliations of much of the printed press are clearly apparent and although some may pay lip-service to Boyer's principles of objectivity, such commitment is by definition both partial and inconsistent.

Broadcasting, as we have noted, constitutes a different case. Because, historically, governments were involved at their inception of these new media forms this century, they have been subjected to more direct and persistent government attention than the printed press. Nevertheless the degree of objectivity in the presentation of information practised by European broadcasters varies significantly from country to country. Until comparatively recently the French television services were regarded as the 'voice of France' ('la voix de la France'). In consequence there was between 1958 and 1982 pressure applied to broadcasters to represent government policy in a favourable light. Only in recent years have regulatory bodies been established to encourage media independence (and by extension, objectivity).

In Italy, the media have been traditionally associated with the political establishment and divided along political spheres of influence following a widespread Italian tendency known as 'la lottizazione'. Such politicisation must inevitably place pressure on principles of objectivity and neutrality regarding the treatment of news.

In the United Kingdom the BBC is required by its charter to operate with 'due impartiality' and in the opinion of many has succeeded in exemplifying the objective/neutral approach to broadcasting. Even so such 'flagship' news programmes as *Newsnight* (BBC 2) and the *Today* programme (Radio 4) achieve impartiality more by adopting techniques of devil's advocacy, even-handedly applied to all sides,[2] than by strictly neutral presentation.

We prefer to take the view, in the light of these observations, that the media in Western Europe is at best unevenly committed to the principles of neutrality and objectivity but that this lack of commitment is not necessarily in itself socially subversive, provided (a) this attitude towards neutrality is understood by the public, and (b) that other conditions prevail (for further discussion see below).

This is the appropriate moment to explore further the arguments supporting the view that the media neither are, nor can be, neutral in a democracy. This argument takes as its basic premiss the view that the media, by the act of producing and distributing information, provide the citizenry not just with objective information, but also with the ideological perspectives within which to form opinions, and by so doing, they play an important role in the development of citizenship itself.

Thus, in these circumstances, where the media hold one of the keys to the formation of public opinion, it would be misleading to see them as neutral instruments of communication. Indeed, far from being neutral, they are deemed to offer the public a range of opinion from which to choose and by so doing reinforce their membership of a particular socio-political group. The concept of public opinion may be usefully defined as the totality of mediated information by which the citizens of a nation construct their socio-cultural (including political) relationships with the society at large. Or, to extend this idea further: public opinion is the totality of mediated ideas, beliefs and principles required by the citizenry in order for them to construct their socio-cultural relations with the city, region or state, through a process of choice (Lamizet, 1992).

As we have already suggested, it is misleading to speak about neutrality with regard to mediated communication and it follows from this that neutrality would constitute a rejection of choice and a denial of the opinion-forming process which in turn would have harmful consequences for democracy. By adopting a neutral stand the media would be failing to fulfil the obligation to accept the democratic responsibilities which they have assumed by historical process. But this non-neutrality of the media is conditional upon a single and important assumption relating to their operational context: it presupposes the quality of pluralism. Media pluralism is the way of guaranteeing the simultaneous presence in the public sphere of a mixed discourse derived from different media sources and comprising a range of differing opinions. Currently in Europe the democratic condition of pluralism is required to operate within three geo-political contexts: the regional, the national and the international. Daily and weekly newspapers, local radio stations and television channels currently serve the interests of the region, whilst the national interests are met by the national dailies, periodicals, books, the national radio stations and the main (terrestrial) TV channels. Satellite television, film and transnational radio services offer information and other services to Europe at the international level (Sánchez-Tabernero, 1993:30). The extent to which these services are truly pluralistic is a matter of considerable debate and we shall return to this issue later in this chapter and in the Conclusion.

It should also follow from these observations relating to the essential non-neutrality of the media that it is equally misleading to assume that they are dedicated to the pursuit of truth and objectivity in the usual sense of those terms. As we have already pointed out above, the media represent society and its activities to their public from a known ideological point of view by which, it is assumed, they (users and media) understand and make sense of the external world. If we can use the concept of truth in relation to the media, it is in somewhat different sense of designating a process of opinion formation by the mediated voice of a particular socio-political group. In other words it could be said that the media *construct* truths rather than express them in any universal way. The construction of truth by a western, pluralistic media is realised by the mediation of different, often conflicting, socio-political views culminating in an act of choice by the citizen to belong or not to belong. Where media function is concerned, the truth is always a matter of choice, not so much between the meanings of words, but between one form of socio-cultural affiliation and another. As odd as it may appear, the media do not tell the truth for the simple reason that the truth is not theirs to tell. Instead they offer to their public a range of mediated information from which the latter construct their own truths and by which they consolidate their social allegiances, quite literally to the best of their knowledge.

To sum up, media truth is the end product of a process of persuasion and argument wherein a certain perspective makes sense. The truth, therefore, when used in relation to the media function, should designate a construct and not a revelation (Lamizet, 1992). Finally, and very importantly, 'media truth' should exist not as a single construct but as one among many within the pluralistic context already mentioned.

II The development of the media post-1945

Two phases of development

The development of the post-war Western European media can be usefully divided into two overlapping periods. The first is the phase dating from 1945 to approximately 1980, and the second from 1980 to some time in the next millennium. The need for the western democracies to reassert their liberal ideologies upon the turbulence created by the defeat of fascism offered to the media a major role in the creation of a new order. As a first step in this direction, the fascist and by definition, non-pluralist media of war-time Germany and Italy, as well as the collaborative press of the French Vichy régime, were purged and reconstructed along lines approved of by the western allies in 1944–5. Simultaneously the media of the so-called Eastern Bloc countries were undergoing a purge of a different kind designed to mediate a different kind of reality. In the West the radio and newly emerging television services were developed along the lines of the public service model inherited from the BBC whose wartime performance had won for it the admiration of liberated Europe. This need to rebuild nations and to stabilise the European community was reflected in the process of mediation which had now been reinforced with a new mode of communication, the television. In the immediate post-war years the media actively represented to the peoples of Europe a mediated image of themselves as nations existing in a new, more united Europe within a new world order dominated by the two superpowers of the United States and the Soviet Union.

The role of the media in this first phase, 1945–80, can be summarised in diagrammatic form in Figure 1.3.

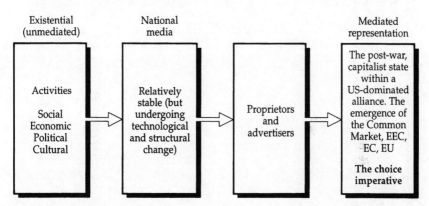

Figure 1.3   The development of the media in Western Europe Phase 1 1945–80

Such a broad outline is in our view a useful and necessary one for the development of further arguments in this chapter, but it is obviously a simplification. As we have already indicated, not everyone agrees that the western media is a force for the democratic promotion of social order. Some see them as a force for social *control* (see Habermas, 1989). This is an appropriate point at which to examine the characteristic structures of the post-war media 1945–80, and in particular the so-called public service tradition.

The public service tradition

Significant sectors of radio and almost all of the television services of Europe[3] were until the early 1980s the inheritors and the practitioners

Table 1.1 State funding of television services

Country	Public funding	Licence funding	Public channel advertising	Number of channels funded	Total licence funding 1992 ($ million)	As a % of European total
Austria	√	√	√	2	210	2.5
Belgium	√	√	√[2]	2	265	3.2
Denmark	√	√	X	1[5]	130	1.6
Finland	√	√	√	2	200	2.4
France	√	√	√	3[1]	995	11.9
Germany	√	√	√	3	2,790	33.5
Greece	√	√	√	1	70	0.8
Ireland	√	√	√	2	45	0.5
Italy	√	√	√	3	860	10.3
Netherlands	√	√	√	3	220	2.6
Norway	√	√	√	1	95	1.1
Portugal	√	X[3]	√	2	0	0.0
Spain	X[4]	X	X	2	0	0.0
Sweden	√	√	√	2	345	4.1
Switzerland	√	√	√	3	310	3.7
UK	√	√	X	2	1,800	21.6
Total	–	–	–	–	8,335	100.0

Source: Industry, GEAR, Kagan World Media, Morgan Stanley Research
[1] Includes Arte
[2] Advertising only allowed on French-speaking RTBF
[3] Licence fee abolished 1990
[4] Although government subsidies are available in 'emergencies'
[5] Although commercial network TV did receive a small public grant between 1988 and 1993
Key:
√ = Yes
X = No

of the public service tradition. Public service broadcasting (PSB) developed a mission of programme provision based on such principles as diversity of content, universal access and quality programming. Until recently their status within the full range of European media has been unique by dint of their having been largely protected from the pressures of commercialisation to which the written press and some European radio channels have been exposed. This freedom from market forces has been the determining factor in their organisational structure, their perceived missions, and the means by which they have sought to fulfil them. Free for the most part from the need to generate their own revenue (they were funded, and mostly still are funded, by licence fee: see Table 1.1), they could ignore market pressures and pursue their own aims of 'educating, informing and entertaining' the people. Indeed the direction taken by the post-war television and most radio services in Europe is in sharp contrast with that of the USA which, from their inception, had been dominated by commercial interests.

Arguably, the public service broadcasters in Europe have been highly effective in representing to the people an intelligible experience of their respective cultures. Acting simultaneously as entertainers, keepers of folk memory, interpreters of events, and guardians of the national conscience, they have offered to the peoples of Europe a mediated reflection of themselves as national communities. With the reservation already made above regarding this achievement, it could be argued that public service radio and television in Europe have been able to resist the process, apparent in the written press, known as the 'commodification of information' and its resulting restrictions. By so doing, it is argued (see Scannell, 1989), they have been able to widen the horizon of public awareness through a diverse range of informational and cultural programmes (news, current affairs, documentaries and drama). They have, at the same time, introduced the ordinary citizens of Europe to the national sphere via a range of activities from soap opera and game shows to participation at a national level in spectator sports. Notwithstanding this service rendered to the democratic processes of post-war Europe, public service broadcasting is currently undergoing a major re-evaluation. The reasons for this review are wide-ranging and involve social, political, economic and technological factors.

Ironically, however, there is another, unexpected quarter from which PSB is coming under attack. According to some contemporary thinkers, public service broadcasting was conceived within the final phases of what has come to be known as the 'modernist era'. By this they mean that PSB developed in a time of clearly defined national identities as well as of strongly held views of historical destiny (i.e. Marxist and capitalist theory). It is currently a *fin-de-siècle*, post-modernist argument to assert that such cultural and ideological certainties, which gave the states of Western Europe their sense of mission, were illusory. If this is the case, then a large part of that illusion, as we have seen, was reinforced by the media and by public service broadcasting in particular. There are many reasons, as we shall see, why the principles which underpin public service broadcasting are under threat across Europe. But, in so far as public service broadcasting may be seen, until recently, as an aider and abetter of the 'modernist illusion', its continuation in its current form, from a post-modernist point of view at least, can be questioned. In other words, not only can the future of PSB be challenged on social, economic, political and technological grounds, but its self-confessed commitment to permanent or semi-permanent social values may also be questioned by the prevailing currents of intellectual thought at the end of the twentieth century.

The second phase of post-war media development, 1980–2020?

The second phase in the development of the western media begins around 1980 and continues through the present into the next millennium. The choice of this date is somewhat arbitrary, but there are at this time sufficient indicators of a diverse nature to suggest that the media, and perhaps their role, are undergoing a major transformation. These new factors will be discussed in greater detail later in this chapter but at this point we can broadly restate them as being socio-economic, political and technological in nature.

The questions to be asked relating to this second phase and to which there are no clear answers are threefold. How will the media continue to develop over the next two decades in this second phase? Will they continue to function as forces for social cohesion within the wider European context? If not, what are the implications for Europe as a mediated reality beyond the year 2000? Inevitably, the second phase of media development is more difficult to plot than the first.

It could be argued that there is at least a theoretical possibility of Europe being represented (mediated) as a socio-cultural community in the post-1980s in a manner comparable to that of the post-war nation-state in the first phase. As we mentioned briefly previously, the most significant addition to the established modes of delivering information has been the development and the commercial application of television technology. If we can briefly characterise media trends during this period it could be by claiming that the predominantly emerging influence in the field of communication is that of the image (as opposed to the word). This domination of the image in the communication of the late twentieth century is apparent in three striking ways. The first is the predominant use of the image as the preferred mode of communication in the field of advertising. The second is the predominant use of the image as the preferred mode for the communication of information throughout Europe. Thirdly, as proof of the two foregoing features, is the perceivable 'spectator culture' which has developed among users arising from this mode of information delivery (see Lamizet, 1992).

In theory at least, the stage would again seem to be set for the next historic phase of the mediation process: the representation and interpretation through the filmed image of the European Union, of its institutions, activities and major players and their many voices all collected and presented within the new, enlarged European public sphere. On the surface at least, the same processes of mediation that allowed the citizens of the various nation-states in the post-war period to establish their socio-cultural allegiances are still available to them. Indeed, any anecdotal check on the content of programming reveals that the amount of broadcasting time (including radio programming) devoted to the presentation of European institutions, issues and its major players has significantly increased over the last fifteen years. This programming is wide in scope, ranging from news content, documentaries and special reports, on the one hand, to Euro-entertainment on the other. The same holds true for the written press too. All major European newspapers, including the noisy and notoriety-seeking tabloids of the UK and Germany, reserve space in their weekly output for the mediation of Europe.

But as we have suggested already, the second phase of the development of the European media has been, and will continue to be, played out against the background of social, political and economic turbulence accompanied by extraordinary technological advance. It would be useful to consider these factors in a little more detail at this point, because we shall argue that they have played and will play a vital role in shaping the future role and function of the European media.

Forces of change: The socio-cultural factors

If the role of the media in the first phase of their post-war development served to revitalise democratic principles and reinforce the national identities of the newly liberated European nation-states, then to a large extent they did so by setting an example themselves and embodying those same principles and identities. This they achieved in two ways; firstly, by the organisation and structure which they adopted and, secondly, by the way in which they interpreted their post-war mission towards their respective governments and peoples. Thus generally across Europe, with the exception of Franco's Spain (see Chapter 6), the written press was never more pluralistic than it was in the immediate decade after the war. The existence of literally hundreds of daily newspapers and periodicals in Europe has in retrospect come to be seen as a 'Golden Age' of the post-war press.[4] Since then the trend has been inexorably downward in the direction of fewer and fewer titles.

With regard to the broadcasting media, having experienced the extraordinary power of the radio, and a little later of the television, sometimes to their cost, all European governments seized the opportunity to regulate (or re-regulate in the case of France, Italy, Spain and Germany) their broadcasting services. Sometimes confusing the concept of state sponsorship with that of state control[5] governments took the opportunity to impose upon their broadcasters varying degrees of social and political acquiescence *vis-à-vis* their respective plans for national reconstruction. But in addition to these grand designs of government which the media dutifully represented to the public, the public services of radio and television as well as the written press also presented images and discourse which suggested that Western Europeans, whilst for the most part distinguished and separated by their respective cultures, did hold in common certain cultural and moral values related to family, social behaviour and working practice.

These assumptions on the part of the media were well founded in fact. The pre-war class divisions, the clear cultural and economic distinctions between the working class and the bourgeoisie, still remained intact throughout post-war Europe. The war had changed little if anything relating to social stratification or the holding of traditional (non-fascist) class values. The European working class emerged as the peacetime 'army' (reinforced by substantial immigrant labour) by which the old continent would be reconstructed. American aid in the form of the Marshall Plan was to be the driving force. The peoples of liberated Europe demanded social and economic reform and political stability. For almost thirty years, until the first oil crisis of 1973, relatively speaking, that is what they got. These demands, however, were made within the context of the existing traditional social and moral values and assumptions about class attitudes which, like the media which had helped to create them, were not to endure.

Hobsbawm (1994) writes authoritatively about this first phase up to about 1970, referring to the period as the 'Golden Age'. He offers a penetrating analysis of the social and cultural changes which occurred in the period 1965 to the present. The changes he identifies are far-reaching and have served to create a Western European society which, to anyone born in the first quarter of the century, has changed almost beyond recognition. Whilst this period between 1965 to the present does not exactly coincide with the second phase of media development that we have proposed, it is necessary to understand the changes which were taking place at a slightly earlier time because their later social manifestations (post-1980) clearly have a bearing upon the development of the European media in its second phase.

Hobsbawm identifies two main currents of change post-1965. The first is of a social nature and the second cultural: both currents he qualifies as revolutionary. Under 'social revolution' he proposes five major areas of dramatic development which can be summarised as follows:

The decline of the peasantry as the consequence of the capital-intensive modernisation of agriculture. In 1990 no country in Western Europe except Spain, Portugal and Ireland had more than 10 per cent of its working population employed on the land. In some countries the figure is much lower than this (i.e. less than 3 per cent in the UK and in Belgium).

The corresponding post-war urbanisation of Europe as the rural poor move from the farm to the factory in search of a livelihood.

The improved educational standards and in particular the sharp increase of entry to higher education to include the children of the lower middle and the working classes. Hobsbawm points out that the scale of the student uptake of the new opportunities offered in higher education far exceeded the expectations of the planners and that this in part explains the great student revolts of the late 1960s.

The subsequent decline in the post-1980s of the industrial working class following the collapse of the traditional 'rust-belt' industries of coal-mining, iron- and steel-making, textiles and clothing manufacture. Hobsbawm attributes the breakdown in working-class solidarity directly to the turbulence of the labour market wherein 'new industries replaced old ones but not in the same place and differently structured' and where 'Prosperity and privatisation broke up what poverty and collectivity in the public place had welded together' (Hobsbawm, 1994:307).

Hobsbawm suggests that the decline in working-class solidarity has resulted in the fragmentation of the whole social stratum, the top 10 per cent of the workers having adjusted more easily to the methods of high-tech production whilst at the bottom end there has been the emergence or re-emergence of an underclass, partly or wholly dependent on the welfare state and unknown in Europe in the post-war era. It was the first group, the top 10 per cent of workers, who for the first time in the UK became the potential supporters of the political Right.

To this process of social fragmentation may be added the phenomenon of immigration, which accelerated in the immediate post-war era in response to the European labour shortage and has resulted in the current presence of significant numbers of ethnic minorities – North Africans, Asians, Turks and Afro-Caribbeans – residing and working in Europe. As we have seen in the UK and more recently in Germany and France, their presence alongside indigenous white workers has often led to tensions in the workplace as well as in the community itself.

Finally under the category of 'social revolution' Hobsbawm underlines *the importance of the mass entry of women into the labour market* and their emergence as an economic as well as a political force in the 1960s. Politicised in the aftermath of the student revolts of 1968, they have progressively since then gained ground in matters sexual (contraception and abortion rights), marital (divorce laws relaxed) and economic (access to jobs and equal opportunities).[6]

Under the title 'cultural revolution' Hobsbawn suggests that this phenomenon is best approached 'through the structure of relations between the sexes and the generations'. He identifies three major trends which can be summarised as follows:

The weakening of family ties and the decline of the nuclear family, mostly evident in the spiralling European divorce rate and the increase in the number of single-parent families.

The new climate of sexual freedom for both heterosexual and homosexual persons.

The emergence since the 1960s of a youth culture as a new, major and independent financial group in western society. Young people in the late twentieth century are, he notes, 'a separate social stratum' and constitute a 'concentrated mass of purchasing power' (Hobsbawm, 1994:326). Notwithstanding the paradox of their transitory condition, he points out, somewhat wryly, that they behave as if they occupied the final stage of human development. They have in common their internationalism, their blue jeans and rock music, as well as the language of the urban lower classes and the apparent rejection of moral restraints.

Hobsbawm concludes that the cultural revolution of the late twentieth century 'can be best understood as the triumph of the individual over society . . . the breaking of the threads which in the past have woven human beings into social textures' (Hobsbawm, 1994:334). Such a conclusion has resonances beyond those of the social historian. It is, for example, clearly the espoused view of the neo-libertarian Right (to recall Margaret Thatcher's oft-quoted comment) that 'There is no such thing as society, only individuals'. Indeed much of the liberal market credo in the 1980s has been founded on a consumer view of individual freedom which appears to lend support, encouragement and strength to the claims of Western European youth culture.

Such claims to individualism, as we have already mentioned, also find favour in fashionable, post-modernist writing. As a significant postscript to Hobsbawm's analysis consider the following as a possible fitting tribute to youth culture at the end of the twentieth century:

> But the post-modern nomad-like activity is predicated on the abundance of resources in the present. The groups of post-modernity can in principle satisfy every want and therefore they quite lack any purpose in linear time. They do not need to struggle to satisfy their wants since the resources of satisfaction are simply supposed to be available in the here and now (not least thanks to the technology, which in a kind of Faustian pact, satisfies previously unimagined wants and desires . . . . (Tester, 1994:141)[7]

The aim of this section on the social and cultural changes in Europe since 1945 (but in which we have particularly focused on the period post-1960) has been to identify the nature of these changes and to propose that they are linked causally to recent developments in the media. As we have seen, from the so-called 'Golden Age' of the immediate post-war period down to the present, Europe has experienced a social and cultural revolution of a most profound and far-reaching nature. We have taken the view that the media have played a major role in the formation of public opinion, but paradoxically it must be acknowledged that the forces of influence cut both ways. The media have both influenced and facilitated social and cultural change, and, in turn, been themselves influenced by them. This phenomenon of reciprocal influence is not difficult to understand if we consider that, as social actors in their own right, the media, like any other institutions, are susceptible to the same forces of social and cultural change as the people for whom they act as mediators.

The social and cultural changes which we described undoubtedly have produced a society in late twentieth-century Europe with very different lifestyles, aspirations and attitudes from that of the first two decades of the post-war period. The media, as we have already pointed out, have also been swept along by these changes. With the possible exception of some of the UK tabloids, the content of the written press has become more sophisticated, more expensively packaged and more diversified in readership.[8] Commercial and regional radio have developed in serious competition to national stations and, most strikingly of all, television has undergone, and is still undergoing, a profound metamorphosis. All of these changes in some measure are in response to the post-1960s social and cultural revolution which Hobsbawm has described and we have summarised above. If we add to the influence of socio-cultural factors others of an economic, technological and political nature, we can further understand current trends in the media and in particular in broadcasting. It is to these other factors which we shall now turn.

The economic factors

The fact that the European communications industry is a multi-billion dollar player in the world market clearly underlines the importance of economic factors in explaining current developments in the media. In 1992 European governments themselves invested over 8.3 billion dollars derived from licence fees (see Winnington-Ingram, 1994:2) in their respective broadcasting services. But the real investment in broadcasting has come not from governments in the last decade but from the private sector, where it is estimated that advertisers alone invested 60 billion dollars in 1993 (Sánchez-Tabernero, 1993:124).

The communications/media industry in the 1980s has been characterised by the following four major economic trends.

The first is the phenomenon of globalisation of the communications industry led by the American and Japanese conglomerates and facilitated by the deregulation of the world's money markets. Europe is already a major purchaser of American software and Japanese hardware but it also has important production and manufacturing potential of its own in both these domains. Much of the turbulence in the European communications market is attributable therefore to the strategic manoeuvring of European and other conglomerates aimed at both consolidating and improving their position in the world market. The phenomenon of globalisation has created an irreversible increase in the size and importance of the communications industry. The deregulation of the money markets has also brought about a corresponding reduction in the power of national governments to regulate an industry whose structure is becoming increasingly internationalised.

The second economic trend, which is associated with the first phenomenon of globalisation, is that of the expansion of the activities of certain players within the European communications industry. This expansion is in part made possible by a general increase in audience (see Sánchez-Tabernero, 1993:45–50) accompanied by an improved technological capability for programme delivery, but the underlying causes are primarily economic in nature. This is because the media industry is a high-risk investment and extremely capital-intensive. The most successful players therefore are inevitably those with sufficient capital to invest in the costly technology of cable and satellite in markets where the returns, whilst potentially very lucrative, may materialise in the longer rather than the shorter term. Such conditions encourage media corporations tactically to merge and expand in order to better spread the load of investment, reduce the risks associated with media enterprise and, above all, improve their market position. Expansion is a natural function of the market and, in such an important one as communications in the 1980s, was inevitable.

In addition to the 'critical mass' factor described above where expansion is an obligatory tactical policy designed to spread the costs and risks between more players (but fewer groups) overall, there is also the strategic imperative which we touched on under 'globalisation' above. The European communications industry, if it is to defend its own home market from the predatory thrusts of the Americans and the Japanese, must itself possess strong corporations and conglomerates with economies of scale capable of matching those of the other world players. This trend towards reinforcement is illustrated by events in 1994 where out of the top fifteen mergers and acquisitions of European corporations, four (i.e. 26 per cent) were involved in the communications market. The total value of the mergers amounted to 4.5 billion dollars (*European*, 4.1.95:18).

Whilst expansion alone does not necessarily lead to media concentration (and the resultant loss of pluralism), it is associated with the process and this would be an appropriate moment briefly to look at the phenomenon a little more closely. Sánchez-Tabernero proposes four principal kinds of media concentration which he characterises as mergers, acquisitions, the launching of new media and deals between companies. These four categories of concentration together with the conditions which promote them and their consequences are summarised in Table 1.2.

Thirdly, these associated trends of expansion, concentration (and possibly diversification) of the media can be more precisely characterised by a further process which may be termed integration. Sánchez-Tabernero identifies five separate kinds of media integration: vertical, horizontal, international, multi-media and multi-sectoral (see Sánchez-Tabernero, 1993:62–96).

Vertical integration relates to the control by a single company of several related activities in the communications industry. Thus in the current world market where there is a shortage of programming, due to the recent sharp rise in demand, many large media companies are

Table 1.2 Process of media concentration and diversification

System of media concentration and diversification	General conditions required	Effects (companies and market)
Mergers	– crisis in the industry	– decrease in level of competition in the market – more favourable conditions for the companies
Acquisitions	– financial, industrial and commercial superiority (buyer) – need to improve competitive ability (seller)	– quick growth of the companies that invest large sums of money – less 'voices' in the market
Launching of media	– markets changing, growing or with new possibilities (i.e. new media)	– slow growth of the company – more diversity in the market
Deals between companies	– maturity of the industry and considerable entry barriers	– dangerous competition in the market avoided – power sharing

Source: Sánchez-Tabernero (1992), European Institute for the Media

engaged in 'upstream' purchasing of production companies in order to gain access to and partial control of the programmes market. An example of this activity is the current trend in the United States for media corporations to seek access to programme production through acquisitions such as Columbia by Sony and Twentieth Century-Fox by News Corporation. Vertical integration is also characteristic of public service broadcasting in Europe. The BBC, for example, although obliged to purchase a part of its productions from independent producers, is still strongly structured on vertical lines.

Horizontal integration relates to the expansion or concentration of ownership of the same kind of media in different markets. In the UK, for example, Rupert Murdoch's News International possesses a significant number of daily and weekly newspapers. In France Hersant owns the maximum share permitted by law of the daily and weekly newspaper market (see Lamizet, Chapter 3, below).

International integration is often the natural extension of the horizontal kind described above but with the difference that it crosses international frontiers. The main causes of this kind of international expansion, as Sánchez-Tabernero points out, are due

19

to the saturation of the home market, the imposition of legal restraints upon media ownership in the home country and the overall effects of the deregulation of the world money markets. A detailed account of this process with regard to the German magazine market is given by Hickethier in Chapter 4.

Multi-media integration describes the ownership of various kinds of different media by one media company. Again, News International, with interests in television and the printed media, is a good example. Bertelsmann in Germany, with an even wider range of activities in publishing, radio, newspapers, records and film production, is another (see national chapters for further examples).

Multi-sectoral integration refers to holdings in media companies by other corporations whose major interests and activities lie outside the media in, for example, such areas as banking, insurance, construction and retail selling. Examples of this kind of integration include Fininvest in Italy which, among others, has interests in television and a national chain of supermarkets (see Figure 1.4) and Bouygues in France, a construction company with a majority share in TF1.

The principal questions raised by this expansionist trend in the media industry are twofold. Does a specific case of expansion amount to concentration or to diversification?[9] And, if the former, what are

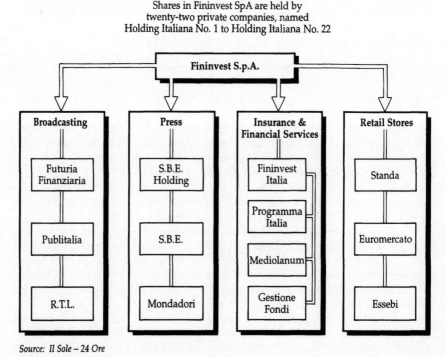

Source: *Il Sole – 24 Ore*

Figure 1.4   Berlusconi's Fininvest empire

the likely effects of this phenomenon upon the democratic process which the media are supposed to serve? As we have already pointed out, pluralism – the availability to the citizen of a range of sources of information and opinion (discourse) – is a pre-condition of a democratic society. If, by any of the processes described above, the net effect of media integration and expansion in any part of Europe is to reduce the number of information sources by placing formerly independent media within a single, larger group, then the effects upon society will be negative even if it makes sense economically.

It is extremely difficult to evaluate the precise effects of media concentration upon the quality of information flow within Europe. However, the trend towards concentration with the resulting reduction in pluralism must remain one of the prime causes of concern in any debate of a wider nature, where a deterioration in media performance is alleged to have occurred. The implications that such concerns have for the democratic process are potentially very serious. We shall return to this issue towards the end of this chapter.

Finally, the fourth element of the economic trends affecting the media in the post-1980s is that of commercialisation. Above all other, commercialism is the characteristic feature of media development at the end of the twentieth century. We have already touched upon the nature and consequences of the changes in the external organisation of the media. In addition to the external regrouping of companies and the possible effects of these changes on the essential pluralism of the media, there are other organisational consequences which economic integration imposes upon the internal organisation of the media. McQuail has described these changes as 'the fragmentation and functional disaggregation of different organisational activities: ownership, management, production, editorial, distribution, research' (McQuail, 1992:305).

One important consequence of disaggregation is the possible effect that it can have upon such key areas as editorial control. Weaver and Mullins (1975), in a study of editorial distinctiveness within chain ownership, concluded that the majority of chain newspapers had similar editorial policies (cited in McQuail, 1992). An example of imposed editorial change of direction occurring as the result of a change of ownership is the curious case of the *Today*[10] newspaper in the UK. From its right-of-centre politics under its first sole proprietor, Eddie Shah, it has emerged, in its new home of News International, as a supporter of the Labour Party. Such a change is no doubt dictated more out of a desire on the part of Murdoch to create a competitor for the *Daily Mirror*, owned by the rival Mirror Group, than out of any political conviction, but the turnaround in editorial direction is no less remarkable.

Advertising is clearly one of the major driving forces of both the old and the new media. As we have already noted, advertisers spent 60 billion dollars in the European market in 1992 alone. Such massive financial interests are having, and will continue to have, profound effects upon the organisational structure as well as upon the perceived mission of a large section of the media, for whom advertising is the main source of revenue, and perhaps even their very reason for being.

One of the consequences of the growth of a multi-billion dollar industry in advertising has been the radical restructuring of the advertising industry itself. Sánchez-Tabernero points out that the sector has been characterised by two specific trends which we can summarise briefly as firstly, the globalisation of commercial strategies and of the advertising of companies on a European scale, and secondly, the increase in number and the strengthening of the role and influence of media space buying companies (Sánchez-Tabernero, 1993: 123).

The increase in advertising revenue, encouraged by deregulatory policies implemented by European governments, has re-invigorated commercial broadcasting as well as boosted the fortunes of the European printed media. Indeed the expansion of the commercial interest in broadcasting is on such a scale that it is argued that the balance between the public service and the private sector activities has been irretrievably broken. This imbalance, if indeed it has occurred, will have qualitative as well as quantitative implications for the media in Europe. In general terms these implications are linked to the two distinct missions of the public service and the commercial broadcasters. The objective of the former is to deliver a wide range of quality programming to the public whereas the objective of the latter, it could be argued, is to deliver audiences to advertisers. This is to state the distinction somewhat crudely because not all public service broadcasting is deemed to be of consistent high quality whilst some commercial broadcasters quite definitely do produce programming of a high standard. This general truth underlying this distinction is nevertheless helpful and one to which we shall return later.

Commercial attitudes towards broadcasting places broadcasters in all kinds of dilemmas relating not just to questions of editorial independence, as we have already noted, but to others of an equally serious nature. We shall deal with these questions in some detail towards the end of this chapter but for the moment they can be broadly characterised as follows: commercialisation of the media raises issues concerning:

- the influence of proprietors upon editorial control;
- the influence of the advertisers on programme content;
- the quality and range of programming;
- the right of public access to mediated national events;
- the interests of vulnerable groups;
- the interests of minority groups;
- the democratic need for a pluralistic media.

As we noted at the beginning of this section, commercialisation is above all others the driving and most influential force behind the

Table 1.3 Introduction of television advertising

Country	Public channels	Commercial channels
Austria	1957	–
Belgium[1]	1953	1989
Denmark	–	1988
Finland[2]	1957	1987
France	1948	1986
Germany	1953	1984
Greece	1967	1990
Ireland	1960	–
Italy	1954	1980
Netherlands	1960	1989
Norway	–	1992
Portugal	1956	1992
Spain	1956	1989
Sweden	–	1991
Switzerland	1955	–
UK	–	1955

Source: Carat International, Morgan Stanley Research.
[1] Advertising only allowed on French-speaking RTBF
[2] Advertising previously only allowed during breaks; MTV programming for YLE

changes which have taken place in the media since the 1980s. In our earlier account of the social-cultural revolution, we drew attention to the major change in European society in the last quarter of the century which Hobsbawm and others have characterised as social fragmentation. The intensifying processes of commercialisation, of which one manifestation has been the abandoning of a diversity of programming in favour of satisfying more specialised, individual tastes, may be seen both as a cause of, and a response to, a parallel trend of audience fragmentation which is currently occurring across Europe. Table 1.3 shows the dates for the introduction of advertising and for the establishing of commercial channels in Europe.

The technological factors

The rapid and dramatic progress made in the field of electronics in the post-1980 period has had an important bearing upon the programming, structure and organisation of the media. The upshot for the communication industry has been revolutionary and, arguably, television has become one of its first beneficiaries or victims, depending on the perspective from which these events are viewed. The principal effects of the application of the electronic technology to broadcasting are most in evidence in the modes of delivery, the use of satellite, cable and video text as well as in the exponential increase in frequency space gained from the digitisation of frequency band-widths. These advances in electronics have been instrumental in increasing the number of channels operating in Western Europe from 35 in 1975 to over 150 today (Dawson, 1994:30). Commensurately, the number of programme hours generated by this upsurge in channels has risen from 200,000 in 1985 to over 500,000 in 1994 (Dawson 1994:30). In short there are more pictures, more distributors and more media discourse than ever existed before in the first period of terrestrial broadcasting. This growth in programming space has created a sharp increase in the demand for programmes, as well as an increase in competition between the media corporations, all over Europe. It is the nature of the content of the new programming that is causing concern in some quarters.

For many reasons satellite broadcasting will be one of the most revolutionary influences upon the shape of the future media landscape in the next century. Its seemingly effortless capacity to cross national frontiers, thereby escaping the particular national media legislation of its target audiences, raises all kinds of issues of a socio-cultural nature concerning the relationship between the media and national governments and between public service and commercial broadcasters. From the commercial standpoint it again potentially has the opportunity of reaching new, restratified audiences in Europe for the purposes of either advertising or pay-per-view television broadcasting, or both.

The importance of the new technology and its implications for the European market and for the movement towards ever closer union has been noted by the European Commission and policies have been developed to anticipate and harness the possible effects (see 'European legislation' section below). The important interim report by the Commission, *Realities and Tendencies in European Television: Perspectives and Options* (1983:5) offers the following view on the impact of the new technology:

> The new telecommunications technologies, and especially direct broad-casting by satellite (DBS), will inevitably lead to a proliferation and an internationalisation of television broadcasts in Europe by the end of the decade (. . .) In global terms, the new technological developments will enable Europe to make a greater impact compared with its major competitors, both industrially and culturally – provided a common policy is launched without delay.

Satellite technology of the future has still to resolve the problem of covering large distances at relatively low costs. Currently its cost of transmission per programme hour are substantially greater than those of its terrestrial rivals. Not only is the rocket-launching technology hugely expensive, it is also unreliable. In addition satellite transmission depends on the purchase of a dish aerial or cable; the first is more expensive than the terrestrial aerial to the subscriber and the second involves the cable company in extremely costly investment in cable-laying. Nevertheless, the alliance between satellite and cable

Table 1.4 The uneven distribution of the new technology in Western Europe

Country	Pop. (millions)	TV homes (millions)	VCR homes (millions)	Cable connection (millions)	Cable penetration (%)	Dish total
Belgium	10.1	4.1	2.1	3.7	91.6	15,000
Denmark	5.2	2.2	1.4	1.2	56.5	125,000
France	58.0	20.8	12.3	1.0	4.7	360,000
Germany	81.2	33.0	16.2	14.4	43.9	6,000,000
Greece	10.4	3.1	1.3	Nil	Nil	2,500
Ireland	3.6	1.0	0.61	0.44	41.6	60,000
Italy	57.2	20.3	9.1	Nil	Nil	110,000
Luxembourg	0.4	0.14	N/A	0.17	81.4	2,000
Netherlands	15.4	6.3	4.5	5.6	87.9	250,000
Portugal	9.9	3.1	1.9	Nil	Nil	110,000
Spain	39.2	11.6	6.3	1.2	10.3	180,000
UK	58.4	22.2	16.0	0.77	3.8	2,800,000

Source: Based on data from *Cable and Satellite Europe* January 1995.

is, and will increasingly become, the strong source of a new television delivery system which is bound to compete with the traditional terrestrial mode.

It is estimated that 25 per cent of Western Europe will be cabled by the year 2000 but that the cable distribution will be very uneven with significant national differences (see Table 1.4). For example, as early as 1984, 81 per cent of all homes in Belgium subscribed to cable television. This is because Belgium along with other smaller countries such as Holland, Switzerland, Ireland, Norway and Denmark installed narrowband cable to receive and relay terrestrial television from neighbouring countries (Collins, 1992). In the larger countries of the EU such as France, Germany and the UK, all of which already possess their own substantial terrestrial services, the rate of cabling has been less pronounced, ranging from 44 per cent in Germany to almost nil in Italy (*Cable and Satellite Europe*, 1.95) (see Table 1.4).

The implications of cable and satellite for the terrestrial television systems of Europe are mixed. In countries where the latter are strong, well established and innovatory, their impact will be less pronounced than in countries with systems more dependent on imported programming. Nevertheless, throughout Europe, part of the audience which formerly had no choice but to watch the available terrestrial channels will now be absorbed by the new cable and satellite broadcasters, thus continuing the trend of media and social fragmentation which we have already noted.

The legal factors: European legislation

There can be few areas of policy-making since the early 1980s which have more profoundly exercised the collective mind of the European Commission than that of broadcasting. Motivated partly out of necessity – the impending reality of transnational broadcasting via satellite, not all of which was desirable – and partly out of a conviction that the time was right for a European initiative anyway, the Commission has had to confront some difficult and at times intractable issues. One of the most serious of these is without doubt the fact that for the most part European radio stations and television channels serve political systems and socio-cultural groups whose boundaries are coterminous with a national language and physical frontier. In the context of such linguistic and cultural diversity the question of the nature and function of a single European broadcasting policy was bound to be highly problematic.

Indeed the problems raised by the European broadcasting initiative in the early 1980s in many ways went to the heart of the wider debate seeking to advance the cause and identify the modalities of European integration itself. The policy-makers had to address not just the economic and technical issues relating to the creation of a single broadcasting market, but others also of a more fundamental nature concerning the political and socio-cultural identity of the Community itself. The economic facts were the least disputed. The Community constituted a vast but segmented broadcasting market, occupied for the most part by large European public and private corporations, but in which the Americans, Japanese and other external players were making significant inroads. Its secondary markets (transnational deals in productions and technology of European origin), hampered by restrictive national legislation as well as by underfunded distribution systems, were insufficiently developed. In addition, at the technical level, there were significant differences in transmissions standards throughout the Community.

Ultimately the economic arguments in favour of addressing the weaknesses of the European market were to prevail as the chosen ground for Community action, but this course was not decided on until others had been proposed and deemed to have failed. As we have already mentioned, the advent of satellite technology was interpreted, in some quarters of the Commission, as a threat to future broadcasting unity, and as such it acted as a spur to preventative action against an upsurge in the number of broadcasters in the private sector. However, what was good for the private sector, it was held, could also prove beneficial to the public sector too. The arrival of satellite television for some cultural lobbyists in the Commission was welcomed as the opportunity to strengthen and disseminate a new, mediated image of Europe via a dedicated European channel.

Such commitment to the dissemination of a kind of Euro-Culture via satellite was predicated on two assumptions: the first was the existence of 'common cultural denominators' which transcended linguistic barriers and national cultures and which would form a partial basis for programming; the second was that the political, economic and developing socio-cultural spheres of Community activity would also constitute a natural and necessary focus of attention of a new international audience.

The first Hahn Report (1982) and the Commission's interim report *Realities and Tendencies in European Television . . .* (1983) both underlined the importance of the mission of a common European television service in forging the socio-cultural identity of the Community: 'The situation now emerging, though certainly not without risks, will afford the citizens of Europe greater opportunities to learn about, appreciate and participate in the cultural unity of our continent' (Interim Report to the European Parliament, *Realities and Tendencies in European Television: Perspectives and Options*, 1983:5). To this end, guided by these reports, the European Parliament gave its support to the two satellite channels, Eurikon (experimental) and Europa, created by the European Broadcasting Union (EBU) and dedicated to pan-European broadcasting along public service lines. In the event, neither channel succeeded in winning the hearts and minds of European viewers and both closed down in the mid-1980s. Collins (1994:45) sums up the failure of the cultural lobby in the Commission thus:

Advocates of television as a vehicle for creation of a unified European culture were quickly disabused of their beliefs. Attempts to establish

27

pan-European services (whether commercial or public service) in the 1980s failed. The conception of a unified culture (which was thought necessary to sustain a European polity) thereby became hard to sustain as differences in the tastes of European viewers were revealed.

The second phase of policy-making began in 1984 and marks a significant change in the Commission's attitude towards European broadcasting. The Green Paper, known as *Television Without Frontiers*, whilst reiterating the importance of the cultural issue, also asserted that the Commission's rights in exercising power in the media domain rested primarily on economic factors. Significantly this assertion specifically acknowledged the importance of advertising (and by implication the private sector) as a facilitator of broadcasting: 'It serves a broad range of interests . . . provides the revenue on which broadcasting organisations increasingly depend . . . it can be an important means of informing consumers' (*Television Without Frontiers*, 1984a:8).

The economic priorities of the Green Paper were to determine the policy-making in this field for the Commission in the post-1984 period, culminating in the Directive of 1989 on television broadcasting which is the single most important policy-making document of the Commission in this field. Its overall objectives were for the most part economic and they can be summarised as follows:

- the creation of a single common broadcasting market (unhindered by national legislation;
- the promotion of the growth of European production companies;
- the establishment of common (minimum) standards of advertising and the prohibition and regulation of certain products;
- the establishment of a quota system for programmes designed to protect European productions;[11]
- the protection of individual freedom via the right of reply;
- the protection of minors. (Collins, 1994:69)

Except to note the general lack of impact on the European market, it is difficult to assess fully the effects of the Directive upon European broadcasting. In theory at least, a single television market exists now that the legal obstacles to transnational transmission have been dismantled; but in reality other barriers to the free interchange of programming remain and they appear to be linguistic and cultural in kind rather than judicial (a fact some may have claimed to have known from the start). European viewers, it seems, wish to watch their own indigenous programmes first, imported programmes mostly from the USA second, and only then turn to programmes originating from other European states.

The conclusion to be drawn from this brief review of major policy proposals and their implementation in the 1980s must be that attempts at the dissemination of European culture via dedicated channels have not succeeded for the reasons already mentioned. Similarly attempts to create a single European market have also encountered obstacles of a serious nature. Ironically both initiatives have fallen foul of that once much vaunted quality – European cultural and linguistic diversity. Historically the source of Europe's rich creative (and destructive) energies, its cultural and linguistic diversity is now, in these new times, an underlying cause of the partial disfunction of the single market, and of the communicative deficit between the supra-national Community and its constituent parts.

The European Commission's initiative may have had less than the desired or anticipated impact upon the creation of a single market, but this is not to suggest that the European market has not developed. On the contrary there have been very significant moves in almost every sphere involving media groups in mergers, takeovers, collaborative deals in co-productions and diversification into new media fields. But the point is that these developments have occurred for the most part, firstly, in spite of the legislation, and secondly, the targets of the expanding media activities are today still national rather than transnational in nature (with the exception of the Franco-German channel ARTE, see national chapters). Moreover, whilst the need for transnational market dealings in software is clearly acknowledged, it often manifests itself as the need to sell to the American market rather than to the European one.

As an important coda to this section, it would be useful here to examine briefly the past and present role of the European Broadcasting Union (EBU), since its role as a pan-European broadcaster is important and potentially will be even more so in the coming decade. Founded in 1950, the EBU currently has over sixty members made up for the most part of European PSB operators. Originally set up as an exchange system for news, sport and cultural programmes (Eurovision), the EBU now has a European-wide satellite and terrestrial system for both radio and television transmissions. As Collins points out, the EBU comes nearest to what might be considered as a 'shared European mass medium of communication' (Collins, 1994:45). However, its large membership has meant, in the past, that policy-making has been somewhat cumbersome, and slow to come to terms with the changes which individual PSB services are experiencing in the new, market-sensitive contexts in which they are operating. Its pan-European public service bias has brought it into conflict with the European Commission, in particular with the Commission's Competition Directorate over concerns that the EBU's programme rights acquisition policy is allegedly anti-competitive (Collins, 1994: 45). There are signs that the EBU is facing up in a positive manner to the challenges confronting its members from the commercial sector. It is competing aggressively, on their behalf, with the new cable and satellite operators for world and European sporting rights. In 1994 it successfully acquired exclusive coverage for its members of the Football World Cup, and has obtained the exclusive rights for the broadcasting to Europe of the Winter Olympics in Japan in 1998 (Short, *European*, 3.3.95). The EBU is also active in the important area of technical research – and, significantly, adopting a higher profile in the taking of policy initiatives – making proposals which, among others, exhort its members to establish global broadcasting systems in the future, which integrate both terrestrial and satellite systems (EBU Consultation Document, 1995).

Potentially, as we have said, the EBU represents a powerful intermediary for further developments in programme exchanges and co-productions, as well as in technical collaboration and political lobbying at the European level.

III New media for a new era

The arguments for and against

For all the reasons mentioned above it can be seen that the European media have undergone profound changes since 1945 and have entered upon a marked new phase in their development since the early 1980s. They are becoming more diversified in form and content, serve more fragmented user groups and engage with these users in new ways. All the indications are that this trend will continue and become accentuated towards the end of the century. The question which now has to be posed is the very important one relating to the likely impact that this change may have upon the expanding community of nations situated within the newly named European Union.

Attempts by the Commission to create a single media market and facilitate the transmission of common cultural values through a 'European' public service or private sector initiative have either failed or, at best, met with limited success. The expansion that has occurred therefore is in the main the result of market forces exploiting the massive financial potential of the communications industry in general (and of the media in particular); a process made possible by the advent of new technology together with the deregulation of the media and money markets. It follows from this that the developments in the media which have occurred already, and which will extend into the future, will be characterised by a new set of values derived from the commercial rather than the public sector. This is not necessarily a cause for alarm but it is certainly the source of much debate in media circles. It is to the issues raised by the prospect of the increasing commercialisation of the European media that we shall now turn, because by a closer study of the nature of this process we may best be able to evaluate the impact of the future role of the media in the creation of the supra-national community.

It would be useful at this point to recall the earlier claims made in this chapter that the media (all kinds) have played a seminal role in defining and promoting the respective identities of the national states within the new world order. For the most part this role was performed by the printed press and increasingly post-1945 by national public service broadcasting agencies. The essential difference between the newspapers and the broadcasters, other than their modes of delivery, was that the former had already developed fully into commercial ventures whereas the latter were mostly a part of a state monopoly outside the magnetic field of market forces.

Indeed it was the European written press, as Habermas and others have pointed out, which first adapted to the concept of information as a commodity resulting in the development of the newspaper industry. It subsequently also accepted the financial lure (together with the ethical dilemmas) proffered by the advertisers to the point today where revenue from this source is a pre-condition of viability. Such dependence on the commercial priorities of the market by the written press was already established early in this century and stands in marked contrast to the relative isolation from those same forces enjoyed by the public service broadcasters for a half-century after the mid-1920s.

Such is the diversity in form and concept of the written press that there is a real problem in arriving at a satisfactory 'European' definition of a daily newspaper. They vary significantly in price, frequency and time of publication and, most importantly of all, in content matter. Predictably, Europe itself divides into a northern zone characterised by high newspaper readership and a southern zone where the habit is much less pronounced. The Germans and the

Table 1.5 Daily newspaper circulation in Europe (in millions)

Country	1975	1990	% variation
Austria	2.4	2.7	+12.5
Belgium (Fl)	1.9	1.2	−36.8
Belgium (Fr)	1.2	0.9	−25.0
Denmark	3.0	3.2	+6.7
Germany	**21.5**	**20.3**	**−5.6**
Finland	2.1	2.8	+33.3
France	**9.6**	**8.6**	**−10.4**
Greece	0.9	0.8	−11.1
Ireland	0.8	0.8[1]	−
Italy	**4.6**	**6.4[2]**	**+39.1**
Netherlands	4.2	4.6	+9.5
Norway	1.5	2.5	+66.7
Portugal	0.7	0.5	−28.6
Spain	**2.7**	**2.9**	**+7.4**
Sweden	4.9	4.9	−
Switzerland	2.5	2.7	+8.0
UK	**22.7**	**22.3**	**−1.7**

Source: Sánchez-Tabernero (1992) European Institute for the Media
[1] 667,000 copies of Irish newspapers plus an estimated 100,000 copies of British newspapers
[2] 1989 figures

British read more newspapers than are read in Spain, Italy and France put together (see Table 1.5). However, this superiority in number is almost certainly not matched by a corresponding level of information quality. Germany and the UK also account between them for half the advertising revenue within the European newspaper market (Pilati, 1993:61).

One explanation for this numerical superiority resides in the fact that the process of commercialisation is also the most advanced in Germany and the United Kingdom, where the tabloid press with its characteristic features of trivialisation, sensationalism and xenophobia occupies an important place in the market. Such characteristics contrast sharply with the more measured tones and content of the Spanish, French and Italian written press.

The Western European press in general, and that of the five largest countries in particular, have been subject to a process of commercialisation which has had at least two consequences: first, a movement, promoted by market forces, towards the reduction of titles and the concentration of ownership, and second, the development in the two largest user countries of a populist tabloid journalism which has very successfully recruited a strong readership and following. We shall delay drawing any firm conclusions from these consequences until we have examined other more recent developments in broadcasting to which we shall now turn.

If the written press this century has been characterised by a strong tendency towards commercialisation, the broadcasting media, with the exception of some European radio and the commercial ('independent') television of the UK, have been conspicuously free from market influences. However, this commercial-free status is double-edged and whilst it may be construed as a blessing by some, in retrospect it may also be seen as the partial cause of the problems which some public service broadcasters in Europe are now encountering.

Public service broadcasting, as we have seen, untrammelled by the need to attract 'audiences as revenue' since there was no competition, was able to develop a unique organisational structure and a wide socio-cultural mission which exposure to market forces would have almost certainly impaired. On the other hand, this special protected status which the state monopolies enjoyed did little to protect them from the hot breath of the market when, by the coincidence of circumstances already described, the winds of change turned against them late in the twentieth century.

We have already identified the socio-economic, political and technological factors which have undermined the status of public service broadcasting in the period leading up to the 1980s. A summary of the unified argument to emerge from this complex set of circumstances in favour of a shift of broadcasting initiative from the public to the private sector runs as follows.

Socio-cultural: There is a declining vision of the traditional institutions which formerly made up the constituent parts of the nation-state. In consequence allegiances to the mainstream national religions, political parties and trade-unions have become weakened in favour of a socio-cultural realignment in the form, for example, of single-issue pressure groups and parties (Blumler, 1992). From the market perspective there is a perceived social fragmentation and corresponding 'market opportunity' to which, it is alleged, public service broadcasters have been slow to adapt.

Economic: The market is the only viable financial player in the future European landscape. The state monopolies have dwindling resources and cannot possibly hope to undertake the heavy financial investment needed for the future. Also public service broadcasting is costly, inefficient and constitutes a restrictive practice (particularly latterly when it had the quasi-monopoly over advertising). It is feather-bedded and oversized in its production staff as well as in administrators (Keane 1993:53).

Technological: Cable, satellite, high-density television, multi-video distribution systems (MVDS), video recorders and compact discs all undermine the protected position of the state monopolies. Scarcity of transmission space is no longer a reality, hence the state should remove itself from the role of regulator which it has occupied traditionally since the inception of broadcasting earlier this century.

Political: Public service broadcasting restricts the expression of individual needs. It is dominated by powerful elites who are unaccountable to the public and who foist upon the people a systematic censorship. By definition therefore they promote an elitist, middle-class cultural regime which conspires to consolidate and promote both state and capitalist power.

The arguments in defence of public service broadcasting are equally telling and can be summarised as follows.

Socio-cultural: The under-representation of specific groups – children, women, ethnic minorities – by commercial broadcasters is an endemic feature of market-led media. Unrestrained competition, far from increasing choice, actually works against it, producing a narrower range of programmes of indiscriminate mass appeal. On the other hand, the diversity of programming found in the public service sector – news, current affairs, documentaries, chat shows, phone-ins, games, puzzles, children's programmes, drama, soap operas, music, ballet and sport – all play an important role in the social mediation process and form the basis of 'a corporate, public life that persists to this day' (Scannell, 1989:141).

Economic: Advertising promotes consumerism as a way of life. It works in favour of the advertisers and against the interests of the citizen by fostering the undemocratic assumption that unbounded consumerism *is* life (Keane 1993:85) with little emphasis placed on the values of intellectual enquiry, aesthetic experience and public service.

Political: The commercial media of the late twentieth century represents a privileged elite of powerful and rich players (Hersant, Berlusconi, Murdoch, Bertelsmann *et al.*) who are able to buy influence in the public sphere. Supporters of the privatisation of the media often use and deliberately falsify the concept of the freedom of the press which in its original eighteenth-century sense referred to the right of every citizen to receive and publish information as a *personal right* not dependent on wealth. In reality the commercialisation of the media limits access to all but a wealthy few to influencing the public sphere.

By reducing the range and quality of programming, commercial interests first impose their own brand of censorship upon the public (the 'freedom of choice' argument is hereby dismissed) and secondly remove from the people what has been called their 'communicative entitlement', by which is meant the 'right of free assembly, to speak freely and (more often overlooked) to listen, contribute to creating formal minimal guarantees for certain forms of public political and religious life' (Scannell 1989:160).

Whilst these arguments are well rehearsed and commonplace in media circles, we summarise them here because they have a clear but as yet not fully stated relevance for the way in which the supra-national functions of the enlarged European public sphere will be represented in the future by the media to the citizenry of the Union.

Many of the negative aspects of commercialisation – low-cost production, repeats, game-shows, soaps and old films – are already all too apparent in the schedules of the so-called new broadcasters of Europe. It is generally acknowledged that the production standards of the former French public service channel TF1, privatised by the Chirac government in 1986, have fallen. The German satellite channels, RTL plus and Sat 1 offer mixed programming of indifferent quality and Berlusconi's three Italian channels, Canale 5, Italia 1 and Rete 4, mostly put out an unashamed mish-mash of populist entertainment. In Spain it is much the same story: none of the recently established private channels, Antena 3, Tele 5, Canal Plus, have schedules which are comparable in range and production quality to the existing public service channels.[12] The commercial channels in the United Kingdom constitute, for the moment at least, a different case. Commercial television was established in Britain in 1955 in circumstances which contrast starkly with those in which most private television in continental Europe has developed in the post-1980s period. Created at a time when the influence of public service broadcasting was riding high in the UK, the commercial operator, ITV, was obliged to adopt the BBC model of programming and production standards. However, in the post 1980s climate of more aggressive commercialisation there has been a perceivable reduction in quality in some areas of production.

Developments of these kinds, which are occurring throughout Europe, are the legitimate causes for concern among those who see in them a dangerous shift away from an informational axis, essential to the democratic needs of the people, towards one of 'info-tainment'. In short, there is a danger that the development of a kind of pervasive 'tabloid television' will do the same for that medium as tabloid journalism has done for the written press (see Chapter 2 for further discussion).

At this juncture in the historic movement towards closer European union, the prospect of a weakened public service broadcasting sector, coupled with an 'underperforming' private sector alternative, gives rise to justifiable concern. As we have seen already, *dirigiste* attempts at transnational broadcasting via a dedicated European channel were unsuccessful in the 1980s. The lesson which has to be drawn from this failure must be that the mediation of supra-national Europe, if it occurs, will take place primarily *within* the respective national media and not outside them. But if the fundamental issues relating to the modalities of further social, political, economic and cultural integration are of little interest to the new media (whose priorities and mission lie in a different direction) then the prospects for the creation of a dynamic European public sphere are not encouraging.

Nevertheless, as is often pointed out, the process of media commercialisation is an inexorable one (Silj, 1993:15–48). Private broadcasters will play an increasingly important role in European affairs and therefore the commercialisation of a large sector of the broadcasting media is the future reality for Western Europe. Any solution, therefore, to the 'information deficit', if indeed a solution exists, will have as much to do with pragmatics as it will with principles. It will turn on the issue of how best the 'new broadcasting' can be integrated with the old in a manner which sustains the communicative rights of the people to be informed at a European level as well as at the national one, and by so doing participate in the construction of a European public sphere.

Notes

1. Few French, British or German citizens would have difficulty in placing *Le Monde, Le Figaro*, the *Sun*, the *Guardian* or *Bild* on either side of the Left–Right divide, even if they could not associate them directly with a political party.
2. By the technique of the interviewer adopting alternately the views of the opposing political party.
3. The UK is an exception; commercial television was introduced in 1955.
4. Except for Germany where part of the press was located in the Eastern Zone.
5. This is true of the attitude of successive French governments towards the television from 1958 until comparatively recently.
6. The parenthesis and contents are ours.
7. This is intended to apply to a more general, less socially identifiable category than youth but its relevance to the latter may be considered as striking.
8. I.e. The sharp increase in the number and variety of magazines in Europe targeting particular socio-cultural groups.
9. Expansion by diversification may not necessarily lead to a reduction in the number of information sources.

10. At the time of this book going to press and too late for detailed commentary in the main text of this chapter or of chapter 2, *Today* ceased publication. The demise of this paper is ironically the result of the price-war initiated by its owners, News International, against the *Daily Telegraph* and the *Independent*. It would appear that the considerable losses of *Today*, rumoured to be in the region of £11 million in 1994–5, have served to aggravate the even greater losses sustained by the *Times* as the result of the reduction in its price in the same period. The disappearance of *Today* not only depletes the number of national dailies in the UK, but also further weakens the voice of the left-of-centre in the British written press. This development should be bourne in mind when reading Chapter 2.
11. France has been particularly insistent on protecting the European production industry via a quota system.
12. Although Vilches in Chapter 6 reports a crisis and a loss of quality in the Spanish public service channels too.

CHAPTER 2

The media in Britain

Anthony Weymouth

I Introduction

The development of the mass media in the United Kingdom has been fashioned by influences which distinguish it from the rest of Europe in two important respects. First the written press has enjoyed (if that is the right word) an uninterrupted commercial progression since the nineteenth century. This fact accounts in part for its strengths as well as for some of its serious weaknesses. Secondly, the British government introduced a commercial channel to UK television services much earlier (1955) than any other country in Western Europe, with far-reaching results.

Whilst the keyword in both media sectors is 'commercial', the consequences in each case have been dramatically different. The commercialisation of the written press has led, in significant areas, to a reduction in both the quality and quantity of information, whereas the same process in television, occurring when it did in 1955, has proved to be a blessing in disguise for British broadcasting. As we have said, the consequences of these two historical factors have been far-reaching and we shall examine them briefly here before returning to them later in this chapter.

The process of commercialisation of the written press was greatly accelerated with the creation by Lord Northcliffe of the *Daily Mail* in 1896 – the first truly mass-circulation popular paper in the UK. This process continued at a gathering pace in the 1930s, was restrained only by the shortage of newsprint during the period 1939–45, and quickly refound its momentum in the news-thirsty post-war decade. Unlike the experience of Germany, Italy and France, the British written press was not ideologically purged in the aftermath of the war, nor was it subject to the control of an authoritarian regime of the kind imposed on the Spanish press until 1976. In consequence it was free to pursue unchecked its pre-war course of market-led development. With regards to broadcasting, the UK was also unique in Europe in introducing a national commercial channel in 1955. The result is that commercial television in the UK still bears the unmistakable imprint of a public service tradition under the influence of which it fell in the late 1950s.

Putting the matter briefly in relation to these two factors, the commercialisation of the written press has produced, as one of its extreme manifestations, the mass tabloid *Sun* whereas the process with regard to television has produced the admirable Channel 4. The differences between the two media in performance terms are striking and we shall examine the reasons which underlie and explain them later in this chapter.

Table 2.1 National dailies: changes in circulation 1955–95 (in thousands)

Quality broadsheets	1955	1995
Daily Telegraph	1,055	1,061
The Times	222	631
Financial Times	80	305
(Manchester) Guardian	156	400
The Independent	–	290
Total	1,513	2,687
Middle-market (tabloids in 1995)		
Daily Express	4,036	1,292
Daily Mail	2,068	1,794
Daily Herald	1,759	–
News Chronicle	1,253	–
Today[1]	–	549
Total	9,116	3,635
Mass-market (tabloids in 1995)		
Daily Mirror	4,725	2,476
Daily Sketch/Graphic	950	–
Sun	–	4,134
Daily Star	–	741
Daily Worker/Morning Star	90	?
total	5,765	7,351
Overall total	**16,394**	**13,673**

Source: Seymour–Ure 1992 and *Media Guardian* (ABC) 24.4.95
[1] *Today* ceased publication in November 1995. See Note 10, p. 36.

II The development of the written press in the UK 1945–95

Whilst comparatively speaking the written press in the UK is among the strongest and the most dynamic in Western Europe, it has like all the others succumbed to an overall decline in circulation (see Tables 2.1 and 2.2), a political realignment towards the Right, and a sharp inclination towards concentration in the ownership of titles.[1]

Table 2.1 indicates an overall decline of approximately 2.7 million copies in the national daily press since 1955. Within this context of decline, it shows an increase of over a million in the circulation of the quality broadsheets as well as a massive decrease in the middle-market circulation of nearly 5.5 million (with the significant disappearance of two left-of-centre titles). It also shows an increase in the mass tabloid market, although the fortunes of the left-of-centre *Daily Mirror*

Table 2.2 National Sundays: changes in circulation 1955–95 (in thousands)

Quality broadsheets	1955	1995
Observer	564	462
Sunday Times	606	1,238
Sunday Telegraph	–	694
Independent on Sunday	–	324
Total	1,170	2,718
Middle-market (tabloids in 1995)		
Reynolds News	579	–
Sunday Chronicle	830	–
Sunday Dispatch	2,549	–
Sunday Express	3,235	1,446
Mail on Sunday	–	1,933
Total	7,193	3,379
Mass-market (tabloids in 1995)		
Empire News	2,049	–
News of the World	7,971	4,716
People/Sunday People	5,075	2,085
Sunday Graphic	1,220	–
Sunday Pictorial/Mirror	5,539	2,479
Total	21,854	9,280
Overall total	**30,217**	**15,377**

Source: Seymour–Ure 1992 and *Media Guardian* (ABC) 24.4.95

are clearly in decline compared with those of the right-wing *Sun*. In summary, within the context of a declining overall readership, there has been a significant shift of political alignment towards the Right. Table 2.2 again indicates an increase in the number and circulation of the quality broadsheets. A large decrease, similar to that of the daily press, is recorded for the middle market (again with the disappearance of two left-of-centre titles and the addition of one right-of-centre paper). By far the largest fall is recorded in the mass market (12.5 million) with the disappearance of two titles and a significant reduction in the circulation of the rest. The political shift of emphasis towards the right is also apparent in the national Sunday press. A more comprehensive list of factors which characterise the post-1945 period are the following:

- Decline in overall circulation, in particular the national Sundays and the regional dailies.
- The domination of the national dailies and Sunday papers over the regional press.
- Technological adaptation.
- The weakening of the powers of the print and journalist unions.
- The intensifying trend towards concentration of ownership.
- The change of political alignment.
- The emergence of the 'new era' tabloids.

The overall reduction in circulation for national dailies and Sunday newspapers between 1957 (the post-war peak year) and 1995 is approximately 30 per cent. As can be seen from Table 2.2, it is the Sunday editions which have been by far the hardest hit by the falling trend (see Tables 2.3 and 2.4 for further comparisons from 1988–95).

The regional press

The regional press too has been another victim. Whilst there have been some notable exceptions such as the *Glasgow Herald* and the *Scotsman*, both of which have increased their circulations since 1945, the overall picture is of decline both in the numbers of titles and in circulation figures. There are currently in the UK approximately 90 regional dailies, mostly appearing in the evening but 16 of which technically appear in the morning. Their total circulation is 5.6 million. In addition there are 10 regional Sunday papers which have a collective circulation of 2.5 million (Peake, 1993:18) It is worth noting in passing that this domination of the British national (London-based) press over the regions is in marked contrast to the press in France, Germany, Spain and Italy, all of which have strong regional sectors.

Technology, industrial relations and take-overs

From a recent historical and market perspective, three factors explain the continued commercial resilience of the British written press. The first relates to the speed with which it adapted to the new technology emerging in the early 1980s, and the second to the winds of change in industrial relations created by the Thatcher government in the post-1979 period. The third concerns the increase in market activity in the form of important takeovers of established titles as well as the launching of new ones in the 1980s.

The Royal Commission on the Press of 1974–7 had acknowledged that, in the national press in particular, manning levels were over-generous and wages significantly high (1974–7:42). It also noted that the cause of this impediment to financial viability in the post-oil-crisis era was a combination of 'easy profits and weak management' in the earlier post-war days which had led to 'the exceptionally high earnings of print workers and a disposition among publishers to yield easily to the threat of unofficial action' (1974–7:5). Such is the fragility of news, and so inexorable the rhythm of production of a daily paper, that the power of the trade unions was mostly triumphant in obtaining lucrative concessions from the owners in the 1945–75 period.

This situation was dramatically changed in the 1980s by two forces: first the increasing pressure upon owners to take advantage of the new technology which offered greater efficiency and lower costs, and second, the introduction by the Thatcher government of new legislation on industrial relations which severely weakened the bargaining power of the unions. Encouraged by the sympathetic findings of the last Royal Commission in favour of cost reductions, emboldened by Mrs Thatcher's new industrial relations laws, and enticed by the economies promised by the new technology, the owners at last struck decisively against the perceived restrictive practices of the unions. These moves were above all spearheaded by Eddie Shah who successfully launched the new daily *Today* using the new technology, and by Rupert Murdoch, who moved the printing of *The Times* from Fleet Street to Wapping literally overnight in one of the most audacious and violent industrial manoeuvres of the Thatcher years. Other papers were quick to follow the lead set by Shah and Murdoch, in the abandoning of the old 'hot metal' type-setting in favour of computerised methods, massive reductions in the workforce, union de-recognition and renewed confidence on the part of the owners in the future commercial viability of the industry.

Concentration of ownership

As already mentioned above, the pronounced trend towards concentration of ownership is a strong characteristic of the British press. As early as 1947 five major groups owned 52 per cent of the national dailies and Sundays. However, the extent to which this state of affairs has deteriorated may be judged by the fact that in 1995 four large companies – News International; Mirror Group; United Newspapers; Daily Mail and General Trust plc – between them own 87 per cent of the British national daily and Sunday press.[2]

Concern relating to the harmful effects of the trend towards concentration in the British national press is not new and indeed was being expressed at the outset of the post-1945 period. It is significant that all three post-war Royal Commissions on the Press have devoted a considerable part of their time deliberating on this issue. The first Commission (1947) was unequivocal in its views:

> the monopolist, by its selection of the news and the manner in which it reports it, and by its commentary on public affairs, is in a position to determine what people shall read about the events and issues of the day and to exert a strong influence on their opinions. Even if this position is not consciously abused, a paper without competitors may fall below the standards of accuracy and efficiency which competition enforces. (Royal Commission on the Press, 1947:para 247).

The second Royal Commission on the Press (1961–2), recommended that the General Council of the Press extend its powers to include the public reporting on changes of ownership, managerial control and patterns of press development.[3] The third Commission, 1977, set up by the newly returned Wilson government, was also required as part of its brief to examine the implications for the public interest of further media concentration. Indeed in its final report the third Commission expresses the view that any further concentration of ownership from the then nine owners of national titles and the seven owners of Sunday titles 'would be regrettable' (1974–7:para 14:38). As can be appreciated from our comments relating to the four biggest owners in 1995, the situation has indeed deteriorated quite significantly since this last pronouncement of disquiet from the Royal Commission in 1977.

Realignment and depoliticisation

The effects of this trend towards concentration of ownership have been further aggravated by progressive depoliticisation of the national press since 1945, which is now particularly apparent at the most popular end of the market. In the 1939–45 period and for some time afterwards the British popular press was both radicalised and politicised with the presence of such left-of-centre titles as the *Daily Mirror, Daily Herald, Daily Worker, Reynolds News, Sunday Pictorial* and the *News Chronicle*, enjoying between them a circulation of nine million readers. Of these predominantly working-class papers, only the *Mirror* and *Sunday Mirror* (the successor to the *Sunday Pictorial*) remain as mass circulation papers on the Left. The *Morning Star* (previously the *Daily Worker*) still lives on but is only a pale shadow of its more working-class forbear. As an example of the highly politicised and radical tone of the working-class *Daily Mirror*, consider the following editorial written in 1942:

> Let it be remembered, however, that the Trades Union Congress represents the organised labour movement in this country, and, consequently, speaks with great authority on all matters where general principles are involved. At the present time, it can, for instance, help substantially in the delicate,

difficult but highly important task of linking up the widely different labour movements of Great Britain, The United States and Soviet Russia . . . Then there is another matter of principle on which the Congress should make its pronouncement. The Labour party has already demanded, without any effect whatever, the withdrawal of the ban on the *Daily Worker*. Perhaps if the powerful T.U.C adds its voice Mr Morrison will at last be impressed by the depth of democratic feeling in this matter. (*Daily Mirror*:26.8.42:3).

There are many reasons, not the least the historical moment in time, why the *Mirror's* politicised rhetoric, its international perspective and its passionate plea for the freedom of the press strike us with the kind of eloquence unknown in the mass circulation tabloids of today. It is unlikely that we shall ever see its like again.

Over the last fifty years, but in more pronounced fashion over the last twenty, the popular papers of the Left have either disappeared completely or have adjusted their tone and content to meet the needs of a new generation, allegedly less interested in the so-called serious issues of the public sphere – politics, international affairs and socio-economic development – than they are in other matters of lesser import. Indeed this adjustment is true not just for the left-wing press but for all the so-called popular mass-circulation papers of the United Kingdom. The resulting pattern in the 1990s is one which is preponderantly right-wing in its political leanings. Of the eleven national dailies only the *Guardian*, the *Daily Mirror* and *Today* support the left-of-centre. But even this support should be tempered by the fact that the *Mirror's* ability to deliver a convincing political message is severely limited since it became embroiled in a life-or-death struggle with the *Sun*, and *Today's* political allegiances, as we have already noted in Chapter 1, are curiously changeable, and for this reason, suspect. The only major daily title, therefore, which consistently supports the left with 'in depth' coverage is the *Guardian* (circulation 406,000) a broadsheet with a staunch middle-class, professional readership.

The movement away from the 'public interest' coverage towards stories of less taxing 'human interest', always apparent in the post-war press, has intensified over the last fifteen years. In its most pronounced form this trend has led to a kind of journalism that is uniquely British, and we shall examine it in the next section.

The tabloid phenomenon

The tabloids represent an important aspect of the process of commercialisation of the British press and because, as we have already noted in Chapter 1, this process is of particular relevance to new developments in the media generally in Europe, it is worth a small digression here to speculate on the reasons for its extraordinary manifestation in the British market. The term 'tabloid' used in the relation to the press has both a neutral and a pejorative sense: in the first it denotes a single, vertically folded newspaper or newspaper section, allegedly easier to read on public transport than the double folded (vertical and horizontal) broadsheet. The second meaning is more contentious and overlaid with a social and attitudinal significance which, for many, has come to designate (though not perhaps by tabloid readers themselves) the purveying of sensationalism, voyeurism, trivia and xenophobia in the name of news reporting. Such a view needs placing in perspective. There has always been in the British popular press a strand of journalism which has traded on exposing the moral peccadilloes and sexual proclivities of the famous, as well as the crimes, virtues, fortune and misfortunes of the ordinary citizen. The *News of the World* and the *People*, to name but two titles, were notorious in the 1950s and 1960s for the priority given to 'human interest' stories (a euphemism for sexual titillation) over the other more mundane stuff of public life. The complaints in recent years, however, relate to the intrusion of this kind of journalism into the national daily press and in particular in such papers as the *Sun*, the *Star*, and the *Mirror*.

Whilst the precise reasons for the growth and the extraordinary success of the mass tabloids in the UK have yet to be satisfactorily identified, we suggest that any plausible explanation of this phenomenon will have to take the following factors into account.

The powerful effects of commercial continuity and current market conditions. First, there is the historical fact mentioned earlier that the process of commercialisation in the British press has experienced an unbroken line of development from the nineteenth century up to the present day. This is in contrast to the written press of most other Western European countries for which 1945 was a major point of restructuring and political re-orientation. This means that the process of tabloidisation, so well harnessed by the owners of the *Daily Mirror* in the mid-1930s, was firstly enhanced by the huge demand for a people's paper during the period 1939–45, and secondly, the process continued totally unhindered by outside intervention in the post-1945 period. Such a head-start on the rest of Europe should not be underestimated when accounting for the current state of the British press. The industry is famous for its circulation battles – not just restricted to the tabloids, as was demonstrated by the price war between the *Times* and *Telegraph* in the mid-1990s – but fought, at the lower end of the market, on a 'tooth and nail' basis. The daily scramble to catch and keep the fickle and declining attention of the public has meant a relentless invasion by the tabloids of individual privacy, involving not only public figures (particularly politicians and members of the royal family), but ordinary people to the exclusion, at times, of almost all other news. Although the commercial factor and the cut-throat competition that it engenders are probably paramount in determining the nature of the mass tabloids, there are others which may also have played their part. For example:

Patterns of press ownership and editorial influence: the intensifying patterns of concentration of ownership increase the influence of the proprietors over editorial content. 'If Murdoch falls out with an editor he sacks them' (Ecclestone, 7 April 1994, in Franklin, 1995:7). Writing for a tabloid often means adopting an obligatory house-style and attitudes towards news coverage which is likely to be imposed either by the editor or the owner. Failure to comply usually means the departure of the journalist concerned.

De-recognition of the trades unions: the de-recognition by the employers of the professional trades unions, and of the National Union of Journalists in particular, has had the effect of removing professional standards and restraints from editors and owners. Franklin describes a growing tendency, for example, in the local press to produce what journalists contemptuously call 'advertorial', that is to say editorials which are designed specifically to attract advertisers (Franklin, 1995:8). Such practices, if they were to occur in the national press, would undoubtedly result in a lowering of journalistic standards.

Marketing by social class stratification: Britain was and still is one of the most inflexibly stratified countries in Europe in terms of social class membership. Such clear-cut divisions were, and still are, the targets of well marketed and appropriately pitched newspapers. Whilst in the 1930s, for example, there were other popular papers which represented the cause of the working classes, it was the well marketed tabloid *Daily Mirror* which outstripped them all in representing the people to the people. At the end of the century, the *Mirror* has been joined by two other mass-circulation daily tabloids, the *Star* and the *Sun* (and greatly outshone by the latter in terms of readership) and they have between them a circulation of 7.3 million predominantly working-class readers. However, as we mentioned in Chapter 1, this social group is significantly more fragmented than it was earlier this century. Thus while the socially defined market is still being accurately targeted by the mass tabloids, the clear-cut political allegiances which once distinguished the post-war working-class press from the rest have become increasingly blurred.

Education: if the quality of a national education system is to be judged by its results, then the public sector system in the UK does not emerge in a favourable light compared with its major European and other world competitors. In 1991, 56 per cent of young people in the UK between 16 and 19 years were engaged either in full-time or part-time education and training. This figure compares with 76 per cent in France, 79 per cent in Germany and 94 per cent in Japan (Green and Steedman, 1993:16). The point of drawing attention to these statistics, in the context of the tabloid phenomenon in Britain, is to suggest a possible link between relatively low educational achievement at the post-16 level and strong social class adhesion on one hand, and a strong, commercial drive to market a product appealing to both these characteristics on the other. Such a view, though, is less plausible if we try to apply the same arguments to explain the success of the German tabloid *Bild*, since in Germany educational achievement at the post-16 level is significantly better.[4] However, *Bild's* extraordinary success may be the consequence of a tabloid paper being imposed on Germany in the immediate post-war period. If its success can be explained in

45

this way then it is further evidence of the predominant role of the commercial factor in accounting for the 'tabloid phenomenon' over any other.

The behaviour of the 'new era' tabloids and their relentless pursuit of the sensational, particularly over the last few years, has provoked a heated debate in the UK about the need or otherwise for legislation specifically to curb their intrusive and distorted presentation of news. As far as intrusiveness is concerned, there can be few more intrusive newspapers in the Western World than the British mass-market tabloids. But it is the distortion factor in news presentation which gives ground for more serious concern. The failure of the mass tabloids to meet acceptable standards of professional behaviour in this area is related to the very restricted range of news items and the inadequate quality of debate on matters of public interest which they present to their readers. Thus, far from constituting a pluralistic range of opinion spread over a diverse coverage of news, they set their own very limited agendas of predominantly scandal, sport and cash competitions, intermixed with a meagre portion of national and international news. This limited agenda actually contributes to an 'information deficit' among the readers of the mass tabloids, which, fortunately, for the moment at least, is compensated for by the public service broadcasters of the BBC and ITV.

The arguments for and against the introduction of legal curbs on the excesses of the press are complex and vociferously expressed on both sides. There appear to be no easy solutions. The press generally in the United Kingdom, as we have seen, is dangerously concentrated. It could be the case that legislation designed to protect the individual from intrusion from the tabloids works mostly in favour of the powerful, in which case attempts to curb the investigative abuses of the 'new era' tabloids may also exert restraints upon the wholly desirable and legitimate investigations of other newspapers and broadcasters. In the current climate of media concentration, legislation intended to curb the tabloids but used instead to restrain other sectors of the media would be an outcome that the democratic process in this country can ill afford (see below for a more detailed discussion under 'Legislation and regulation').

The press in 1995

The national daily press in the United Kingdom can be divided into three principal categories (Seymour-Ure 1992:30) as follows:

- The so-called 'quality' broadsheets – the *Guardian, Times, Independent, Daily Telegraph* and *Financial Times.*
- The 'middle-market tabloids' – *Daily Express, Daily Mail* and *Today.*
- The 'mass tabloids' (also referred to as the 'new era' tabloid in this book) – *Sun, Daily Mirror, Daily Record* (Scotland only) and the *Star* (see Table 2.4 for Sunday titles).

The three categories are distinguished one from the other mainly on criteria relating to the range of content and its conceptual level (including length of articles) and to social group distribution. Generally speaking (and therefore to oversimplify), the broadsheets are read by the better educated, the wealthy and the relatively wealthy, whereas the new era tabloids attract the less literate and the less socially privileged. The middle ground is occupied by three titles, the *Daily Express*, the *Daily Mail* and *Today*, which attract readers from both the other categories, but the *Daily Mail* also targets women readers, and the *Daily Express* has difficulty in shedding a middle-aged image. *Today* has recently changed its political colours and has been successful in modestly increasing its readership as the result.

In Tables 2.3 and 2.4 each national daily and Sunday paper appears under the appropriate category and its circulation figures between 1988 and 1994 are compared. The spectacular increase in the circulation of *The Times* compared with the fall in circulation of the other broadsheets (with the exception of the *Financial Times*), and in particular of the *Independent*, is explained by a price war, initiated by Rupert Murdoch's News International, which reduced the price of *The Times* by half in 1994, obliging the *Telegraph* and the *Independent* to follow suit. The fall in the circulation of the *Express* is allegedly due to the current

Table 2.3   Comparative circulation 1988–95 (dailies) (in thousands)

Category	Title	1988	1995	%±
Quality	*Telegraph*	1,128	1,061	–6
broadsheets	*Times*	436	631	+45
	Financial Times	279	305	+9
	Guardian	438	400	–9
	Independent	387	290	–25
Total		2,668	2,687	+1
Middle-market	*Daily Express*	1,637	1,292	–21
tabloids	*Daily Mail*	1,759	1,794	+2
	Today[1]	548	549	0
Total		3,944	3,635	–8
Mass-market	*Sun*	4,219	4,134	–2
tabloids	*Daily Mirror*	3,157	2,476	–22
	Daily Record	–	748	NA
	Daily Star	967	741	–23
Total		8,343	8,099	–3
Overall total		**14,955**	**14,421**	**–4**

Sources: Seymour–Ure 1992 and *Media Guardian* (ABC) 24.4.95
[1] *Today* ceased publication in November 1995. See Note 10, p. 36.

Table 2.4   Comparative circulation 1988–95 (Sundays) (in thousands)

Category	Title	1988	1995	%±
Quality broadsheets	Independent on Sunday		324	NA
	Observer	722	462	–36
	Sunday Telegraph	693	694	0
	Sunday Times	1,314	1,238	–6
Total		2,729	2,718	0
Middle-market tabloids	Sunday Express	2,033	1,446	–29
	Mail on Sunday	1,919	1,933	+1
Total		3,952	3,379	–14
Mass-market tabloids	People	2,743	2,085	–24
	Sunday Mirror	2,953	2,479	–16
	News of the World	5,360	4,716	–12
Total		11,056	9,280	–16
Overall readership		**17,737**	**15,377**	**–13**

Sources: Seymour–Ure 1992 and *Media Guardian* (ABC) 24.4.95

ageing readership which is not being replaced at the younger end of the market. The declining fortunes of the *Mirror* are due in part to its recent disastrous experience under Maxwell and in part to its ongoing battle with News International's *Sun*.

Legislation and regulation

The position of the written press with regard to the law is problematic from several viewpoints and may be characterised by two principal features. First, there is an absence of a specific body of legislation enacted to deal with the written press *per se*, and secondly, and partly as the result of this, there is provision for self-regulation in the form of a Press Complaints Commission (PCC). Critics of the current situation argue that neither of these arrangements is satisfactory.

There is then no specific legislation relating to the status, function and obligation of the written press in the United Kingdom as exists in other European countries. Viewed in a positive light it could be argued that this absence of legislation, also constitutes a *de facto* absence of censorship. But whatever surface attractions such arguments may possess, they should be quickly dispelled by reference to the consequences of the current legal and regulatory arrangements. These are, as we have already noted, a worrying over-concentration of ownership on one hand, and on the other, a mass tabloid section of the press whose professional standards and general behaviour appear almost to be out of control.

With regard to the issue of concentration, takeovers and mergers of the press are monitored by the Office of Fair Trading (OFT). Sections 57 to 62 of the Fair Trading Act (1973) specifically deal with press mergers and the latter may be referred to the Monopolies Commission in cases deemed to be prejudicial to the public interest. But, as we have already noted, recent interpretations by the OFT of what appears to be a loophole in the law relating to takeovers and mergers, have particularly favoured prospective buyers of newspapers at the expense of the public interest requirement of a pluralistic press. Thus it has been possible for Rupert Murdoch's News International to acquire five national titles – *News of the World, Sunday Times, Today, The Times* and the *Sun* – without ever having been referred to the Monopolies Commission!

In addition to what appear to be these ineffectual laws relating to monopolies, Franklin (1995:6) identifies no less than forty-six other Acts which indirectly impose restrictions upon the press, ranging over such diverse fields as the Criminal Justice Act (1988), the Prevention of Terrorism Act (1989) and the Children's and Young Persons Act (1969). What is absent from this miscellaneous body of law, which indirectly controls the British press, is legislation, at the level of the commercial organisation of the newspaper industry, which effectively deals with the issue of press concentration.[5] Similarly, at the professional level, there are no laws which explicitly set standards of professional conduct, by, among other means, prohibiting (a) the falsification of news; (b) the invasion of individual privacy or; (c) the imposition of a 'commercial censorship' in the form of human rather than public interest stories.

In place of statutory controls of such matters, the British press industry reluctantly accepted the recommendations of the first post-war Royal Commission (1947) which proposed that the sector should be self-regulating under a Press Council and, to this end, a General Council of the Press was established in 1953. It is this body which, in theory at least, for nearly four decades was the guardian of the newspaper industry's conscience and the arbiter of its ethical standards and general professional behaviour.

In reality, the evidence suggests that self-regulation of this kind, operated by the Press Council and latterly by the Press Complaints Commission, has not achieved its objectives. The reasons for this failure are not difficult to perceive. Firstly, the original Press Council, as we have seen, was imposed upon the industry which for the most part rejected the need for self-regulation. Secondly, it was financially dependent upon the very newspapers whose conduct it was supposed to monitor and regulate. Predictably, in such circumstances, the Press Council was too weak to deal with its unruly patrons, and unable to impose upon the industry the standards of conduct called for by successive Commissions. In the words of its successor, the Press Complaints Commission (itself the object of much recent criticism):

'The Council never achieved sufficient authority or respect to impose its standards on all newspapers and refused persistently over the years to frame a Code of Practice though one was adopted belatedly in 1990' (PCC November 1994).

The continuing unruly behaviour of the mass tabloids which had begun in earnest in the 1980s 'failed to observe the basic ethics of journalism' and prompted many people to call for the establishment of a statutory press council possessing legally enforceable sanctions. In the event, the government commissioned an investigation into the alleged malpractices of the press under the direction of David Calcutt QC. In 1990 Calcutt recommended that the Press Council should be scrapped and be replaced by the Press Complaints Commission, which would be required to demonstrate over an eighteen-month period that non-statutory press regulation could be made to work. In 1993 a second Calcutt Report found that the PCC had not fulfilled its mission and proposed the setting up of a Statutory Complaints Tribunal and the creation of three new criminal offences relating to the acquisition of information by trespass; the using of surveillance equipment on private property or the taking of photographs on private property without the owner's consent (Calcutt 1993:51).

Calcutt's recommendations of 1993 have not been implemented. The reason for this unwillingness to act is presumably that the dangers of political interference in the running of the press potentially constitute a bigger threat to democracy (or perhaps to the interests of a political party) than the current state of unruliness that exists in some areas. As Franklin says: 'Some MPs offer a generalised support for the idea of statutory press controls but their conviction crumbles when the detail of particular recommendations are unravelled' (Franklin 1995:13).

The PCC has survived, then, on the principle of 'better the devil you know'. When evaluating its recent performance as well as its future as a regulatory body, two factors should be borne in mind: firstly, it is still funded on a voluntary basis by the newspapers that it is supposed to regulate. Moreover, this funding is commonly held to be insufficient for the task that the PCC is supposed to fulfil. Secondly, the distribution and the nature of the complaints received by the Commission in 1994 strongly suggest that the mass tabloids are as determined as ever to accept nothing more than the absolute minimum level of regulation, and indeed frequently break their own agreed Code of Practice. This is true particularly when they are in pursuit of public figures. Since 1989 there has been a constant pursuit by these papers of members of the Conservative government, and several ministers and government officials have been forced into resignation by revelations of alleged sexual or financial misdemeanours. There appears to be no let-up in the tone and intentions of the tabloids to seek out and to reveal the most intimate secrets of the great and the good. In May 1994, for example, no less than five complaints were received from Buckingham Palace alleging serious breaches of the Code by five separate tabloids obtaining photographs of Prince Andrew using long-lens cameras. All, perhaps unsurprisingly, were upheld. Despite loud calls for statutory control of the media in this area, from both the main political parties, neither is likely to advocate the taking of the legal steps necessary to implement the Calcutt proposals in the near future, not just for the reasons already outlined above, but also because neither wishes to antagonise the rowdy tabloids further in the run-up to the next election.

In addition to the Calcutt proposals for the statutory reform of the press, there are others which have been put forward from all political parties as well as sections of the media themselves. These proposals can be summarised as follows for the written press:

- The strengthening of the PCC Code of Practice and the removal of ambiguities in it relating to key areas of journalistic behaviour.
- The obligatory inclusion of a statement of adherence to the Code of Practice to be included in all journalists' contracts.
- The legal protection of journalists' rights of independence from editorial and other outside influences.
- A statutory right of reply for injured parties resulting from media misrepresentation, to be given equal prominence as the offending article in the newspaper concerned.
- A new Freedom of Information Act, not just at national but also at a European level of government.
- A new, reformed libel law.

On the issue of press ownership and multi-media concentration,[6] there are proposals which call for:

- The reform of the Fair Trading Act, with particular reference to the sections relating to press ownership.
- The introduction of a points system by which points are attributed to media owners according to an established set of criteria relating to the power and influence which is calculated to accrue from a particular combination of media holdings. Once the maximum number of points were recorded no further media ownership would be permitted (whilst an interesting proposal, the difficulties in establishing the criteria for points allocation are potentially very great).
- One owner, one title. A wholly effective answer to press concentration but impracticable within western, liberal democracy, currently dominated by market forces.

As far as the future is concerned, the prospect of a change of government has received a mixed reception from those who campaign for the reform of press policy. Fifteen years of *laissez-faire* policies have allowed major groups to consolidate their position in the market and indeed, the issue of the concentration of one medium, the written press, has been superseded by a growing concern relating to cross-media ownership (see below in 'III Broadcasting media'). The extent to which a new government of the Left would go in the direction of media reform is not clear. A front-bench spokesman[7] from the Labour Party is on record as reaffirming the party's determination to take action on cross-media ownership, but at this stage its commitment to tackling the question of the current ownership of the written press is unclear. On the question of professional standards, a future government of the Left would be more inclined to support and reinforce the arm of the PCC (by, for example, strengthening the terms of the Code of Practice) than by introducing statutory controls. At the same time, it is likely that the libel laws would be modified to permit cheaper and easier access to compensation. It is likely too that there would be a new Freedom of Information Act, as well as a new Bill of Rights.

The magazine sector

In keeping with a European trend, the magazine sector in the United Kingdom has experienced an almost unbroken period of expansion over the last two decades of the century. There are currently over 70 publishing houses or their subsidiaries operating in Britain, accounting between them for nearly 7,000 professional and consumer magazines. These publishers vary in size from the relatively small, specialising in titles of an academic, legal, medical or technical nature, to the massive international conglomerate, the largest of which in Britain is Reed/Elsevier (the result of merger between the British and Dutch publishing giants in 1992). As the result of this merger, Reed/Elsevier now ranks among the world's largest magazine publishers such as Bauer, Burda and Gruner Jahr who are operating in the British market as well as extensively elsewhere in Europe.

Consumer magazines derive approximately 50 per cent of their revenue from advertising, and despite the predictions in some quarters of the demise of certain consumer magazine titles as the result of increased commercial competition from television, the majority have survived albeit with reduced advertising revenue into the 1990s. This survival is due, firstly, to the tenacity of individual titles to hang on to their readership in the face of greater competition, and secondly, to the growing tendency on the part of magazines to serve 'niche' markets in which they target specifically identifiable socio-economic groups, particularly, of late, young, single men and women.

In the consumer category, the leading titles are the mass circulation *Radio Times* (1.6 million), the *Readers Digest* (1.5 million) and *What's on TV?* (1.4 million) (Peake, 1993:55–6). As elsewhere in Europe, women's magazines are a dynamic and aggressively contested area of the market. Titles of the more traditional kind such as *Woman's Own* and *Woman* have experienced a serious decline in circulation since 1987, whereas, relative newcomers, trading on a more assertive, more open and candid image, such as *Marie-Claire*, have achieved dramatically increased circulations, particularly among young professional women. The popular end of the women's market is now firmly occupied by two relative newcomers, *Take a Break*, and *Bella*, both owned by the German publisher Bauer and with circulations of over a million each. The latter is an example of the significant penetration of the British market by a German group, and it well illustrates the kind of horizontal expansion across national boundaries we referred to in Chapter 1. In one important sense (the economic) it represents a kind of Europeanisation of the media and progress towards a single market in this area at least. For the most part, this phenomenon is, as we have said, economic in nature, involving the investment of foreign capital in a national market. However, as Lamizet points out in Chapter 7, the advertising activity of these 'glossies' frequently promotes the consumption of 'Euro-products' (perfume, cosmetics, tourism, cars, food, etc.) and is accompanied by a socio-cultural exchange of information which is both European and transnational in nature. A detailed account of the major European players (the German media groups) in this sector is given in Chapter 4).

III The broadcasting media

We have already discussed in Chapter 1 the phenomenon of social fragmentation which has characterised Western European society during the second half of the twentieth century and noted its interrelationship with the media. We have pointed out that this process is reflected in the written press, of which one good example is the spectacular growth and diversity of titles to be found in the magazine sector. In radio too we find a similar process of audience fragmentation taking place throughout Europe, and the United Kingdom is no exception to this trend. To give some idea of the extent of this process, in 1950 the BBC possessed a virtual monopoly of radio broadcasting in the UK, with three main programmes, the Home Service, the Light Programme and the Third Programme; today it has lost more than half its listeners to commercial operators which between them possess over 150 stations.

BBC radio

It is worth noting briefly here that it was BBC radio under the extraordinary influence of its first director, John Reith, which laid the foundations of public service broadcasting both in the UK and subsequently elsewhere in the world. Notwithstanding attempts by British politicians to influence its policies and its programming, it was Reith, variously described as 'authoritarian', 'illiberal' and 'meglomanic' (see Curran and Seaton, 1988:142 ff) who imposed upon the new corporation his own personal vision of public service. This vision was translated into reality by the creation of a national broadcasting service which attempted, at least, to be impartial in politics, enriching in cultural content and, above all, accessible to all of the people. According to Curran, by the mid-1930s 'radio was a central component of British culture' (Curran and Seaton, 1988:144). By 1941 it was, according to the same authors, 'the most important medium for information in Britain'.[8] The status of the BBC as the major source of information declined in the post-war period, firstly because demand for news itself was less intense, and secondly because its supremacy in this field was soon to be challenged by the new medium of television. Nevertheless, at the end of the twentieth century, BBC radio occupies an affectionate, prestigious and influential place in the everyday lives of the people. In the space of the last fifty years, however, this status has had to be constantly fought for, renewed and modified, in the face of several developments which threatened it, not the least of which emerged from the commercial sector.

As we have mentioned above, radio had already established itself as a medium of mass communication in the pre-1945 period. After 1945 two factors especially were to intervene in its fortunes which would help guarantee its future but, at the same time, bring about a partial and significant change in direction. The first was the coming of age in the 1960s of the so-called 'baby-boomers' of the immediate post-war generation. The development of this group of young people into a separate socio-economic stratum in the early 1960s, with their own tastes in clothes and music, created a special demand which, at first, went unrecognised by the BBC (or, if recognised, unacknowledged), to its cost. The second was the technological advance made in electronics which enabled manufacturers to produce a cheap, attractive, and highly portable radio which was to become the ubiquitous emblem of the 'swinging sixties': the transistor. The BBC was slow to meet the new demands created by changing socio-cultural behaviour and the new technology, and the opportunity was seized, initially at least, by the so-called 'pirate stations' transmitting from ships outside British territorial waters. Their schedules were relentlessly aimed at the young, and had the distinct advantage of being free to broadcast the innovatory and exciting music of the emerging youth culture, unheard, or banned even, on the BBC. Whilst a startled government contemplated the implications of pirate radio transmissions (and ultimately found the means to close them down), the BBC made belated but effective moves to set up its own 'pop' station aimed specifically at the younger generation, resulting in the launch of Radio 1 in 1967.

In retrospect, the development of commercial radio, which had been inaugurated in the early 1960s by the pirate stations, was inevitable and its progress was only halted temporarily by the creation of Radio 1. The BBC, after all, was not in the business of selling records (or indeed anything else) at that time, and yet the significant difference between its Radio 1 audience and the rest of its listeners was that, to some extent, young people perceived the programming of the new station as 'product' (i.e. records, cassettes, musical instruments) which they subsequently purchased along with other associated by-products such as cosmetics, clothes and other lifestyle commodities. With such a unique relationship between programme content and commodity it was inevitable that commercial broadcasting in its own right would develop in competition with Radio 1. This happened in 1973 when the first legal commercial station began transmissions in London. Before returning to the current public service/commercial broadcasting division which neatly bisects the listening habits in the United Kingdom, this would be an appropriate moment to examine a little more closely the programming profiles and latest developments in station activities of BBC radio.

As we have already noted, it was in BBC radio that the public service concept of broadcasting was first developed and nurtured. This tradition presupposes the provision of information, education and entertainment, possibly in that order of priority, to an audience universally capable of receiving the transmission regardless of geographical location. To this day much of this tradition of public service is still intact, albeit in a modified form, in the Corporation's radio schedules. Radio 4 still retains a wholly mixed range of programming which includes high-status news coverage – *Today*, *The World at One* and *The World Tonight*; in-depth programmes of national and international political analysis; quizzes; chat shows; drama, phone-ins and musical events. Radio 4 is predominantly a talk programme with a strong, partisan and possessive audience, and a quality of news coverage that is deemed to be second to none in up-to-the-minute, informed reporting. It has high status, not only among the listeners of so-called 'middle England', but also among the great and the good – if, that is, their eagerness to be interviewed for *Today*, in particular, is any measure of its reputation. Radio 4 currently has 11 per cent of the radio audience in the United Kingdom (see Figure 2.1).

If Radio 4 is the epitome of high quality and highly successful public service broadcasting, Radio 3 is singularly less successful in its bid for a place in the broadcasting arena. Never intended as a mass-audience station, it is essentially a classical music programme,

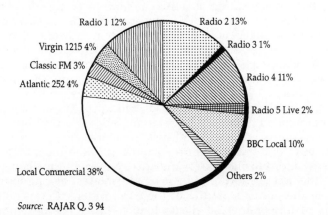

Radio 1 12%
Radio 2 13%
Virgin 1215 4%
Radio 3 1%
Classic FM 3%
Atlantic 252 4%
Radio 4 11%
Radio 5 Live 2%
BBC Local 10%
Local Commercial 38%
Others 2%

Source: RAJAR Q, 3 94

Figure 2.1   Current share of radio listening

but has inherited the high-brow image and cultural baggage of the educated middle classes which, by definition, leaves it remote and isolated from the majority of listeners. Despite recent attempts to make the programming more listener-friendly, Radio 3 has lost ground recently to the national commercial channel Classic FM. The latter has over two years gained an audience that is three times greater than the BBC station.

Radio 2 remains the BBC's most popular station and retains its place ahead of Radio 4 as the United Kingdom's most listened-to national programme. Radio 2 is a music-plus-talk station which targets the non-adolescent listener with a schedule comprising mainstream, popular music, light entertainment and news. It is the antithesis of Radio 3. Self-mocking in its preference for the ordinary, it projects an up-beat and cheerful image of itself. Above all else, it is easy on the ear and undemanding on the brain. Its place in the BBC's future plans for radio must be assured, if for no other reason than it consistently heads the ratings, and in many ways delivers to its audience an apparent casual mix of popular programming which belies what is, in reality, a finely tuned response to listener demand.

Radio 5 Live is the newest comer to the BBC's radio family of stations. Originally conceived as a young people's station featuring sport, programmes for schools and news, in 1994 Radio 5 changed its name slightly, and moved in a different direction to become a 24-hour news and sports station. Its educative programming was moved to Radio 3 and its target audience enlarged to include the non-adolescent news-hungry insomniac. Radio 5 Live initially met with opposition from the newly established Radio 5 audience as well as from the opponents of a rolling news programme. This case appears to have been lost, however, as Radio 5 Live continues to consolidate a modest place among the partner stations of the BBC.

The area of greatest concern for BBC radio is the one surrounding the future of Radio 1. As we have already noted, this station targets what must be the most volatile of the BBC's radio audiences, the teenage/early twenties age group. Yet during its life-span of nearly three decades, it has enjoyed the unswerving loyalty of huge audiences of young people dedicated to its trend-setting music and its celebrity disc jockeys who audibly sparkle with vernacular wit, cheeky familiarity and cultural 'street cred'. Faced with the increasing competition from the commercial sector in 1993, the BBC decided to reorganise Radio 1 with the appointment of a new controller and the removal of many of its established disc jockeys. These changes were no doubt intended to increase the station's appeal to the young but the policy was controversial and high-risk in nature. The BBC was seen by many to be attempting a major re-shaping of Radio 1 at a time when it could least afford to alienate its audience. No doubt the planners were prepared to accept short-term losses in the interest of long-term gains, but given the dramatic nature of the current defection of millions of listeners to its commercial rivals, it looks as if the BBC may have miscalculated in its strategy. Between January 1994 and January 1995,

Radio 1 lost almost 5 million listeners. Some moved back to Radio 2 but the majority abandoned Radio 1 for pastures new in the commercial sector. It is most unlikely that Radio 1 will ever command audiences of the size it enjoyed in its heyday of the 1970s.

BBC local radio

In addition to its populist, new national station, Radio 1, the BBC, following the recommendations of the Pilkington Committee, launched itself into local radio in 1968. As Seymour-Ure points out, in the beginning, the setting up of local radio was a 'shoestring operation' which had to be paid for out of the existing licence fee (Seymore-Ure, 1992:79). Today the local radio of the BBC has expanded to 38 stations with, in addition, three major regional networks for Scotland, Ireland and Wales, and has a 10 per cent share of the total radio audience. BBC local radio distinguishes itself from local, commercial radio in several important ways, not the least of which is that 60 per cent of its audience is in the 55+ age group which, significantly, is the one of least interest to the advertisers. It also distinguishes itself more positively in the provision of superior news and information service as well as by a wider range of speech programmes. The BBC has attracted much criticism over the last decade for allegedly neglecting the local and regional side of its operations in favour of a distinct metropolitan, southern bias. In response to this criticism, the BBC has embarked on a new policy of reinvestment in regional production which, if they succeed, will have undoubted benefits for local radio particularly in the area of news and information. In the meantime the BBC claims to have increased further the proportion of speech content in local radio from 70 per cent to 80 per cent in 1993–4, as well as to have increased the reach of local radio from 20 per cent to 22 per cent of the population (BBC Reports and Accounts 1993–4).

The BBC World Service

On the other extreme of radio broadcasting activity from local radio, the BBC is also one of the major international broadcasters worldwide with an estimated audience of 130 million, 12.5 million of which is located in Europe. The World Service, which broadcasts in 39 languages, is funded directly by the government and targets six main world regions (audience in brackets): Americas (8 million); Europe (12.5 million); Africa and the Middle East (42.5 million); Former Soviet Union and SW Asia (7.5 million); South Asia (52.5 million); Asia Pacific (7.5 million) (source BBC World Service). The World Service is a curious historical mixture of British altruism and self-interest. On the one hand, true to its public service tradition, it provides an impartial but nevertheless British perspective on world events whilst, on the other, it seeks to enhance British standing, diplomacy and trading position throughout the world. The government grant which finances the World Service has been progressively reduced over three years from 1995, thus necessitating considerable efficiency savings. For the first time the World Service will be exposed to the controversial 'Producer Choice' system already operating in the rest of the Corporation, designed to open it up to a more market-oriented approach to production.

Commercial radio

The autumn of 1994 was a landmark in the history of radio broadcasting in the United Kingdom. At this point the size of audience listening to commercial radio surpassed for the first time the number of listeners tuning in to the BBC. In retrospect it can be seen that the turning point in the fortunes of commercial radio dates from the early 1980s, when, encouraged by the entrepreneurial zeal of the Thatcher administration, stations began experimenting in earnest in 'narrowcasting'. This they achieved by transmitting different programmes on FM and AM frequencies respectively, targeting different social groups, whereas previously they had 'simulcasted' the same programme on both frequencies. They also began to encroach on each other's territories but with distinguishing, specialised schedules. This expansion was subsequently given added impetus by the provisions of the Broadcasting Act (1990), which removed the obligation previously placed upon commercial radio to provide a range of programming, as well as loosening the restrictions relating to advertising itself (Peake, 1993:110). The Act also provided for the setting up of three national commercial radio stations (INR) which has resulted in the granting of licences to Classic FM, Virgin Radio and Talk Radio.

The result has been impressive, both in terms of the number of new local stations (ILR) which have been created since the early 1980s – there has been an increase of approximately 100[9] – and in terms of advertising revenue, which has risen from £60.8 million in 1982 to £178.5 million in 1995. However, despite this significant increase, the revenue derived by commercial radio in the United Kingdom, as percentage share of the overall national advertising 'spend', still only hovers between 2 per cent and 3 per cent. Figures 2.2 and 2.3 indicate the development, in both audience and revenue terms, of commercial radio since the take-off point in the early 1980s.

The success of commercial radio in building large audiences in the United Kingdom may be ascribed to many factors, not the least of which must be the ease by which the medium is broadcast and received by its audiences. Compared with television, the capital outlay and running costs of operating a radio station are low. In addition, in contrast to the extra cost involved by the viewer in order to receive cable or satellite television, there is often no additional outlay required on the part of the listener to receive a new radio station. It is estimated that 97 per cent of British homes possess at least one radio with the majority possessing two or more. Radios are also almost a standard provision in motor vehicles of all kinds. If to

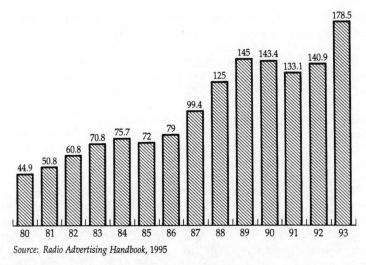

Source: *Radio Advertising Handbook*, 1995

Figure 2.2   Radio advertising revenue 1980–93 (£ million)

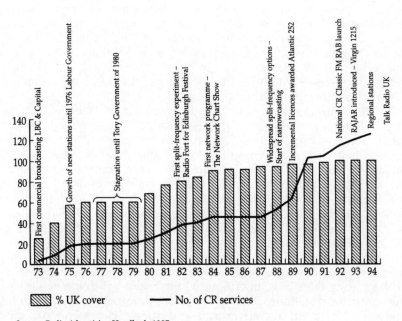

Source: *Radio Advertising Handbook*, 1995

Figure 2.3   The development of commercial radio in the UK

59

these important factors is added the availability of a listening audience culturally disposed to satisfying ever more individualised tastes, then the reasons for the conquest of the air-waves by the commercial stations become more understandable. Even so, as we have already noted, the revenue attracted to commercial radio remains relatively modest at around 3 per cent of the advertising spend for all media, despite its impressive increase in audience. Technological advances, especially in the field of digital radio, will offer commercial operators new possibilities for expansion over the next decade. But stations will be obliged to 'dualcast' using both the existing 'old' technology as well as the new digital kind in order to maintain contact with their audiences during the transition period.

By definition, the exploitation of the 'niche' market by the policy of narrowcasting – the offering of specialised, thematic programmes (jazz, phone-ins, pop-music, religion) to specially targeted audiences (teenagers, compulsive talkers, ethnic minorities) – is a significantly different activity from that of public service broadcasting of the kind found on Radios 2 and 4. It is tempting to draw a parallel between the effects of the entertainment bias in commercial radio and the similar inclination in the tabloid journalism in the written press. Such a comparison would lead to the conclusion that commercial radio listeners will develop an 'information deficit' (and, in consequence, a loss of their democratic rights) resulting from a constant in-put of non-informational biased programming. But this would be to overlook other important factors and, in consequence, to oversimplify the issue. In fact, research indicates that radio audiences, whilst remaining loyal to their preferred stations, do listen to more than one, spread across the public service/commercial divide (see Figure 2.1 above). Radio stations, unlike newspapers, are free and listeners move across frequencies at literally no cost. In these circumstances, radio may indeed be considered to be the most accessible, and by extension, the most democratic medium of them all.

The BBC enjoys, as we have already noted, a formidable experience in programming of all kinds, and its place as a major influence upon British national culture must be considered secure in the foreseeable future. Even so, the proposal, unthinkable two decades ago, to privatise all or parts of the corporation was successfully placed on the agenda of policy options by the Thatcher government. In 1986 the Peacock Report recommended that the BBC should have the option to privatise Radios 1 and 2 (Peacock Report, 1986:Rec. 7a). In the event the BBC has declined the option to sell off two of its mass-audience stations, convinced rightly that its public service mission still finds strong support among its Radio 2 listeners, and that it will ultimately stabilise and even increase its listening share at the cutting edge of competition, where Radio 1 is doing battle with the commercial stations. Putting this issue somewhat crudely from the opposing viewpoint, the advertisers and commercial operators regard the BBC as occupying 50 per cent of the radio landscape, some of which would be more appropriately located in the commercial sector.

For the time being at least, it is on the frontier between Radio 1 and the commercial sector that future losses and gains will be counted.

Regulation and legislation

Commercial radio in the United Kingdom is operated within the statutory provisions of the Broadcasting Act 1990.[10] It is regulated by the Radio Authority (established by a provision of the Act in 1990). The Radio Authority is responsible for the allocation of frequencies, the awarding of licences and the regulation of programmes and radio advertising. It is also the major policy-making body for the commercial radio sector. This statutory regulation of commercial radio stands in marked contrast to the regulation of the written press in the United Kingdom. (For regulation of the BBC see below in the television section.)

The BBC–ITV duopoly

Of all the controversies, political manoeuvres, and shifting alliances in the market which characterised the development of the British media over the decade 1986–96, those relating to television have been the most intense and confusing. The intensity spings from the nature of television itself: its power of influence over the viewing public on the one hand, and the potential glittering prizes for its financial backers on the other. The confusion derives from the complexity of interests which are at stake whose expression does not divide into the conventionally recognisable arguments of the political left or right.

It would be to distort the picture to characterise the situation in the UK, with regard to television, as one in which the BBC alone has been under constant siege from a hostile government over the last fifteen years. This has indeed been the case, but we need to complete the picture by adding that the other (commercial) channels (Channels 3 and 4) have also had to bear the brunt of a government assault culminating in the Broadcasting Act of 1990, and the radical reorganisation of the private sector beginning in 1991.

Thus currently in the UK we find heads and former heads of commercial channels in the unlikely company of left-wing politicians, media specialists, journalists and high-ranking figures from the BBC all making common cause against the government in the alleged interests of public service broadcasting. In the other camp we find neo-Thatcherites, cable and satellite owners, advertising agencies, advertisers and, occasionally, members of the far-Left, exhorting the government to ever more deregulatory extremes in the alleged democratic interest of media freedom. These conflicting attitudes are not of course restricted to the United Kingdom; the struggle between public service broadcasting interests and those of the commercial sector may be found in varying degrees of intensity in all other countries of Western Europe. But the difference in the case of the UK is that the lines between public service broadcasting and commercial broadcasting are not co-terminous with the BBC and ITV (Independent Television) but instead overlap. A strong public service broadcasting responsibility is perceived to be undertaken by all of the four channels – BBC1, BBC2, Channel 3 and Channel 4 – and not to fall exclusively within the remit of the BBC.

The development of the television system in the UK is interesting for its paradoxes and, in one respect at least, for its uniqueness, when compared with its European counterparts. Although the BBC operated an experimental service from 1936 to 1939, it was not until 1946 that the first 'popular' channel began transmissions on a PSB model derived from the radio. The next decade, 1946–56, was one of rapid expansion, firstly in audience which, through the building of new transmitters, increased from 12 million in 1946 to 36 million ten years later (Seymour-Ure 1992:85). Secondly, a new and highly controversial commercial channel was launched in 1955. This event was unique in Western Europe and instrumental in shaping the development of television in the UK for the next forty years. This claim, as it stands, is slightly misleading: it can be restated more clearly perhaps by saying that it was the creation of a commercial channel *at that particular juncture* which was the determining factor, for reasons we shall now examine.

In the post-war decade the reputation of PSB was riding high in the country: the first real consumer generation of the 1960s was still a decade away and any other model of broadcasting, other than the BBC, was either unacceptable (i.e. the US model) or non-existent. The new channel, however, was not intended to be a pale handmaiden of the BBC. In the eyes of its advocates, including Winston Churchill, it was destined to become a 'cultural liberator' which would take television 'out of the hands of the elitist' and by so doing 'challenge the post-war complacency of the BBC' (Curran and Seaton, 1988:209). But despite this intention, stated or covert, to shake up the BBC, the approach to the creation and regulation of the proposed commercial channel was cautious, to say the least. The 1954 Act set down procedures governing production which were designed to guarantee both the range and the quality of programmes, as well as to protect the producers from the influence of advertisers. These procedures were to be enforced by the setting up of the first regulatory body, the Independent Television Authority (ITA).[11] The effect of the 1954 Act was effectively the creation of a second state monopoly which was free to compete with the BBC for audience but not for revenue (since the BBC was licence-funded, and the new channel would be funded entirely from advertising). In the early period, the euphemistically named Independent Television Channel succeeded in outperforming its rival in key areas such as news coverage and entertainment, thus extending its audience appeal, particularly among the working classes. The upshot of the undoubted success of the first commercial channel was the creation of what has come to be known as the 'television duopoly' in the UK. This term designated the development from 1955 onwards of a comfortable co-existence between the public service and the commercial sectors wherein competition was limited to issues of quality, and tacit agreements on mutually beneficial scheduling commonplace. The uniqueness of this development is, as we have said, due to the comparatively early intervention of the commercial sector in a national television system. The consequence is that, unlike the more recent interventions by the commercial sector in Europe in the 1980s, deemed generally to be luke-warm with regard to the public service tradition, the earlier British intervention is now considered to have been distinctly beneficial. Notwithstanding the undoubtedly commercial interests of ITV, it is clear, from any examination of its past or present scheduling, that is has absorbed many of the qualities of public service broadcasting to which it has been exposed for forty years. In reverse token, confronted by the innovatory programme-making of ITV, and the resultant wider audience appeal generated by the commercial channel, the BBC also adapted its style, and approach to scheduling, in the eyes of most observers, for the better.

Deregulation

Tunstall (1992:238) points out that media development in the UK has been characterised by policies of 'gradualism' and that is in contrast to the rapid changes imposed on the media in other countries of Western Europe. This is particularly true of developments up to 1980. After that period it could be argued that advances in technology dictated a faster rate of change, on the one hand, and that the more strident voices of government called for faster and more radical moves against the BBC on the other.

The Thatcher government placed the duopoly of the BBC and ITV under close scrutiny in 1986 when the Peacock Committee was commissioned to investigate alternative funding for the BBC.[12] The Peacock Report, in retrospect, represents what has been recognised as the high-water mark of Thatcherism in relation to broadcasting. Whilst the Peacock Report was to make some radical proposals for the funding of the BBC, it rejected the possibility of advertising on the grounds that this method would reduce consumer choice and divert potential revenue from other fledgeling sectors such as cable and satellite (Peacock Report, 1986:para 617). Instead it recommended that the BBC be funded by subscription in the late 1990s, offering the view that the BBC's success would depend on its capacity to market its services (Peacock Report, 1986:para 673). The cultural in-put to programming, Peacock contended, could be safeguarded by the establishment of a Public Service Broadcasting Council (a kind of Arts Council of the air-waves) which would allocate funding for cultural programming although it would not necessarily be obliged to support the BBC. Partly because such plans were politically highly sensitive (the public was in the main against privatisation), and partly because of Mrs Thatcher's abrupt ejection from power in 1990, the Peacock proposals relating to funding for the BBC were not implemented and all further talk of privatisation or alternative funding has ended. This is not to suggest that the matter is resolved in the long term, and many observers see the reluctance on the part of the government to deprive the BBC of its licence funding, as a temporary state of affairs (Smith, 1991:311). However, the BBC has been guaranteed funding (albeit reduced) for a further five years and its Royal Charter will be renewed in 1996. Nevertheless, since 1990, the government has exerted relentless financial pressure on the BBC which, in response, has undergone major reorganisation involving a large reduction in staff, a shift to short-term contracts, and the introduction of a new system, 'Producer's Choice', by which funding is devolved to the programme-makers who can, if necessary, buy in their technical and other production needs on the open market. According to the BBC, the result has been increased efficiency to the tune of £100 million, half of which has been re-invested into programming and the improvement of regional services. However, the price paid in corporate morale, particularly among the programme-makers, appears to be a heavy one.

Somewhat ironically, it is the commercial sector (ITV) which was most affected by the Peacock proposals. The Report recommended that the ITV franchises should be put out to competitive tender (Peacock Report, 1986:para 655). This recommendation was implemented by the Broadcasting Act of 1990, and in 1991 the existing entirety of the ITV franchises were auctioned to the highest bidder. All the incumbent ITV companies placed bids for the new franchises involving, as one observer put it, nothing more than 'a chain of guesses' taking into account other bidders, potential revenue from advertising and other economic factors. Some like Border Television bid astonishingly small amounts (£2,000) whilst others like Carlton were obliged to offer much larger sums (£43.1 million) (see Figure 2.4). Since 1993 the way has been cleared for the exposure of the successful television companies to the full rigours of the stock market and the possibility of hostile takeovers either from other ITV companies or from outside bidders wishing to enter the commercial television arena (Alvarado *et al*, 1992:333). The map showing the originally successful franchise bids of 1992 (Figure 2.4) has indeed changed as the result of takeovers and mergers. There have in fact been four takeovers since 1992 – Carlton has taken over Central; Granada has taken LWTV, Meridian has Anglia, and Yorkshire Television merged with Tyne Tees.

The upshot of government policy from 1986 to 1996, beginning with the Peacock Report and continuing with other White Papers, both before and after the passing of the Broadcasting Act of 1990, has been to focus the minds of the BBC and ITV upon the strictly business side of broadcasting, relegating issues of quality, content and programming policy to the margins of the debate. As one former head of London Weekend Television put it: 'The problem is that the 1990 Broadcasting Act effectively told the ITV companies that being a business was more important than being a broadcaster . . . There has been a significant shift of power' (Dyke, 1994). This shift of power away from the broadcaster and towards the accountant will

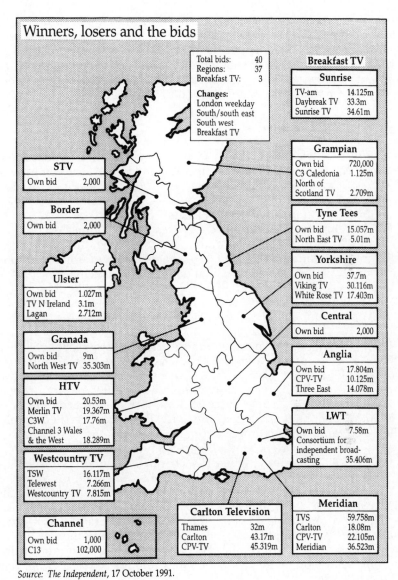

Winners, losers and the bids

Total bids:	40
Regions:	37
Breakfast TV:	3

Changes:
London weekday
South/south east
South west
Breakfast TV

Breakfast TV

Sunrise	
TV-am	14.125m
Daybreak TV	33.3m
Sunrise TV	34.61m

STV	
Own bid	2,000

Grampian	
Own bid	720,000
C3 Caledonia	1.125m
North of Scotland TV	2.709m

Border	
Own bid	2,000

Tyne Tees	
Own bid	15.057m
North East TV	5.01m

Yorkshire	
Own bid	37.7m
Viking TV	30.116m
White Rose TV	17.403m

Ulster	
Own bid	1.027m
TV N Ireland	3.1m
Lagan	2.712m

Central	
Own bid	2,000

Granada	
Own bid	9m
North West TV	35.303m

Anglia	
Own bid	17.804m
CPV-TV	10.125m
Three East	14.078m

HTV	
Own bid	20.53m
Merlin TV	19.367m
C3W	17.76m
Channel 3 Wales & the West	18.289m

LWT	
Own bid	7.58m
Consortium for independent broadcasting	35.406m

Westcountry TV	
TSW	16.117m
Telewest	7.266m
Westcountry TV	7.815m

Meridian	
TVS	59.758m
Carlton	18.08m
CPV-TV	22.105m
Meridian	36.523m

Channel	
Own bid	1,000
C13	102,000

Carlton Television	
Thames	32m
Carlton	43.17m
CPV-TV	45.319m

Source: *The Independent*, 17 October 1991.

Figure 2.4   The ITV franchises 1991

have a subversive effect upon the BBC and ITV which some say is intentional. The BBC is directly beholden to the government for funding and it is alleged that this dependence has been exploited to browbeat the Corporation into making decisions across a range of issues which risk compromising its production and editorial policies. ITV, on the other hand, is dependent on the government in other ways. The lobbying system, by which powerful interest groups make their wishes clear to the political classes in the UK, is widely used by the commercial television companies. In the new harsher financial context, as Dyke says: 'It will take a brave broadcaster to make or broadcast a controversial programme about government, if, by so doing, it seriously threatens its chances of persuading the government to change a particular piece of legislation' (Dyke, 1994).

The terrestrial channels

The terrestrial television system in the UK currently comprises four channels equally divided between the BBC and ITV. A new commercial channel (Channel 5) will be launched in 1996. The principal role and most recent achievements of each channel can be briefly characterised as follows (first transmission in brackets).

BBC1 (1946): the flagship public service channel of the Corporation. It carries a wide range of programmes, including the main news bulletins, documentaries, quizzes, game shows, films, drama, situation comedy, soaps, sport and ballroom dancing. In 1994 it also acquired the exclusive rights to present the weekly draw of the National Lottery, attracting an audience of 17 million viewers. BBC1 is the main competitor in the eyes of the commercial sector with a 33 per cent audience share.

BBC2 (1964): a less populist, more thought-provoking channel, BBC2 has been particularly successful recently in dramatising such works as Eliot's *Middlemarch* and Dickens's *Martin Chuzzlewit*, thus maintaining the BBC's reputation for high-quality literary productions. It has also produced some successful and original comedy series of which the predominantly female *Absolutely Fabulous* is a good example. BBC2 also carries the nightly in-depth news programme *Newsnight* and has an audience share of around 11 per cent.

Channel 3 (1955): the original ITV channel, Channel 3 consistently attracts more viewers than BBC1. It built its reputation on a diverse range of popular programming with an unashamed bias towards the give-away game-show and light entertainment. However, it has also developed a reputation for high-quality news coverage which rivals that of the BBC. Recently it has also been outstripping the BBC in the area of popular modern drama. ITV was instrumental in introducing morning television to the UK in the 1980s. Channel 3 has a 41 per cent audience share.

Channel 4 (1982): in many ways, Channel 4, with its experimental mission to seek out minority and other neglected audiences, was a most unlikely proposition for support from the Thatcher government in the early 1980s. Over the last decade it has established a reputation for itself as a provider of diverse and distinguished programming with audience ratings of 11 per cent which rival those of BBC2. Since 1991, it has become a stand-alone corporation (formerly it was managed by ITV/Channel 3) with responsibility for attracting its own advertising revenues. Channel 4, whilst still providing a broadly based schedule in news, current affairs, education and general entertainment, also caters for the interests of minority cultures such as gays, ethnic minorities, feminists, and alternative youth, as well as for the obsessions of serious jazz people and film buffs. In addition its news coverage is well rated and competes successfully with the bulletins of the BBC.

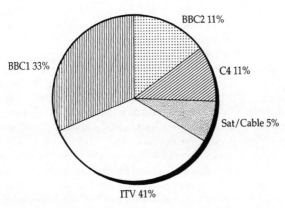

Figure 2.5   TV audience share in UK
Source: Sound Vision/Barb 1994

The BBC goes commercial

There is an interesting coda to this section which relates to a surprising development with regard to the activities of the BBC. Since 1991 it has been operating a commercially funded television channel – World Television Service – targeting the Far East, and in 1995 the Corporation, in partnership with the Pearson Group launched two new satellite and cable channels targeting a European audience – BBC Prime (entertainment), and BBC World (news and information). All three satellite channels have been relocated under a new umbrella group, BBC Worldwide. BBC World will reach 8.4 million homes across Europe whilst BBC Prime (a subscription channel) will have an estimated 2.8 million viewers (Short, *European*, 3.2.95). The BBC and Pearson are no doubt banking on the novel attraction for advertisers of associating their products with one of the world's most prestigious broadcasters. Nevertheless, the future of BBC Worldwide will depend on its capacity to deliver audiences in competition with existing terrestrial and other satellite and cable channels. What of course is noteworthy here is the move by the BBC towards income-generation derived from television advertising. It could be argued that this is a shrewd move on the part of the Corporation, demonstrating to a critical government its acceptance in principle of advertising as a source of income. Whatever view we take on the matter, it is one which will be monitored with interest from all sides in the next few years.

Legislation and regulation

The long-term policy-making of the BBC and ITV is undertaken by special committees on behalf of the government, of which there has been four since 1945 – Beveridge (1951), Pilkington (1960), Annan (1974) and Peacock (1986). Of these the Peacock Report was potentially the most radical although most of the proposals for the BBC have been shelved. The BBC is a self-regulating corporation whose compliance with the conditions of its Royal Charter and the overseeing of its scheduling policy is the responsibility of its Board of Governors. The ITC (Independent Television Commission) is the regulatory body for the commercial sector and is the successor to the former IBA (Independent Broadcasting Authority) as the result of the 1990 Broadcasting Act.

In addition to this first level of regulation, there is a second at which the activities of the BBC and the ITV are jointly monitored by two separate bodies. The responsibilities of the first, the Broadcasting Complaints Commission (established in 1981) are principally directed towards the maintenance of the just and fair treatment of information and of individuals resulting from public and private television and radio broadcasting. The BCC is also charged with the monitoring and adjudication of alleged infringements of privacy in the obtaining of programme material. The responsibilities of the second body, the Broadcasting Standards Council, are somewhat broader in scope. Established in 1988, the BSC was given full statutory powers under the Broadcasting Act of 1990. It deals with complaints and public concern relating to the portrayal of violence, sexual behaviour, and other matters of taste and decency including the treatment of disasters, use of bad language, and racial and gender stereotyping. The BSC is also charged with the monitoring of programmes received in the United Kingdom from external broadcasters and advises the government about unacceptable standards when they occur in this area. One conclusion which may be drawn from this brief outline of broadcasting regulation and monitoring in the United Kingdom is that the British broadcasting system is certainly one of the most closely regulated systems in Europe.

It is widely rumoured that the BCC and BSC will be merged into one body in the near future, a move which, viewed objectively, would protect broadcasters from incurring 'double jeopardy' penalties in the event of them falling foul of both bodies simultaneously.

Cable and satellite

Of the 22.2 million TV households in the UK in 1994, only 3.8 per cent are connected to cable with a further 13.5 per cent receiving satellite transmissions via dish aerials (*Cable and Satellite Europe*, January 1995:52). The sale of dish aerials and the cabling of households is currently mostly driven by the broadcasting initiatives of Rupert Murdoch's News Corporation's BSkyB subscription channels which in 1994 had 3.6 million subscribers, 2.6 million of whom received by satellite using dish aerials, and the remaining million by cable (Bell, *Observer*, 20.11.94). The cable industry is investing in the UK at the rate of £2 billion a year and by the year 2003 it is estimated that 11 million households will be connected to cable (Bell, *Observer*, 27.11.94). Cable and satellite transmission raise common issues for all national television systems in Western Europe. They are perfectly adapted to the needs of the commercial sector in so far as the technology that they use facilitates 'narrowcasting' to particular socio-economic group. This narrowcasting is partly in response to, and partly the reinforcement of, the process of social and audience fragmentation we have noted already in Chapter 1. As Bell points out, cable is the realm of the technical expert, the engineer and the accountant, and not of the broadcasting visionary. It is the carrier of news, facts, entertainment and the facilitator of interactive services. As such, it stands astride the two major areas of television broadcasting and telecommunications which have in the past remained culturally and legally separate. Cable and satellite, as we have noted, are perfectly suited to the new socio-economic climate and their effects upon the major creative mainstream broadcasters of the BBC and ITV are likely to be mixed. On the one hand, they will become major purchasers of their material (repeats of all kinds on cable and satellite will be promoted as a positive service, if not a virtue). On the other hand, they will attract audiences away from the major, creative broadcasters. This new phase of fragmentation raises important issues of a higher order than the financial implications for the major broadcasters, facing more competition in the market. Satellite and cable broadcasters will target smaller socio-economic groups than the mass channels of the BBC and ITV, with thematic packages of entertainment (old films, repeat series, sex, music, sport, etc.) or services (shopping, financial advice, fast food, video-on-demand). BSkyB is both the precursor and good example of one of the first thematic channels to be transmitted in the UK. It is of interest for many reasons, not the least of which is the manner in which it could alter the balance that has existed between television broadcaster and audience for the last forty years. This is because the conditions in which it operates differ from those of the public service duopoly in striking ways.

Firstly, for technical reasons BSkyB is not universally accessible – only 3.6 million viewers receive it out of a possible 22.2 million. Equally it is not universally accessible for financial reasons. In order to receive BSkyB (or other satellite channel) viewers must first purchase either a dish aerial or pay for cable installation and then subscribe to the channels of their choice. In terms of programming, unlike the BBC and ITV, BSkyB is a thematic broadcaster, currently offering nine channels ranging from general entertainment to news, travel and soaps. The approach of a subscription channel of this kind to broadcasting is characterised by exclusiveness at many levels which distinguishes it sharply from the PSB tradition. As we have noted above, the majority of viewers are excluded either on technical or financial grounds (or both). This aspect of its exclusiveness is important in a system where previously television broadcasting was a public experience, accessible to all (except in the case of regional programmes which by definition are restricted) upon payment of a single fee. It is worth recalling that a comparable development in commercial radio does not require either new equipment or a subscription in order to receive transmissions. Satellite and cable television will therefore discriminate between those who can afford their services and those who cannot. A thematic channel is also exclusive in its programming policy. BSkyB, for example, caters for individual choice by encouraging its subscribers to build their own thematic clusters of channels from a total of nine. The choice on offer is limited to films (3 channels), soaps (1 channel), sport (2 channels), travel (1 channel) and news (1 channel). This narrow range of programming is determined by what is deemed to be the most popular and, presumably, the most saleable products. But it hardly constitutes real choice when compared with what is on offer on the BBC or ITV schedules. This point is important because the advocates of deregulation have argued strongly for such a policy in the interest of extending viewers' choice. If it can be demonstrated that, in reality, deregulation merely extends the viewers freedom to choose between more channels, all offering similar thematic packages, then this argument loses much of its force since real (programme) choice will be reduced.

In addition to operational exclusiveness of the kind we have described above, and the risk of reduction in programme choice, there is one further social implication from BSkyB's involvement in a sports channel. It has acquired exclusive or semi-exclusive rights on sporting events hitherto considered to be located in the public domain and therefore accessible to all via the public service channels. That assumption has been proven to be false. Premier league football may now only be viewed on Sky Sport. In a similar fashion Ryder Cup golf, and the creation of a new Super Rugby League competition, promoted by BSkyB, will erect fresh barriers between a nationally 'owned' sport and its mass audience. This exclusive commodification of elements of British cultural life, as in the case of national spectator sports, must have repercussions on social attitudes which will detract from the otherwise beneficial effects such activities bestow upon the people.

The overall impact of cable and satellite broadcasting upon the televisual landscape, as well as upon British viewing habits, will be considerable over the next decade. However, it is too early to offer a prognosis concerning the effects that this kind of television will have upon the future viewing public, and through them, upon our national culture. Traditional viewing habits across existing national channels are well documented, but these habits will change as cable and satellite operators absorb a greater audience share. If the public service channels remained the central cultural elements of the British television system, with cable and satellite offering optional, extra and complementary schedules, the outlook need not give rise for concern. If, however, satellite and cable succeeded in occupying the ground currently occupied by the BBC and ITV (the estimates are that 50 per cent of all TV households will be cabled by the year 2003), then important issues are raised for British society which need to be addressed sooner rather than later. It is doubtful whether, in the latter event, the democratic rights of every citizen of access to information could be sustained in this new communications landscape where certain paths, either by ignorance or design, have been wrongly signposted or have disappeared altogether. Whether or not the public service tradition can be sustained over the next decade will depend on two major factors. The first is the capacity of the BBC, in particular, to maintain a dynamic policy of innovatory production and imaginative scheduling which, by their nature, will capture the interest of the public for 'first time' viewing. By so doing the BBC would demonstrate superiority of production expertise and imagination to capture its audience over the commercial approach of commodification, and the speculative re-running of previously successful programmes. The second is the introduction of legislation which recognises the centrality of the public service tradition in the British television system as an essential mediator of the public sphere, and which imposes upon every government the obligation to protect and enhance that tradition in the interests of democracy.

Multi-media ownership

In the first part of this chapter, we mentioned the trend towards the concentration of the written press in the UK which, in the view of many observers, has reached a level where the continued existence of free speech, underpinned by a pluralistic press, is at serious risk. Superimposed upon this concern, and to some extent superseding it, is the issue of cross-media ownership. By this we mean the increasing tendency among the large media groups to acquire simultaneous holdings in the written press, radio and television. The time has long passed since the principal media operators restricted their business to a single sector. The same groups which are causing concern through their holdings in the written press also have holdings in radio, publishing and television. Moreover, the Broadcasting Act of 1990 imposes a 20 per cent limit upon the permitted holdings of newspaper groups in terrestrial television which the supporters of deregulation wish to see either abolished completely or raised sufficiently to allow national newspapers to own at least one ITV franchise (but see new proposed legislation below). The three following examples well illustrate the nature of cross-media ownership.

The *Daily Mail and General Trust Plc (DMGT)*. This group owns the *Daily Mail* and the only London evening paper, the *Evening Standard*,

8 regional dailies, 27 regional free papers and a controlling share in Channel One, the new London cable-channel. It also has shares in 8 local radio stations and interests in Reuters and Teletext.

News International. Rupert Murdoch's group controls 5 national newspapers, a major publishing house (Harper/Collins), has a controlling or important interest in 6 national magazines and a controlling interest in BSkyB.

Pearson. This group owns one national newspaper (*Financial Times*), a major regional newspaper group, one national magazine (*Economist*), 4 publishing houses, and shares in 3 television companies (Williams, *New Statesman*, 24.3.95).

The most recent thinking on the part of the government on the issue of policy-making in the field of multi-media ownership is contained in a consultative document, *Media Ownership: The Government's Proposals*, (1995). In this policy document the government announces its intention to introduce legislation which will allow newspaper groups with less than 20 per cent of national circulation to hold up to 15 per cent of the total commercial television market (this effectively would allow those newspaper groups which qualify to own a maximum of two commercial ITV or Channel 5 channels) and 15 per cent of the commercial radio market. The immediate consequence of these proposals would be to exclude two of the biggest multi-media groups – Mirror Group newspapers, and News International – from owning ITV franchises (they would be limited to two strictly minority holdings). Whilst this policy document has received a cautious welcome in some circles (it explicitly recognises the need for pluralism of the media), in one area, that of the written press, it unaccountably proposes to relax the regulations for mergers and takeovers such that a further reduction of separately owned titles could occur in a market which is already heavily concentrated.

Traditionally, as Williams points out, the radio and television with their regulated output and commitment to impartiality have provided a useful countervailing force to the loosely regulated and highly partisan written press in the UK (Williams, *New Statesman*, 24.3.95). If that counterbalance is lost through a concentration of cross-media ownership, or by a further concentration of the written press, then the existence of a pluralistic media will be further subverted, and their capacity to deliver a range of opinion and information relating to the public interest significantly curtailed.

The European dimension

The answers to the question, 'to what extent are the British media Europeanised?' are somewhat mixed and, when applied to some sectors, highly negative. To a large extent, the commercial trends which characterise the development of the media in the UK since the 1980s – deregulation, concentration, cross-media ownership, internationalisation of activities, market segmentation – are all commonly discernible as a European phenomenon. In this narrow but important sense, the patterns of media development in the UK are similar to those of its European counterparts. We have tried to gauge the effects of these commercial trends on British society only in the most general terms. Nevertheless, these effects give grounds for serious concern. The extent to which the concept of Europe as a supranational society and political force is successfully mediated, within the new context of media change in the UK, is difficult to assess. It is best approached from the standpoint of the current representation of Europe in the British media. For at least a decade, as we have already noted, all the media in the UK have devoted significantly more time and space to the coverage of the proceedings of the major European institutions such as the European Commission, the Parliament and the European Court. But in the case of the written press, this representation is often negative or, in the case of the tabloids, openly hostile. Increasingly over the last twenty years, traditional rallying points of the tabloids around the royal family, the political parties, the trade unions, the Commonwealth, the Welfare State and others, have either seriously weakened or disappeared altogether. Certainly Europe of the supranational kind is not a popular representation in the tabloids. When a European 'story' is unavoidable and therefore imposed upon them, its treatment is often distorted, misinformed and rarely comprehensive. This tabloid treatment is of special importance in the UK from the point of view of attitude formation. We mentioned in the introductory chapter the imperative of media pluralism for the promotion of opinion formation within a democracy. In the UK today approximately 23.3 million readers take one or more of the daily or Sunday, mass or middle-market tabloids owned by one of the four principal newspaper groups. It is difficult to perceive, given the lack of alternative choice, and in the light of the cursory, and mostly hostile, treatment European issues receive, how any informed opinions can be constructed on this basis.

The situation is considerably better from the point of view of the so-called quality broadsheets. Whilst no British broadsheet can match the quality and comprehensiveness of European news coverage of the kind featured in *Le Monde*, nevertheless the coverage is adequate and informed. The case of the *European* deserves particular mention here, since, as its name suggests, it was conceived as a newspaper with a European mission. In recent times the *European* has established offices in London, Belgium, France, Germany and Russia and increased its circulation to between 180,000 and 200,000 in 1995. The *European* has increased the range of its coverage and added business and leisure supplements and frequently carries special thematic editions. Given the potential circulation of the paper in continental Europe alone, its circulation is modest and this is due no doubt to the language barrier, and the paper's lack of an identifiable cultural 'home'. Even so, the *European* is an historical 'first' in so far as its operations are conceived to be placed directly in the service of the positive mediation of a more unified concept of Europe.

If for various reasons the majority of the written press in the UK is considered to be at best indifferent, and frequently hostile to the coverage of European issues, Europe receives a better, more comprehensive treatment at the hands of the broadcasters who have devoted increasing airtime to Europe over the last decade. The coverage of these issues, with the possible exception of their coverage in the World Service, is usually initiated by British national interest and represented from a national standpoint. Regular reports of the proceedings of the Commission or of the Parliament, in their own right, are rare. In short, Europe, as represented by the British media, still largely remains an unintegrated space, maintained at a distance. It is mediated as existing 'out there' rather than as an integral and significant influence upon British national life and culture.

Conclusion

The British media have undergone a period of extraordinary upheaval in their development over the last fifteen years. In keeping with trends all over Europe, all sectors have been subjected to the processes of increasing commercialisation and fragmentation. The question of ownership, not only of the written press, where it is particularly concentrated, but also of the cross-sector kind, has become a *cause célèbre* because of the consequences that non-pluralism has for the democratic process of opinion formation and social group membership. These trends of commercialisation and fragmentation characterise the development of television and radio broadcasting in special ways and may be expected to become more pronounced as the century draws to its close. On the commercial side in particular there is an increasing tendency towards 'narrowcasting' as opposed to the more traditional form of broadcasting over a range of programme types. The consequences of increased commercial activity inevitably mean that a significant part of the audience share will be absorbed by this sector, away from the former duopoly. These developments suggest a paradox in the context of contemporary Western European politics: within the latter framework, the member states of the EU are cautiously committing themselves to the path of ever closer union, and the enlargement of the powers of supranational government. But, on the other hand, in the UK, as elsewhere in the European Union, these political ambitions are being played out against a background of social fragmentation, and its parallel manifestations in the media, the break-up of traditional broadcasting patterns. The likely outcome of the conflicting currents is not easy to predict with accuracy. But over the next decade, at least, it is likely that the concept of the European Union, as a political, social and cultural force, will not be successfully represented to the British people through the media as might have been hoped for or anticipated in the past.

Notes

1. Only Ireland and Greece have higher levels of concentration.
2. This move towards concentration was pronounced between 1981 and 1987 when the government's interpretation of the monopolies and mergers legislation and the guidelines of the third Royal Commission on take-overs was particularly relaxed. See Royal Commission on the Press (1974–7:para 14.15).
3. Not implemented.
4. According to Hickethier there is a current decline in the fortunes of tabloid journalism in Germany (see Chapter 4).
5. Although new proposals have been made by the government (1995) to limit multi-media ownership.
6. See recent new government proposals (1995) under 'Multi-media ownership'.
7. Chris Smith, shadow Heritage minister, CPBF Conference *The Media Versus the People*, London, 18 March 1995.
8. It is estimated that at this time 15 million people tuned in to the evening news bulletin.
9. Bringing the total to 3 national and 150 local commercial stations.
10. New legislation is proposed relating to multi-media ownership. See *Media Ownership: The Government's Proposals*, London, HMSO (1995).
11. Succeeded by the Independent Broadcasting Authority (IBA) in 1973 and the Independent Television Commission (ITC) in 1990.
12. In the event Peacock decided that the BBC could only be examined in the wider context of the 'duopoly'.

CHAPTER 3

The media in France

Bernard Lamizet

I Introduction

In order to understand the dynamics and structures of the media and other forms of mediated communication in France, it is important to bear in mind the fundamental lines upon which communication is organised in this country. Indeed, mediated communication in France may be approached in a somewhat special way compared with that of other European countries which we are currently examining in this book. This distinctive quality of the French media has its origins in the country's history. France is a country whose existence as a community rests on the fundamental roles played within it by political and institutional forms. In France, the sense of social cohesion, the sense of belonging, together constitute a political experience derived from the citizen's contact with national institutions such as, among others, the school, local government, public health, the law, and the communications services (from the roads and railways to telecommunications). In fact this process of development of social cohesion and social group membership comprises three major elements. Firstly, there is the existence of a people bound together and unified by law and common institutions. Secondly, there is the permanent existence of national institutions and social players that guarantee the continuity of the political as well as the physical 'space' that constitute the Republic. Finally, the third element – and it is here that the media and the school play an important role – there is the existence of a folk-memory and a culture which give a kind of symbolic consistency to socio-cultural identity. The importance, then, of mediated forms of communication in France is very considerable. The role and responsibilities of the media are both immense and specific. The French media have four principal characteristics which, we would argue, are more closely interrelated than is the case in other European societies.

Firstly, by their pictures, information and analyses, the media create a common culture: a common cultural response to events, to the present, and to the development of social life. The dissemination of information plays an essential part in the process of cultural development and the formation of public opinion. The tradition, initiated by the school under the Ancien Régime, and subsequently reinforced during the Third Republic by the policies of Jules Ferry, is one which transforms the existence of information into a process of mediation. This process is both necessary and essential for the creation of French citizenship. Today that tradition has been renewed and developed in the media by their active presence in the public sphere. On a daily basis, we find numerous examples in the media of news reports, features and historical parallels, all of which amplify the event or item of news, bringing to it a whole range of supplementary information and creating what may be called a 'documentary consistency of discourse'. Thus, for example, the majority of French cable channels (untypically when compared with trends elsewhere in Europe) offer programmes of a documentary nature, and in the same way public service radio and most of the local private stations put out complete and well informed magazine programmes with educative as well as entertainment objectives. Indeed the French media as a whole undertake considerable responsibility for education and training of the public (particularly in further education), which is required for the re-equipping and modernisation of the economy.

The second characteristic of the media is the one already discussed at some length in Chapter 1. They represent a kind of symbolic mirror in which the French can observe themselves and their behaviour against the backdrop of national life. In this respect the French media send out a kind of double image to their public. The first is one of the public as actors occupying a political space, and the second is of the people as users of information systems. From this double image stems the tradition, which is well established in France, of political and social commitment (*engagement*). French television, for example, has frequently been seen to alternate between the role of the neutral presenter of information, on one hand, and one with a strong commitment to the defence of French government policy, on the other. This characteristic of *engagement* explains, among others, the centrality of public service broadcasting in France. It also explains the importance of the regional press (it is a regional paper, *Ouest-France*, which has by far the biggest circulation in France). It is the regional press which, for better or worse, successfully offers to the French people an image with which they can identify and recognise themselves.

The third characteristic relates to the way in which the media relay information (in written, broadcast or other form), thus creating a kind of territorial organisation or network. To restate this in a slightly more amplified way: the manner in which information is relayed itself becomes a kind of socialised space and, by extension, a political domain. A good example of what we mean is the way in which the organisation of local radio, or that of the regional press, complements and reinforces the activities of local government. *Ouest France*, which is widely read in Britanny, has made a strong contribution to the forging of the contemporary identity of the whole region. Elsewhere, in the urban context, the so-called 'free radios' (*radios libres*) have made a significant contribution to the creation of neighbourhood solidarity and self-assertive identity (for example, Radio Aligre in Paris, and Radio Utopie in Marseilles).

The final characteristic relates to the fact that the media industry in France is an emerging economic force. Communications in the wider sense are currently developing into a new culture of post-industrial modernity. This development is due to two factors; the first is commercial and concerns the way in which the communications sector has opened up to competition both internally and externally, involving the streamlining of existing players and the participation of new ones such as the Compagnie Générale des Eaux and the Lyonnaise des Eaux (in the cable sector). The second factor is the state-led initiative to modernise and develop the French communications infrastructure, especially in the field of telecommunications. The speed with which the media and communications have developed into a contemporary, industrial, commercial and economic force is very striking. This rapid change in France has been achieved by massive investment, advances in the management of communication companies, and the increasing professionalism of the staff. The information and communications industries constitute together in France an activity which, whilst it has currently reached a plateau, is, nevertheless, one of the most dynamic sectors of the economy.

The state and the role of legislation

In France, the state is a primary force in the economic and institutional life of the nation, and its presence manifests itself in communications, as well as in other key areas. In the media and communications sector it has a triple role as legislator, regulator and initiator in its own right.

With regard to legislation, because of the economic, political, social and moral issues at stake, the state has always exerted a strong statutory control over the media. Between 1974 and 1995, for example, no less than five separate, major Acts have been introduced, each of which has influenced the media in distinct and significant ways (see below). Before 1984 the activities of the written press were largely determined by the *ordonnances* of 1945 which reorganised the written press at the end of the war (and before this, by the famous law of 1881). Broadcasting, on the other hand, was conceived and set up as a state monopoly from its inception in the 1920s and 30s. This monopoly situation led to the establishment of private commercial radio stations located just outside French territory (in Luxembourg, Andorra and Monte Carlo) and appropriately named *radios périphériques*.

As we have already mentioned above, there have been five major pieces of legislation since 1974 and briefly their influence upon the re-shaping of the French media has been as follows:

- The law of 1974. This law broke up the state monopoly of the Office de la Radio et Télévision Française (ORTF) into several smaller companies covering the national television companies, the radio stations, production, transmission and archives. It opened up broadcasting to competition, although the latter was still in the context of an overarching state monopoly. The 1974 law was an important legislative and regulatory landmark because it prepared the ground for the modernisation of broadcasting which was to follow over the next two decades.
- The law of 1982 ended the state monopoly in broadcasting and paved the way for local, commercial radio. It marked the launch of a subscription channel (Canal Plus) and also provided for a major initiative in communications with Minitel[1] and a national cabling project (for further discussion see below).
- The law of 1984 was essentially intended to control and reduce press concentration and thereby sustain pluralism. Via a mixture of statutory controls on media holdings, and financial assistance to small circulation titles with slender resources, this law was commonly held to be directed against the media holdings of Robert Hersant. To this end it was unsuccessful; the socialist government appeared to back down at the last moment and did not insist that the new law be applied to holdings acquired prior to its coming into force.
- The laws of 1986 and 1988 on the press and broadcasting were designed to further break up the state monopoly (TF1 was privatised) and reorganise the communications market.

It can be seen, by this substantial body of legislation, that the state, through direct political intervention of parliament, has played a leading role in the statutory and organisational control of the media. In this way the written press and broadcasting media have become important arenas of institutional and political activity. The mass of legislation relating to the media which the state has initiated both determines their activities in the public sphere and guarantees their functions as essential poles of political activity.

Regulation

The laws which govern communication in France provide for a regulatory function carried out on behalf of the state by several bodies whose duties have increasingly marked the weakening of government control over broadcasting. The current regulatory body is the Conseil supérieur de l'audiovisuel (CSA) and its functions can be divided into three major areas:

- The safeguarding of broadcasting freedom and the guarantee of competition;

- the safeguarding of the quality and content of programming;
- the monitoring of the development of broadcasting.

The CSA is the regulatory body for all broadcasting activity in France (i.e. both in the public and private sectors). It comprises nine members, one third of whom are appointed by the President of the Republic, one third by the Senate (the upper house) and the rest by the National Assembly (lower house). It has a permanent secretariat and resources, and is responsible for the appointments of the PSB channels and radio stations. It is also responsible for the allocation of transmission frequencies, and the awarding of licences to the commercial television channels and other local radio broadcasters. In addition, it has a monitoring function, and keeps a close watch on the broadcasting performance of the operators to ensure compliance with their obligations laid down in the contracts (*cahiers des charges*). In this manner, the regulation of broadcasting ensures that this essential service for the public sphere is organised and well ordered. Its presence and activity avoid uncontrolled media development and protect broadcasters from state influence which might result in a threat to the freedom of speech. It should be noted, however, that the nature of broadcasting regulation is still a contested political issue in France. The name of the regulatory body has been changed and its role modified three times since 1982, twice by the socialists, and once by the Chirac administration of 1986–8 (for further discussion of the CSA see 'French television' section below).

As we have already noted, the state is an essential player in the activities of the media and communications. It operates primarily through three public or semi-public bodies:

- The public service broadcasters – France Télévision and Radio France. These companies are responsible for the devising, production and scheduling of programmes.
- Télédiffusion de France (TDF) which is the public body responsible for all technical aspects of transmission throughout France.
- France Télécom, formerly the Direction Générale des Télécommunications (DGT), which is responsible for the development and the maintenance of cable networks along with other (private) newcomers to the field such as Compagnie Générale des Eaux.

These activities effectively make of the state an essential partner in both the communication and production industries and establish the centrality of the public sector in the domain of the media and communications. Thus, in this important area we find a continuation of the same historical tradition of state intervention which began with Sully and Colbert in the seventeenth century and was reinforced by Napoleon more than a century later. The positive aspect resulting from the role played by the state in the communications sector is evidently that the latter is recognised as a political-economic and commercial priority. It was largely by a state-sponsored initiative that the use of teletext (originally via Minitel[2]) has become commonplace, just as in former times this century the state undertook to modernise the railways and the telephone system. The negative aspect is that the tradition of state intervention may create an overdependency on the part of the industry *vis-à-vis* the state, which in telecommunications, as elsewhere (Radio France, France Télévision and ARTE), is still a major player.

II The development of the written press since 1945

After the Liberation the newspapers which had continued to publish during the German occupation were banned under the provisions of the new laws (*ordonnances*) of 1944. These new laws sought to guarantee the freedom of the press by introducing, among other things, measures to restrict and identify the ownership of newspaper titles. At this time, too, new bodies such as the Societes des Redacteurs were established and introduced to all newspapers with the object of protecting the freedom and status of journalists.

However, at the end of the twentieth century, the principal characteristic of the French written press is a tendency towards concentration and the emergence of press groups such as Hersant and Hachette controlling both national and regional newspapers and constituting, in some cases, quasi-monopolies. Robert Hersant's Socpresse is the biggest daily newspaper group in France. It owns, or has controlling interests in three national titles – *Le Figaro, France Soir* and *Paris Turf* – and more than twenty regional/local titles in mainland France as well as several others in the former French colonial territories (DOM-TOM). As is the case in other Western European countries, this kind of concentration is now being superseded by a new kind involving cross-media holdings in radio and television (for further discussion see Part III below).

The major characteristics of the news coverage

The so-called *presse d'information*, the daily and weekly newspapers, is characterised by three features which influence the mediation of news coverage in France.

Firstly, there is information as a political element: information is directed towards the public sphere which is dominated by the political debate. News coverage, or to qualify this activity in a more theoretical and general way, mediated communication, represents the event which, in turn requires an act of choice and political commitment on the part of the reader, viewer or user of the information. Thus the media, in their roles as political players, are frequently engaged, on one side or the other, in the nation's political and institutional struggles. In France, with the possible exception of *Le Monde* (and the latter only recently), French newspapers make little pretence in separating factual information from editorial comment. This is precisely because, in France, the bias in the presentation is deemed to be an integral part of the 'discourse' relating to the event in question within the public sphere.

Secondly, there is the importance of regional news: there is no tradition in France of a regional paper with a national readership (as used to be the case, for example, with the former *Manchester Guardian* in the UK). The French national and regional press relate respectively to a different public discourse and to separate objectives, and these interests rarely coincide. Indeed the so-called national press which is exclusively Parisian in origin, systematically avoids coverage of specific events relating to the regions, and by the same token, the regional press devotes little space to the coverage of national or international affairs (four to five pages out of thirty). This explains why there is little competition between the national and the regional press. The readers of *Le Monde* and other national papers are also readers of the regional press.

Thirdly, and finally, there is the nature of information coverage itself: the written press covers a wide range of topics and news events and this wide coverage has two main consequences. Firstly, by its style and approach to the news, it defines what we may term as the 'newsworthy' within the public sphere. Press coverage in France embraces a wide range of topics and events which include items of political, social, cultural, sporting, economic and financial interest. This wide spectrum of topics, represented on a daily basis, and treated in a similar manner, maintains the continuity of news-flow to the public. Secondly, this wide coverage prioritises the importance of information (as opposed to entertainment or other features found, for example, in the British tabloid press) as the dominant element of mediated activity in France. It is therefore the nature of the information contained in the French press, rather than any other service, that determines its relationship with its readers, and reader choice. In short, it is information and news coverage alone which are

Table 3.1 Ten leading dailies in France 1992

Ouest France	749,000
Le Figaro	407,427
Le Parisien	380,468
Le Progrès	375,878
Le Monde	368,970
Sud Ouest	351,885
La Voix du Nord	347,230
Le Dauphiné Libéré	286,145
Nice Matin	244,448
Libération	183,000

Source: SJTI

the most valued assets of the French press. Table 3.1 indicates the first ten national and regional papers by circulation.

Four categories of the written press

The written press in France provides four kinds of information in different formats. These can be characterised as follows: the daily papers (wide-ranging news coverage); the weekly news magazines (news in depth and news digests); professional and business papers (economy, finance and other sectors); and the leisure/entertainment magazine sector (human and special interests). These four kinds of titles are unevenly distributed across the population as a whole, the most common being the newspaper, the traditional source of information in France, and the least common being the professional and business press. Finally, the leisure/entertainment/special interest magazines are, as in all other European countries, an area of considerable growth and socio-economic importance.

This four-fold division of information sources corresponds approximately to the different socio-cultural needs of four broad categories of reader. The newspaper functions to reinforce the political and social group membership of its readers, whereas the appeal of the news magazines is to readers wishing to increase and deepen their personal knowledge and understanding of events. The leisure and entertainment magazines attract readers dedicated to special activities – sports, cars, fashion, cooking, cycling – as well as those seeking mere entertainment and escape from their daily routines. The professional press, (i.e. *Les Echos*, *Le Moniteur*) on the other hand, is used by a small social elite which is, as yet, relatively undeveloped in France.

The freedom of the press: political and economic issues

In theory at least, access to, and the publication of information in France is free. This freedom, established by the famous law of 1881, looms large in the political life of the state. This law is considered to be the permanent, immutable basis of press freedom in France[3] and is only limited by three kinds of restraint – personal defamation and libel, public good taste and moral values (especially those relating to young people), and national security.

In fact there are numerous other constraints relating to issues of ownership and finance which influence the nature of press freedom in France. Despite legislation dating back to the Liberation in 1944 which provided aid for the smaller papers, thus compensating for the lack of substantial advertising revenue, the combination of falling incomes generally from advertising and rising costs has aggravated the difficulties of the daily press, and threatened its plurality, and, in consequence, its freedom. Due in the main to economic factors, as well as to the development of competing sources of information, there has been a significant decline in the written press in France since 1945, when, for example, there were 370 dailies read per 1,000

Table 3.2 Decline of national and regional titles and trends towards press concentration 1914–90

Year	National titles	Circulation (millions)	Regional titles	Circulation (millions)	Total
1914	60	5.5	242	4.0	9.5
1946	27	5.9	175	9.1	15.0
1966	14	4.3	91	7.8	12.1
1986	12	2.8	69	7.2	10.0
1990	11	2.9	62	7.1	10.0

Sources: From SJTI

inhabitants in 1945, whereas that figure had declined to 185 per 1,000 by 1985 (Albert, 1993:125). In terms of actual titles, the national figure has fallen from 60 titles in 1914 to 11 in 1990, and the regional figure from 242 to 62 in the same period (see Table 3.2).

The economic development of the written press

The written press in France underwent four rapid stages of development between 1970 and 1980. This development has directed the written press towards the assumption of a new economic role and status within the context of financial and economic activities of the country. These stages of development can be briefly characterised as follows.

Firstly, the modernisation of distribution methods: this technological progress involving improved methods of telecommunications (in particular the fax machine) has facilitated the publishing and the distribution of newspapers in locations close to their readership (thus reducing transport costs). It is largely as the result of this technological progress that the written press – and especially the regional press – has become a major player in the regional and public life of the country.

Secondly, the introduction of computerised copy-making: the computer has entered the newspaper production process and its arrival has had three consequences: it has greatly influenced the production and the standardisation of journalists' copy; it has brought about a change in the nature of professional skills needed for newspaper production; lastly, it has provided the possibility for permanent storage and retrieval of information in the written press. The computerisation of the techniques of copy-making which were pioneered in such regional papers as the *Le Provençal* and the *Dernières Nouvelles d'Alsace*, and in the national press, in such papers as *Libération* and *Le Monde* is now a widespread feature of newspaper production in France. The computer standardises the process of production and the lay-out, and in consequence, reduces the number of skills traditionally required for this purpose by transferring to the journalist the tasks formally undertaken by type-setters and other skilled non-journalist personnel. As already mentioned by Weymouth in the preceding chapter in relation to the 'battle of Wapping', the computer is also potentially a source of industrial conflict between owners and employees.

Thirdly, the decentralisation of newspaper production: the advances in technology, and in the production and distribution of newspapers has also facilitated the decentralisation of the press. By this we mean the geographic dispersal of different departments which combine in the production of a newspaper. This development is primarily due to the progress in the field of communications such as the fax machine and the computer which facilitate the link-up of points of information in-put with the operational centre of the paper. This trend towards decentralisation has had two principal consequences in France. Firstly, it has promoted the simplification, and therefore reduced cost, of newspaper production. Secondly, it has reinforced the trend towards the concentration of titles within press groups such as Hersant and Hachette which are growing ever larger. This decentralisation of the written press, by reducing overall costs, has turned the daily press into an established commercial activity restrained only by the advertising market and, latterly, by the development of the so-called 'free-press' (the give-away newspapers financed entirely from advertising).

Fourthly, growth of multi-media activities: there are numerous examples of newspaper groups involved in multi-media activities. *Le Monde*, for example, is involved with a radio station RFM, whilst *Libération* is active in a video-production. In all these examples, the written press is taking its place within the context of the trend towards multi-media activity. It is becoming involved with other forms of communication in a developmental process which integrates other kinds of technological mediation, within an overall communications framework. Today, in France, the principal daily papers are simultaneously involved in strategies of diversification into a more segmented market, and in moves towards greater convergence of ownership. This tendency is reinforced by two kinds of investment: those forthcoming from advertisers, and those coming from investments in the technological improvement in production and distribution methods.

Newspaper groups have invested heavily in telephone-computer link-ups (*télématique*) in order to offer to their readers a whole new range of supplementary information services which range from data, archival and other kinds of information retrieval on one hand, to access to small ads and job opportunities on the other. Leaders in this field include, among others, such papers as *Le Provençal* which, in association with *Le Méridional*, founded the data access system SEMITEL, *Les Dernières Nouvelles d'Alsace* which set up a similar system GRETEL, and *Libération*, which created 3615 LIBE. Whilst this process is clearly one of diversification, it should not be confused with pluralism. On the contrary, in most cases, it reinforces the trend towards concentration and monopoly, although, as is so often the case with multi-media activity, the concentration is hidden by the diversity of outlets.

The cultural element

The mediation of cultural life in France is an important function of the media. Indeed this kind of mediation plays a crucial part in the socialisation process that we have discussed at some length earlier in this book. In France, if cultural activities occupy an important place in the media, it is because the French themselves lay great store by the role that such activities are deemed to play in the formation of civic values and social group adhesion. The magazine sector is an important mediator of cultural information. There is a tendency to produce publications of a glossy and generally over-priced variety which have readerships of basically two kinds. The first kind may be termed the enlightened middle classes who seek high-quality editions accompanied by equivalent high-quality and relevant commentary. Examples of this type include such luxury magazines as *Beaux Arts*, *Art-Press* and *Architecture d'Aujourd'hui* which specialise in up-market, high-quality editions. In addition there are other titles of a more general interest, *Le Monde de la Musique* and *Les Cahiers du Cinéma*. In the latter case, this magazine has played a determining role in the development of new concepts within the contemporary cinema.

There is, of course, an element of cultural information contained in the daily written press, either with specific designated sections in each edition (i.e. *Le Monde* and *Libération*), or as is the case with *Le Monde de la Musique* from the same press group. This cultural dimension in the written press fulfils two essential functions. Firstly, it enhances its 'serious' aspect and its claim to serious status by its appropriation of themes and topic deemed to be socially, intellectually and aesthetically worthy, perhaps even elitist. Secondly, cultural information of this kind turns the press into the essential vectors of ideological and aesthetic debate for its readers who share the same cultural and political values. The existence of these two functions explains why cultural information occupies a central place in mediated communication in France, and is not relegated to the margins of press activity. It is this element of cultural information which bestows upon the media a wider dimension than the merely political or institutional, placing it actively within a symbolic framework which contributes to the formation of socio-cultural identity and group membership.

III The broadcasting media

The radio

The first radio services were established in France in the 1930s. The state retained a monopoly over the radio (RTF and then ORTF) until 1981. During this period effectively two systems co-existed: the national radio broadcasting from inside France, and the commercial stations (*les radios périphériques*) which transmitted into the country from locations just outside its frontiers (Luxembourg, Andorra, Monte Carlo). Advertising was not allowed on the public service stations whilst, on the other hand, their commercial rivals were able to develop a strong advertising market. These commercial stations, situated just outside French territory, were to become the catalysts for the modernisation of the public service radio in its programming as well as in its future development as a medium. The quality of the reception of radio broadcasting was significantly improved in the 1960s with the introduction of the FM band. This technological advance was instrumental in the rapid increase in the so-called 'pirate stations', all of which contravened the 1974 law on broadcasting. It was indeed the technological innovation of FM which brought about the liberation of the radio and hastened the end of the state monopoly. The end of this monopoly occurred in the early 1980s and a new kind of broadcasting emerged. In 1981 private local radio was legalised and today it falls into three categories:

- First, the 'associative radio' stations, which are unsupported by advertising revenue and subsidised by the state. These stations are closely linked to non-profit-making organisations and associations such as unemployment and local government agencies.
- Second, commercial radio, which is most frequently built into national networks whose essential revenue derives from advertising and whose schedules are music-dominated.
- Third, a number of other stations of mixed status (see below under 'Private, local radio').

The national public service radio

As we have mentioned above, the radio began as a state monopoly in 1937. This monopoly came about for two reasons, firstly, the desire on the part of the government to monitor information during a period of both diplomatic and political tension, and secondly, for cultural reasons – the traditional presence of the state in all great national investments in communications (i.e. in the media as well as in the railways). Today there is in France a strong public service radio system, Radio France, which comprises three main stations:

- France Inter, which is the principal public service station, broadcasting news bulletins and a wide range of general programming.
- France Culture, which specialises in documentaries, literary and artistic programmes.
- France Musique, which, as its name suggests, broadcasts all kinds of music and concerts.

Other minor stations provide for the needs of specialised audiences. Radio Bleue, for example, targets older people, whereas FIP is a station of continuous music aimed at a younger audience. Public sector radio is of the traditional kind in France and the public service ethos is strong and ever-present. Radio France is the overarching administrative organisation whose head, along with all the other heads of the public radio stations and television channels, is appointed by the CSA. Radio France is directly financed from state funds.

Private local radio

Officially legalised in 1981 after a long period of clandestine existence as 'pirates', these local radios divide into two main categories. The first are operated by local associations and are usually politically or socially committed, having as their mission a cultural project of some kind, and the development of closer relations between people of a defined local neighbourhood. Such radio stations firstly owe their existence to the relatively low set-up costs, and secondly to state subsidies. In consequence a significant number of them exist throughout France.

The second category is driven out of commercial interests and get their income almost exclusively from advertising. The function of local commercial radios can be likened in some ways to that of the regional written press. Indeed, they are often to be found in a formal relationship with a regional paper and their development has been complementary to that of the association radios and the regional press. The commercial stations are less political in tone and, although they provide news, they specialise particularly in musical entertainment broadcast over an extended daily and nightly schedule. They mostly have a wide audience, but some (a minority), which are specialist stations, have a correspondingly specialised audience (see below for further discussion). The allocation of frequencies to radio stations is the responsibility of the CSA.

Commercial radio networks

Historically the development of commercial radio in France can be characterised under three headings: the commercial radios operating just outside the French frontier but transmitting to a French audience (the *radios périphériques*), the local commercial radios, and the network stations. The *radios périphériques* were operating during the period when French radio was controlled by the state monopoly. They set themselves up outside the French frontiers in order to avoid the prohibiting legislation internal to France and appropriately named themselves Europe 1, Radio Luxembourg, Radio Andorra and Radio Monte Carlo. Their schedules were weighted towards light entertainment, music and news and, of course, they carried advertising commercials.

Post-1981 network radio comprises clusters of local commercial radio franchise-holders. These franchises amount to commercial concessions awarded to the local stations (by the CSA) allowing them to broadcast using the network signature, and to advertise products at a national level. Network radio was established at the same time as FM transmission was made available to local, commercial broadcasters and its effects upon the latter have been twofold: firstly, the use of the well known network title or signature conferred a national dimension and status upon the local commercial station, and secondly, network status required the station to amass a considerable stock of programmes. The problem of local commercial radios often centres on their need to occupy a large, daily programming space with a limited amount of material. Today in France the principal radio networks are (number of stations in brackets): Radio Nostalgie (165), Fun Radio (82), Europe 2 (82), NRJ (63), Kiss (59), Pacific (53), FRM (35), Skyrock (32), Hit-FM (8), Chic FM. It is a useful comparison, when considering the network system to draw a parallel with the phenomenon of concentration in the written press. Table 3.3 indicates the percentage audience share of the principal radio stations in France.

Table 3.3 French radio audience share (%) in 1994

RTL Luxembourg	20
France–Inter	13.6
Europe No. 1	12.5
France–Info	9.0
France Culture	2.0
France Musique	3.0
Radios Locales Privées	37.6
Others	2.3

Source: SJTI

French television

French television began experimental transmissions in the mid-1930s but, in mass broadcasting terms, dates from the 1950s (a single channel). In the 1960s two new channels, Antenne 2 and FR 3 were added. A characteristic feature of French television is the extraordinarily slow process by which it achieved separation from state influence and interference. It is worth noting that the first regulatory body, the Haute Autorité, was only established in 1982, and the second, the Commission nationale de la communication et des libertés, in 1987, followed by the current Conseil supérieur de l'audio visuel in 1988. For decades after 1945 French television was widely used by government as an instrument of propaganda in the furtherance of presidential or other official powers. During the events of May 1968 the call for the liberation both of the radio and of the television was forcefully expressed, although the first major steps in this direction were not taken until the early 1980s by the almost simultaneous creation of the regulatory Haute Autorité (with the remit to ensure broadcasting independence from the state), and the introduction of private commercial broadcasting. A significant landmark in the history of French television was the opening up of the broadcasting landscape to commercial channels such as Canal Plus, an encrypted subscription channel, as well as to La Cinq[4] and M6. This 'new television' in France may be characterised by four major features:

- Firstly, a strong cooperative activity between the cinema and television, particularly in the broadcasting of films on the cable networks.
- Secondly, the role of music in the television schedules.
- Thirdly, the development of television news coverage and the increase in television magazine programmes.
- Finally, the development of very short programmes or clips influenced by techniques derived from commercial television.

In addition to the developments outlined above, two new cultural channels were also launched, La Cinquième which specialises mostly in educational programming, and ARTE which is a jointly sponsored German–French channel specialising in programming of a cultural nature (for further discussion see below).

Finally, French television has somewhat timidly opened up to cable. The Plan Câble was launched ambitiously in 1982, driven by the dominant player in the sector, Direction Générale des Télécommunications (now France Télécom). Although a considerable number of French towns have adopted cable, the number of connected television households has remained lower than anticipated at around 5 per cent (*Cable and Satellite Europe*, January 1995). Nevertheless, this represents more than one million households currently cabled and it is anticipated that this figure will rise to 10 million by the year 2004.

There has been in France since 1982 an increasing activity in communications involving telematics (*télématique*) and this activity has also largely been at the initiative of France Télécom which has undertaken the installation of terminals on demand from the public. A whole range of interactive services, including Minitel, has resulted from this initiative targeting professional people but also including a wider user group seeking information of a more general kind such as leisure and entertainment. Today France is entering upon the multimedia era, the beginning of a period of integrated and interactive, computer-aided communication of picture, sound and data systems.

The French television channels

There are four types of television channels in France: first, the national state-sponsored corporation France Télévision, operating the two public channels France 2 and France 3. Second, the private commercial channels, TF1, M6 and Canal Plus. Third, the indirect PSB channels ARTE and La Cinquième. Finally come the cable and satellite operators, as well as some channels broadcasting from outside French territory.

France Télévision comprises two public channels, France 2, the main national channel, and France 3, the national channel with regional responsibilities. Both channels are headed by the same chairman appointed by the CSA. They are typical PSB operators in so far as their programming is of the traditional, wide-ranging kind. TF1 was originally the PSB 'flagship' channel in France and was privatised in 1986 by the Chirac administration. The industrialist Francis Bouygues is the principal shareholder. M6 was created in 1985 as part of the media liberalising policy initiated by the departing socialist government. It is essentially a music channel targeting the urban youth of the country. Canal Plus was launched in 1984 (again a socialist initiative) and was headed by Marcel Rousselet. It is the first French subscription channel. Since transmissions are mostly encrypted, a decoder is necessary for access to this channel which is predominantly a vehicle for the showing of films. ARTE, as we have mentioned above, is the jointly operated Franco-German channel which is shared with La Cinquième, a channel specialising in education and documentary programmes. Finally there are the transfrontier channels such as Télé-Monte-Carlo and the French-speaking Swiss channels as well as numerous other cable operators of the narrowcasting kind – Planète for documentaries, Canal Jimmy for young people, and several other film and news channels. Figure 3.1 indicates the current approximate audience share across the principal channels.

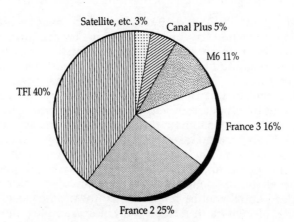

Source: Le Monde, January 1995

Figure 3.1   Television audience share (1995) per cent

The case of ARTE

1984 saw the launch of a new PSB television channel promoted jointly by the French and German governments. ARTE is an innovatory, experimental channel in three ways at least. Firstly, this is the first time that a transnational television channel has been established resulting from cooperation between two countries in this way. Putting aside the political significance that this kind of political cooperation represents, and which points to an active policy of reconciliation between the two countries, this channel has developed production techniques (by which important processes of mediation occur) in two important areas. Evidently, the first is the acceptance of bilingualism on a single channel. This acceptance is manifest in the use both of sub-titles and dubbing. The second is the innovatory nature of ARTE's production and programming. ARTE has succeeded in bringing to its programming a combination of impressive technical innovation and well researched and resourced productions, thus ensuring that the channel provides contemporary, sophisticated material over a range of ideas and cultural issues. ARTE presents a large number of films and TV films in their unedited versions, as well as relaying coverage of prestigious cultural events and concerts. In summary, ARTE is a channel exclusively committed to the broadcasting of cultural programming, and this is a major innovation in transnational broadcasting. In a market-orientated industry, it is also a gamble. Its future lies in its capacity to retain a viable audience given the challenging nature of its programmes, some of which will inevitably be considered élitist in nature. Even so, it should be emphasised that this kind of initiative is probably the only way of increasing the dissemination of transcultural knowledge of this kind.

The modernisation of broadcasting and communications

The period between 1970 and 1990 is one which may be characterised by the modernisation of broadcasting in France and it can be categorised under three principal trends. Firstly, it was a period of intensive re-equipment and very large investment. This trend may be explained by state intervention which has always played a determining role in this domain, and secondly by the participation of a new group of operators and investors from the private sector. The process of modernisation in the broadcasting and communications sectors has been accompanied by a trend towards concentration, a trend which may be partly explained by the need for costly investment in equipment. Two examples will suffice to illustrate this point. Firstly, in the radio sector, the policy of heavy investment explains the growth of network radio as well as the tendency towards concentration in a sector while, elsewhere in Europe (Italy, for example), the possibility of lower levels of investment has created conditions which favour the development of a vast sector of smaller radio stations. Secondly, in the cable sector, the decision on the part of many operators to use fibre-optic cable has resulted in the establishment of networks offering very broad choices of interactivity and, in consequence, multiple services. However, these first routes of the information superhighway significantly increase the installation costs to the network operators, and have thus increased the control and influence of the main financial investors in the cable networks (i.e. Compagnie Générale des Eaux, Lyonnaise des Eaux, Caisse des Dépôts-C3D and others) as well as the weight and influence of France Télécom.

Beyond the illustrative scope of these two examples, the process of modernisation can be characterised by the trend which involves major decision-making, occurring at the centre, and, secondly, the undertaking of experimental and research activity of both a comprehensive and fundamental nature. This activity in the area of information science and communications has produced an impressively strong link between industry, the domestic market and basic research.

Bearing these circumstances in mind, it is interesting to study the process of the modernisation of broadcasting and communications in the light of the likely outcomes. Firstly, in terms of outcomes, it is clear that a gamble was taken relating to the development of communications, which in the case of the Plan Câble was only partly successful (see below). It is also necessary to clarify the issue more precisely by noting that, from the start, this process was conceived as an issue of national proportion and importance, which was undertaken not at the level of local networks or companies but at a national one, involving the direct participation of national and institutional policy decision-makers (i.e. government and telecommunications companies).

Finally, the process of modernisation of the audiovisual sector in France must be viewed within a wider context overall of change in the field of telecommunications itself. The most singular event which truly launched the process (in re-equipment as well as in production) was, without doubt, the Plan Câble which was initiated in 1982 by the then Direction Générale des Télécommunications (DGT). The Plan Câble affected the process of modernisation in three principal ways.

Firstly, by the establishing of cable networks which was mostly undertaken by the municipalities and the local associations. This achievement amounted in real terms to the setting up of a new kind of technological infrastructure with the dual objectives of establishing both active and interactive networks. The cable and associated industries were involved in the building of networks which ultimately would carry, among others, their own products. Secondly, the choice of fibre optic technology led to a great number of operators becoming involved in the process of modernisation which was both long-term in nature and offered multiple opportunities for commercial and other kinds of exploitation. Finally, the increase in the demand for hardware has meant that the French manufacturers have had to produce good quality receiving equipment and satellite dishes in large quantities, and in turn influence the modalities of their use by the French public (there are currently 385,000 operational satellite dishes in France, which is a 10 per cent increase on 1993).

Recent developments in the production sector in France are directly linked to the increase in the number of television channels and production companies at a national level, and to the emergence, at a local level, of cable television companies. The production companies are generally organised on a small scale in France (the so-called *Petites et moyennes entreprises* or PME), or, at the other end of the scale, on a transnational or international basis. However, the kinds of programming and services offered to the public are predominantly linked to the rise in the number of cable networks. Essentially, the nature of this programming has been fashioned by the convergence and integration of a variety of programmes and services within a single cable network, linked to teletext activities, thus transforming both network use and user demand. By transformation we essentially mean the development of services such as teleshopping, telesurveillance, and the provision of practical information linked to the requirements of everyday life and events.

The role and significance of telecommunications in the audio-visual sector

In the 1980s France trailed significantly behind other European countries in the field of telecommunications. This state of relative backwardness was in fact the spur for the modernisation, in a complementary way, of both the audio-visual and the tele-communications sectors. The Plan Câble was instrumental in the modernisation of the French telecommunications system, and it is within this wider context that these two political initiatives should be viewed. Indeed, such was the speed by which France caught up in these fields that it became clear that the national Telephone Directory could no longer continue to exist in its traditional hard-copy form. The cost of producing information in printed form was prohibitive, and its distribution to subscribers problematic. France Télécom resolved this problem by providing subscribers to the new services with a telephone-computer link (Minitel) which gave them access to all the telephone directories for the whole country, and at the same time also accessed all the computer-based public and commercial services available throughout France. From this provision of Minitel by France Télécom, the computer-based services which we have mentioned above have developed into a public service network of considerable proportions, unique in Western Europe. Financially the system works on the basis of a variable tariff, depending on the nature of the service required, and the length of consultation (it is not distance-related). A percentage of the tariff goes to the service provider as payment.

The number of Minitel terminals has increased in France from 3.3 million in 1987 to 6.5 million in 1994. In the same period the number of consultations has gone up from 514 million to 1,100

Table 3.4 Cable and satellite penetration in Western Europe in 1995

Country	Pop. (millions)	TV homes (millions)	VCR homes (millions)	Cable connection (millions)	Cable penetration (%)	Dish total
France	58.0	20.8	12.3	1.0	4.8	385,000
Germany	81.2	33.0	16.2	14.4	43.9	6,000,000
Italy	57.2	20.3	9.1	Nil	Nil	110,000
Spain	39.2	11.7	6.3	1.2	10.3	180,000
UK	58.4	22.2	16.0	0.77	3.9	3,000,000

Source: Cable and Satellite Europe, January 1995

million, and the number of services available from 7,372 to 23,227 in 1993 (France Télécom, in *Le Monde*, 21.3.95). Table 3.4 shows the position of France with regard to cable and satellite compared with the other countries examined in this book.

The role of France Télécom as catalyst in the process of modernisation of the audio-visual sector is both seminal and specific to its development in France. As we have seen, it took the form both of the setting up of teletext networks, and of the development of the nature and use of the services now available. The modernisation of the audio-visual sector has taken a similar route to that of the telephone system in France at the end of the 1960s, when there was a period of technological vacuum followed by a vigorous leap forward, driven by massive state funding. In both cases there was a strong public take-up of the new services provided. It was initially, therefore, the role of France Télécom which determined the shape of the development in the audio-visual sector in France. As we have also seen, there has been a close interlocking of the telephone and teletext systems. The complementary interaction between cable, satellite, computer and telephone technology has produced communications networks which are both highly performative and comprehensive, and which give access to services of an extremely diverse nature. The satellite is the latest development in a technology which, upon the purchase of a dish aerial (this is a growth market in France), opens up local audio-visual communication to a vast number of transmissions and products from all over the world. Such developments as this will reinforce the process of diversification and fragmentation of the form, content and even the concept of communication itself.

Finally, and importantly, the role of France Télécom in the development of audio-visual communications has brought about a transformation in this field from one of passive spectator status to one of interactive participation (the developments in the domain of teletext, i.e. telephone-computer links, serving as the model in this respect). To restate this in a slightly more elaborate way, the extraordinarily significant development that has taken place in audio-visual communication over the last twenty years has moved it from a situation where viewers stared fascinatedly at a series of pictures in the role of spectators, to one in which they can now take part as interactive participants in a whole range of services. The direction in which this revolution is moving suggests a future wherein such services will become commonplace and everyday in France. Nevertheless the first period of wonderment at the technological progress made in this field has given way to one of disenchantment, and as such typifies what we may call 'a phase of modernity'. Modernity can be defined for our purpose not as the moment when a particular technology is discovered, but as the point in time when it becomes fully integrated into our daily lives and social habits. Audio-visual communication is, from now on, as much a part of our daily lives as the telephone.

Audio-visual communication owes its modernisation and its standardisation precisely to the fact that the public have taken to its use on a daily basis. Its services and transmissions have become the simple aids of daily life in the service of the public. For this reason audio-visual communication and the role of France Télécom are the subject of an animated political debate. In retrospect, the predominantly technological power which was exercised by DGT/France Télécom from 1960 to the 1980s has been followed by a period of a more political nature (coinciding with the entrance of new national companies from the private sector) relating to the organisation and regulation of communications. The creation of a body such as the Conseil supérieur de l'audiovisuel is in part the acknowledgement by the state that audio-visual communication has political implications and poses the government with democratic issues relating to the exercise of political power.

Conclusion

The media in France play an essential role in the communication process and in national daily life. The mediating role of the media in France cannot be properly characterised by mere reference to technology or to the manner in which information is collected, processed and relayed to the public. Their most important aspect is indeed the result of this process: the socio-cultural and economic impact which the media have upon French society. The media are the major forces which influence and shape social identification and cohesion. In this respect the media are not mere vectors of information, but have a vital institutional role to play as well. It is this duality of role, especially in its pre-millennium form, to which we shall briefly turn in conclusion.

The media both facilitate and express socio-cultural group membership by giving the latter a kind of almost measurable consistency and intelligibility. In France this process of mediation is characterised by strong political and institutional overtones. The reason for this particular emphasis lies in the fact that French social identity is fashioned by a strong interplay between political and institutional forces. In these circumstances it can be appreciated that the role of the media is a crucial one. They give wide access to particular interpretations of events as well as to comparable, opposed and debatable points of view. It is through the media, for the most part, that the public sphere takes on its existence as a forum for dialogue, confrontation and political manoeuvre. The French media, and the written press in particular, have always constituted a powerful force for the expression of social attitudes and for the sustaining of a dynamic dialogue within the public sphere.

On a specifically cultural level, the media, by the act of mediation, become the carriers of our group identity and our choice. France 'reads' itself through the images which are represented by its media and projected into the public sphere. These images are also a kind of cultural rallying point for the public (readers, viewers, users) and can be categorised into a number of functional characteristics which emerge as the consequence of a careful reading of the media.

Firstly, there is the democratic function: the media represent one of the most advanced forms of democratic debate in France. As such they constitute a forum for the expression, interplay and confrontation of a range of viewpoints within the country. This range and interplay of opinion may be found in the pages of Le Monde and Libération, and in the such television debates and news magazine programmes as Sept sur sept. These are the kind of debates and confrontation of opinions which help create an image of France, through the media, as a democratic and open country. There have been periods of French history when the media have played a very important part in the mediation and influencing of events. For example, the 'events' of 1968, which brought many acute social tensions to the surface, were the object of intense media coverage. Similarly, electoral campaigns are also always the occasion for the media to engage in the drawing of historical parallels, political commentary, face-to-face encounters, and post-electoral analyses by which they remind the public of their political bearings.

Secondly, there is the modernisation function: the media currently play a considerable role in the modernisation of French society. France has committed itself, since the 1980s, to a path of modernisation of its economy, its social structures and its methods of professional training. In this respect, the extension of media representation to industrial, research and social issues has had the effect of reinforcing this trend towards modernisation. We should note, by way of example, the activities of Le Monde in this domain, which publishes weekly economic supplements, and which, on a daily basis, dedicates many column inches to the coverage of social and industrial relations. In addition, magazines such as the Nouvel Economiste and L'Entreprise publish detailed reports on company relations and activities, and others such as La Recherche relay to a wide public the nature of on-going experimental work as well as the results of scientific research.

Thirdly, there is the cultural memory function: the past is an essential element of identity for a country such as France, and in this respect, the media play an important role in both the preservation and the dissemination of the nation's history, as well as acting as pointers to its present direction. Thus, for example, the media played an important role in the festivities organised to mark the bi-centenary of the Revolution of 1789 and, more recently, to mark the fiftieth anniversary of the end of the Second World War.

As we said at the beginning of this chapter, mediated communication is a powerful means of shaping and reinforcing the process of socio-cultural identity and cohesion. The responsibilities of the media in this domain are particularly recognised in France and this recognition manifests itself in the form of responsibilities and constraints imposed by law, especially in relation to the radio and television.

Notes

1. Minitel was first implemented in experimental form in 1978.
2. Using a telephone-modem-computer link.
3. This specific legislation on the written press, together with the *Ordonnances* of 1944, stand in marked contrast with the absence of similar laws in the UK.
4. La Cinq ceased operating in 1992.

CHAPTER 4

The media in Germany

Knut Hickethier

I Introduction

Following the defeat of the Third Reich and the liberation of Germany from National Socialism in 1945, the German mass media were reorganised by the allied victors. The decisive factor was the view that the media, and in particular film and radio, had contributed considerably to the maintenance of the Nazi regime and to the imposition of its inhuman ideology. Therefore the primary objective, especially of the western allies, was to use the media as instruments of democracy, and to prevent their employment for propaganda purposes; above all, the setting up of a re-education programme shaped media policy from 1945 until 1948. This policy also had a formative influence upon the further foundation of the Federal Republic based upon western culture, and its integration into the West in general.

The organisation of the media along lines laid down by the allies was, then, a matter of top priority. Whilst the Soviet Union organised the media in its zone according to the communist interpretation of media function (i.e. as the mouthpiece of the Communist Party), the Western allies agreed upon a single plan of action, in spite of the differences in the organisation of the media in their own countries. The intention was to establish the media as a public supervisory authority, clearly independent of the state, as a kind of 'fourth force'. The freedom and independence of the written press, as well as of broadcasting, was enshrined in the West German Basic Law and therefore was (and still is) a constitutional issue.

Legislation and public expectations

Despite numerous attempts to put political pressure on individual media and to restrain critical journalism, the media today are still viewed as independent channels of popular opinion anchored in the Basic Law and, as such, constitute a fundamental element of contemporary German society. The expectations of society with regards to the role of the media can be summarised as follows:

- The establishment of a public sphere which facilitates the exchange of ideas between institutions and citizens and which at the same time creates transparency in the political process.
- The political socialisation and integration of the individual citizens in their roles, among others, as voters, party members, dissidents and demonstrators.
- The critical monitoring of public behaviour by the constant exposure of political and public institutions, as well as policies, to public scrutiny (the media as the 'fourth estate').
- Political education by which individuals may learn to digest and understand political information and use it in the formation of opinions (see Pürer and Raabe, 1994:308ff).

In order for the media to fulfil these functions people expect them to convey information according to the following principles:

- Thoroughness: the public should be informed thoroughly about relevant social, political economic and cultural events: above all, all interest groups should be allowed a voice.
- Objectivity: the media should present the most undistorted and generally most acceptable journalistic description of reality possible.
- Comprehensibility: news coverage must be presented so that information is readily understood by non-specialists (Pürer and Raabe, 1994:306).

These expectations concerning the media, which are commonplace in media circles in Western Europe (i.e. McQuail 1983:82), are enshrined in several laws relating to the media in the Federal Republic. However, the manner in which the citizen's right to receive information via the media may be guaranteed is the subject of much diverging argument among the political parties of the Federal Republic. On one hand, for example, parties of the political Right such as the CDU and FDP favour freedom of information by guaranteeing a free market in the commercial sphere. On the other, the Left and Green parties prefer that the guarantee of pluralism and diversity be enshrined in public law. As will be noted, the second view – the legal guarantee of journalistic freedom safeguarded by statutory bodies – is a far cry from the first which relies much more on the control by market forces alone.

This debate over media policy is most sharply focused currently within the context of broadcasting in Germany, since the commercial organisation and status of the written press have been long since accepted. Broadcasting, however, because of its nature, constantly forces new decisions upon politicians relating to its status either as a public service body or as a commercial undertaking. Decisions about broadcasting policy in Germany usually have taken place over a protracted period. The debate, for example, concerning the proposal to introduce commercial broadcasting went on from 1976 to 1983 before any decision was reached. Thus the decision, when finally made, could be seen to have taken into account many different interests and therefore stood a better chance of being accepted. The possibility of this kind of protracted discussion within Germany is likely to diminish as media policy becomes less and less determined at national level and has to take account of international factors such as decisions made in Brussels by the European Commission, within the framework of the Single European Market.

The continuation of the media organisation set up in the aftermath of the Second World War, under the jurisdiction of the Federal Constitutional Court, has resulted in the development of a multi-layered structure of regulatory bodies and, to some extent, to the existence of overlapping legislative responsibilities (Jarren, 1994:112). Thus there is a high degree of cooperation between the Federation and the Länder on one hand, and between the individual Länder on the other. In addition to the regulation of the way in which the media represent public events, media policy is increasingly occupied with the task of monitoring its own technical expansion as well as the establishment of economically viable media groups in the individual Länder and regions.

As we have said, in the past there existed in Germany a kind of 'cooperative federalism' which for a long time ensured relatively stable media relations. However, this cooperation has become increasingly more difficult to sustain in recent times (Jarren, 1994:144). In the past, decision-making on media policy was determined by the following factors:

- an extensive division of powers;
- few formalised political connections;
- limited professionalisation of the political administrative system;
- the significant influence of the judiciary, i.e. judgements of the Constitutional Court (Jarren, 1994:116).

This situation has proved to be increasingly problematic to maintain in the current context of recent technological changes which have led to:

- a blurring of the distinction between individual and mass communication;
- a shift in the context of decision-making from a national to the European level;
- a huge clash between (new) economic interests and the traditional cultural mission of the media, due to the interest of new, 'non-media friendly' capital from such backers as banks, insurance companies and manufacturing groups.

Thus the traditionally slow internal decision-making machinery in Germany is becoming increasingly an obstacle to the demand for rapid development in the media. What has proved particularly disadvantageous is the fact that, at government level, no overall plan for a single media policy exists.

Development of the media in the GDR 1949–90

In the former East Germany (GDR), as we have already noted above, media policy was also heavily influenced by the occupying power. This meant that the media were wholly controlled by the Communist Party but, at the same time, there was an attempt to maintain an outward appearance of pluralism. The SED[1] published a main title, *Neues Deutschland*, and numerous regional newspapers. The so-called 'block parties' allied to it in the National Front, the CDU[2] and the Liberal and Farmers' Parties possessed their own newspapers. Nevertheless, all were centrally controlled by the Politbüro of the SED. It is true that other publications did become established, in particular weekly papers and special interest magazines, but they too were influenced by the Party. In consequence they did not provide a public forum for the discussion of official policy or of social issues (see Hickethier, 1994d).

As far as broadcasting was concerned, after a brief pause during which regional radio was established, radio soon became centralised and centred in East Berlin under the direction of the 'State Broadcasting Committee'. In addition to the principal stations serving the GDR, stations aimed at the Federal Republic were also established through which the Cold War could be conducted over the air-waves. In the reverse direction, radio and television channels such as RIAS Berlin and SFB were beamed on the GDR from West Berlin with the result that, almost throughout the GDR, programmes from the West could always be seen and heard. In the long term this situation of almost total transmission 'spill-over' into the GDR led to the creation of a particular consciousness in East Germany with regard to the West, and maintained a bond with the Federal Republic.

East German television, which sent out its first test transmission in December 1952, began regular broadcasting in 1956. The expansion of television in the GDR followed a similar course to that of the Federal Republic. However, as the result of the reception of channels from across its western frontier, television took on the function of a 'window on the West'. In 1971 a second channel was created in the GDR which concentrated mostly on educational programmes. In the eyes of the citizens of the GDR, their own television suffered from a lack of credibility which arose from its obvious links with the state and the Communist Party. For this reason viewing figures were established in secret and not published (Hoff, 1993). During the final phrase of its existence, the GDR was increasingly infiltrated by the influence of western television. Literally during the last days of its existence the GDR channels covered the demonstrations in Leipzig and Berlin and reported the 'floods of refugees crossing through Czechoslovakia and Hungary'. Such reporting without doubt had the effect of speeding up the collapse of the GDR. After a transition period in 1990–1 the Länder were re-established in the GDR and the whole of Germany was placed under the jurisdiction of the Basic Law. Broadcasting corporations were set up in each of the new Länder modelled on those in the West, and the dual system comprising both commercial and private channels was established.

II Development of the written press in the Federal Republic since 1949

As was the case before the coming to power of the Nazis in 1933, the written press remained in private ownership in the post-1949 period, although for the launching, publication and printing of newspapers, publishers required a licence which was only granted to those who had not incriminated themselves by serving under the Nazi regime. As the result of this licensing policy many new national papers were established such as the *Frankfurter Allgemeine Zeitung*, the *Süddeutsche Zeitung*, the *Frankfurter Rundschau* and *Die Welt* in addition to numerous regional and local papers. By 1948, 56 newspapers (with 112 different editions) had been licensed in the American Zone, 53 in the British Zone (with 387 different editions) and 29 in the French Zone (with 174 editions) (Pürer and Raabe, 1994:99).

The press groups which had existed before 1933, which had prepared the way for Hitler, had been expropriated into the ownership of the Party, and what remained of them in 1945 was completely suppressed. Following the foundation of the Federal Republic in 1949, and the lifting of the licence requirement, several other former publishers re-emerged in order to launch yet more newspapers. However, on the whole, they could not compete with the licensed papers which had already established themselves in the earlier period. Indeed as early as the 1950s and 1960s there was a detectable trend towards concentration in which numerous smaller papers and magazines folded or were taken over by others. In particular the 'party newspapers' (papers associated with a political party), of the kind which existed under the former Weimar Republic, were unable to survive, mostly because readers preferred a more independent press. In consequence, political opinions were increasingly presented with an air of impartiality. The strongest press group to emerge from these moves towards concentration was the Axel-Springer Verlag with its tabloid *Bild Zeitung* and *BZ* as well as the *Hamburger Abendblatt* and several others, including the TV listing magazines. In particular *Bild Zeitung* developed a biased presentation of political opinion, disguised as impartiality, into a dangerously fine art. This led to fierce criticism and numerous demonstrations against the Springer Group, especially during the period of student unrest of 1968.

Table 4.1 Overview of written daily press in Germany

Year	Publishers Total	Index 1954 = 100	Year	Titles Total	Index 1954 = 100
1954	225	100	1954	624	100
1964	183	81	1964	573	92
1967	158	70	1967	535	86
1976	121	54	1976	403	65
1979	122	54	1979	400	64
1981	124	55	1981	392	63
1983	125	56	1983	385	62
1985	126	56	1985	382	61
1987	121	54	1987	(375)	(60)
1989	119	53	1989	358	57

Year	Regional local titles Total	Index 1954 = 100	Year	Circulation in millions Total	Index 1954 = 100
1954	1,500	100	1954	13.4	100
1964	1,495	100	1964	17.3	129
1967	1,416	94	1967	18.0	134
1976	1,229	82	1976	19.5	146
1979	1,240	83	1979	20.5	153
1981	1,258	84	1981	20.4	152
1983	1,255	84	1983	21.2	158
1985	1,273	85	1985	20.9	156
1987	–	?	1987	20.7	155
1989	1,344	90	1989	20.3	152

Source: Walter J. Schütz in Media Perspektiven, 1989
NB: Prior to unification

At the peak of this first phase of concentration, which lasted until 1976, the Springer Group had a 32.2 per cent market share of daily newspapers and 83.9 per cent market share of the entire press of the Federal Republic (Pürer and Raabe, 1994:115). Whilst the newspapers of the Springer group practised a markedly national and right-of-centre style of reporting, particularly from the end of the 1950s, other papers such as Der Spiegel, Frankfurter Rundschau and Süddeutsche Zeitung also established themselves and these were more liberal in outlook and adopted a more overtly critical stance (see Table 4.1).

Concentration in the contemporary written press

The level of press concentration in Germany has been described in a nationwide survey into the ownership of German daily newspapers undertaken by Walter J. Schütz in 1994. According to Schütz the total of daily publications in Germany, including the former GDR, has dropped from 158 in 1991 to 137 in 1993 and the number purchased daily has fallen from 27.3 million to 25.4 million in 1993 (Schütz, 1994). Within a very short space of time, German unification has led to the demise of the independent newspapers of the eastern Länder. Almost the only newspapers to survive are those operated by the SED which were sold off to western media groups by the Treuhand.[3] Today it is no longer possible to speak of an autonomous East German newspaper scene. The opportunity to establish a new press structure on the basis of medium-sized groups and, by so doing, preserve pluralism, has been lost. This development has led one media specialist to describe what has happened as 'the lightning colonisation of the media scene' (Holzer, 1993) and another to observe that 'the dangers that threaten media freedom and the diversity of opinions in the old Länder were not avoided during the restructuring of East German communications' (Geissler 1993:26). One consequence for the regional press is that individual titles now have monopoly status in over half of the Federal Republic. This situation is clearly at odds with the public interest principle of media pluralism which we have already discussed in Chapter 1. Furthermore, media research suggests that the establishment of a new paper in the Federal Republic is now practically impossible (Röper, 1993b:403). The last successful attempt to launch a daily newspaper occurred in 1979 with *Tageszeitung*, an alternative newspaper, which still only has a very limited circulation and whose continued existence cannot be guaranteed, even after sixteen years.

Röper has also examined the concentration of media groups in the popular magazine market and points out that, between them, the four largest groups – Burda, Springer, Bauer and Gruner + Jahr – possess approximately two thirds of the market share. In this area it is worth noting in passing that there has been an increase in the number of titles from 519 in 1992 to 554 in 1994. The increases in circulation figures for the four largest groups clearly show the extent to which this specialist magazine market is expanding. This expansion is also discernible in other sectors of the press, and we shall return to this topic again shortly (see Table 4.2).

The social dominance and preference shown for television in the Federal Republic (see below for further discussion) has produced a tendency for the written press to adopt a more 'visual' format. Whilst it is true that papers such as *Bild* have always attracted readers with an eye-catching lay-out, there is now a perceptible trend in many other papers towards the visual image through the use of photographs, colour and varied typescript. This phenomenon is particularly apparent in some of the new magazines such as *Focus*, *Tempo* and *Max*. Also brand new, highly visual TV listing magazines have appeared, enlivened by graphics typifying the changes in lay-out in the 1990s. This tendency towards the increased visualisation of the written press may be interpreted as the development of a new cultural function of the media in which the former distinction between information and entertainment is becoming blurred.

Table 4.2   Popular magazines: developments in the circulation of major publishers[1]

Circulation in millions	1968	1972	1976	1980	1984	1988	1990	1992	1994
Bauer	10.38	12.51	15.98	17.36	19.04	20.52	20.51	24.08	24.04
Burda	7.02	12.52	13.85	10.29	10.71	10.93	9.98	8.29	10.00
Springer	4.99	5.73	6.39	7.14	9.97	10.10	10.44	10.88	10.28
Gruner + Jahr	4.54	6.30	5.67	5.64	5.52	6.89	6.86	7.71	7.73
Total	56.31	62.62	74.85	84.53	94.48	105.14	109.82	121.9	125.96
Index 1968 = 100									
Bauer	100	121	154	167	183	198	198	232	232
Burda	100	178	197	147	153	156	142	118	143
Springer	100	115	128	143	200	202	209	218	206
Gruner + Jahr	100	139	125	124	122	152	151	167	170
Total	100	111	133	150	168	187	195	216	224

Source: Horst Röper in *Media Perspektiven*, 1994
[1] Excluding foreign language editions

The concentration of economic power in the media, which has developed over a short space of time in the Federal Republic, must be viewed as a threat to the public interest requirement of pluralism, the nature of which has already been discussed in Chapter 1. This threat is increasing due to foreign involvement and to mergers with supranational conglomerates. Although such tendencies are increasingly criticised in public debate, the Federal and Land governments do not feel obliged to intervene politically (through, for example, the imposition of upper limits on the media market holdings). This may be because the media conglomerates themselves have political sympathies – the Springer Kirch group favours the CSU/CDU whilst the Bertelsmann CLT group leans towards the SPD. But in addition to politics, economic factors also play a role. Media policy regarding the location of media groups within the regions is increasingly assuming political-economic importance in Germany, in addition to the need to create large groups capable of competing on a global scale. There are real dangers for the democratic process inherent in such policies. On the one hand corporateness often obscures ownership and editorial influence, and on the other the entire balance of interests between the major powerful players in German society risks becoming distorted. So far these dangers have gone unrecognised.

The magazine sector

In the German-speaking world, media concentration is to a large extent concealed through the apparent diversity of choice in the market. As we have already mentioned above, in the case of the written press, the magazine market is particularly significant. Whilst the number of independent newspapers is diminishing in the long term, the number of magazines is constantly on the increase. Between 1984 and 1991 the number of titles rose from 6,817 to 8,740 and their circulation increased from 261 million to 386 million (Medienbericht, 1994:104).

The most noticeable expansion has been in the area of popular entertainment magazines which has experienced an increased turnover from 5,600 million DM in 1984 to 7,600 million DM in 1991. This has been achieved by a process of ever-increasing diversification of existing market segments, so that women's magazines, for example, now target women of specific age groups (older women, young mothers, career women, etc.). In the category 'women, family, fashion, living' there were 35 new titles in 1991 added to the list of those existing in 1984. In the same period magazines targeting young people increased from 55 to 77. Magazines in the category 'general information, culture and politics' increased from 375 to 484 (although their overall circulation also dropped from 5.5 million to 4.7 million). The most diversified category was 'cars, travel, leisure and hobbies' which rose from 221 to 384 titles (again here, the overall circulation fell from 17.2 million to 16.6 million). This phenomenon of increasing titles but falling overall circulation well illustrates the paradoxical nature of diversification. However, the same pattern is not apparent for all segments; in the sports magazine market, for example, the rise in the number of titles is relatively small (212 to 261), but the overall increase in circulation – from 2.6 to 4.1 millions – is significantly higher.

Finally, the number of titles in the 'general entertainment' category has also risen, increasing from 176 to 292 titles, with a rise in circulation from 36.1 to 43.5 millions. In this area, the glossy magazines targeting the youth market, with their emphasis upon entertainment, adventure, sex and consumerism, reflect a noticeable shift in socio-cultural values in recent years. This widening diversity of choice has also resulted in a greater diversity of expectations. The trend in readership is moving away from magazines focusing upon politics or the arts towards those which promote consumerism[4] and its associated lifestyles. Inevitably though, at the same time, the discourse of the public sphere is being lost. In short, the reading public communicates increasingly in fragmented spheres. Isolated, for the most part, people pursue individual desires to the exclusion of other kinds of wider social and cultural importance.

The numerical increase in magazine titles does not necessarily produce a greater variety of choice. Indeed the difference between titles in the same market segment is often so slight that diversity

Table 4.3 Circulation of magazines by category (in millions)

Types of magazine	1984 Titles	Circulation	1991 Titles	Circulation
Political weeklies	109	1.7	97	2.0
Religious titles	313	8.9	347	7.6
Entertainment	1,364	104.8	1,685	142.0
Scientific/	1,268	8.3	1,713	13.4
Academic	1,616	41.0	2,007	69.9
Consumer magazines	87	38.9	124	67.8
Official journals	1,099	2.6	1,276	2.9
Small and magazines	732	42.1	1,207	68.0
Free official journals	46	0.3	166	1.2
Others	184	12.5	118	12.2

Source: Medienbericht 94

often means little else than more of the same thing. It is worth noting here that this trend is also perceivable in broadcasting and, in particular, in television in Germany where the multiplication of channels has led to a limited range of programming. This limited programming can be clearly seen in the screening of similar films and serials which are repeatedly shown by one channel after the other. The cause of this restricted range of programming comes from the need to place on the schedules those kinds of programmes which will guarantee high viewing figures. In this way, lesser known films, unusual documentaries and original dramatic works rarely feature on the schedules. Hence the alleged multiplicity of choice, in reality, conceals its absence.

However, as far as the written press is concerned, while the quantitative reduction of politically and culturally centred newspapers and magazines, as a proportion of the total market, is discernible in the long term, it is not viewed as a threat to socio-cultural values in the Federal Republic. The major quality political newspapers and magazines such as *Die Zeit, Der Spiegel, Frankfurter Allgemeine Zeitung, Süddeutsche Zeitung* and *Frankfurter Rundschau* have been steadily able to increase their circulations in recent years. Moreover, engaging new quality papers such as *Die Woche, Wochenpost* and *Freitag* have either entered the market or already existed in the former East Germany.[5] The influence of the sensationalist press such as *Bild Zeitung* and more recently of *Super Illu* is either declining or, in the case of the latter title, has disappeared altogether.

III Broadcasting in the Federal Republic 1945–95

The radio

In the same way as they had determined the organisation of the written press, the Allies also laid down the basic organisation and form of the broadcasting media. Radio broadcasting was established in the Weimar Republic with government involvement and was already state-operated in 1933. It was reconstructed in 1948 in the form of a public service corporation. The model for public service broadcasting was the BBC and the strong emphasis upon its independence was embedded in German law. Operating broadcasting on commercial lines, using the American model, was out of the question in the immediate post-1945 period because the disaster of the Second World War and the extensive devastation made financing through advertising an economic impossibility. Furthermore the lack of frequency space ruled out radio competition (Bausch, 1980).

Broadcasting today is financed by a licence fee, originally collected by the Post Office, but now by a special licensing centre (GEZ). The fees are fixed by the Land Assemblies which, in consequence, give them a considerable, but an undesirable, political hold over the broadcasting media. The installation of the broadcasting corporations was carried out differently by the individual zones of occupation. The British founded a single station for their zone, the Nordwestdeutscher Rundfunk (NWDR) in Hamburg. The Americans built up several regional stations which became subsequently Bayerischer Rundfunk (BR) in Munich, Süddeutscher Rundfunk (SDR) in Stuttgart, Hessischer Rundfunk (HR) in Frankfurt, and Radio Bremen (RB) in Bremen. The French founded Südwestfunk (SWF) in Baden-Baden as the single station of their zone. Therefore, by different routes, large broadcasting corporations became established which eventually grew to a total of eleven Land-based organisations, grouped into five regional zones, which have increased to seven since German unification. These broadcasting corporations are linked together in the Association of Broadcasting Corporations, the Arbeitsgemeinschaft der Rundfunkanstalten (ARD), which together are responsible for the transmission of the joint ARD television channel, eight regional channels and forty radio stations.

The development of radio broadcasting

In the 1950s, radio was the predominant medium of communication in Germany and the principal element of socio-cultural integration. Its aims were to transmit a comprehensive view of the world by its news coverage as well as providing for the education, cultural enrichment and entertainment of its listeners. Conceived as a 'window on the world', radio helped the German people to become acquainted with the culture of other countries by its news coverage and its documentaries. Radio plays (and later television drama) presented the literature of the western world and, in this unique manner, the ordinary German citizen was brought into contact with the western cultural tradition. Until 1994 the American Forces Network (AFN) and the British Forces Network (BFBS) introduced younger listeners to western music.[6]

The British and American influence on programme content also extended to programming itself in the form of quiz shows, serials and news broadcasts, the style of which was open and critical towards world issues and conflicts. As early as the mid-1950s there was already 24-hour radio broadcasting, but the 1960s and 1970s, in particular, were periods of rapid expansion for radio by the broadcasting corporations of the Länder. The 1970s saw the beginning of the introduction of magazine-type programmes in which the traditional boundaries between information and entertainment became blurred with a resulting reduction in both content and range of broadcasting. Today every Land broadcasting corporation operates between three and six radio stations with some arrangements for shared broadcasts between regions.

The development of public service television

Between 1935 and 1943 there had already been regular television broadcasts in Berlin and the reconstruction of German television, initiated in 1948, resulted in the first test transmission being made in Hamburg and Berlin in 1951, and regular transmissions beginning in 1952. Subsequently the first national channel, Erstes Deutsches Fernsehen (ARD), was established in 1954.

In the composition of its schedules, German television adopted the public service principles, derived initially from the radio, of providing information, education and entertainment. These, together with the principal comprehensive coverage of all significant world events, were, and still are, the guiding principles of the public service channels.

Even more so than radio, television became the window on the world and by this we mean, of course, the West. There was an emphasis upon comprehensive reporting and, by the extensive use of foreign correspondents, attempts were made to get as close to events abroad as possible. It should be remembered that during the first two post-war decades many Germans were unable to travel outside the country, and so it was the role of the broadcaster to bring the outside world into the home. This, then, was an important time for the television reporter specialising in the coverage of world affairs,[7] as well as for the promotion of western culture through the dramatisation of the works of both great and popular literary works ranging from Eugene O'Neill to Francis Durbridge (Hickethier, 1980:107).

The mid-1950s witnessed a constitutional dispute between the Federal government and the regional governments of the Länder when the former proposed the introduction of a commercial channel. This proposal went before the Constitutional Court in 1961 and was rejected. Instead the Land governments set up a second public service channel, Zweites Deutsches Fernsehen (ZDF) which began broadcasting in 1963.[8] The intention was that the two channels should not be in competition with one another since it was felt that this would lead to a reduction in programme quality. The emphasis was therefore on complementarity and, to this end, the two channels regularly cooperated in the coordination of their schedules.

However, in the 1960s, the expansion of channels brought new types of programmes to the small screen. *77 Sunset Boulevard, Bonanza* and *The Avengers* gave the schedules a new flavour. This period also saw the increase in the number of feature films, but these tended to be accompanied by cinema documentaries and biographies of individual directors so that the educational function, as well as that of entertainment, was sustained. Since 1969 a third channel provision has been added, the Dritte Programme. They were intended primarily to have a regional and educational bias as well as, in part, to be produced collaboratively by several Land corporations. Since the 1980s they have increasingly developed into channels offering entertainment whilst still retaining their regional flavour (Ross, 1967).

Commercial television and the creation of the dual system

With the development of new systems of distribution such as satellite and cable in the 1970s, the question of the introduction of commercial channels was again raised in the early 1980s. Supported by the report of a Federal Commission (1976), this time the proposal gained the approval of the Federal Constitutional Court in 1981. As the result of this decision radio and television took similar but separate paths in their development. Following some pilot projects, the first commercial channels began transmitting in 1984 from which RTL (initially RTL plus) and Sat 1 have established themselves as the dominant commercial channels.

In 1987 the Land corporations entered into a new agreement providing for the licensing and control of the commercial operators at Land level with the overall coordination ensured by a new body, the Direktorenkonferenz der Landesmedienanstalten or DLM. The large media groups, in particular those which had become established in the press and publishing market from the early 1950s, were now entering the commercial television business. The media corporations of the Länder could not prevent the emergence of two huge broadcasting groups during the first ten years of the existence of the dual media system (1984–94). The first is RTL Bertelsmann with RTL, RTL2, Vox and Premiere, and the second Kirch Springer with Sat 1, Deutsches Sportfernsehen (DSF), Pro 7 and Kabelkanal.

1984 also saw the establishment of commercial radio stations in the Federal Republic. The relatively low cost of operating a radio station (compared with the very high costs of financing a TV channel) has meant that smaller companies have been able to enter the market. Patterns of broadcasting vary: whilst in some Länder commercial stations serve the whole area, such as Radio FSH in Schleswig-Holstein, in others such as Bavaria and Baden-Württemburg several local stations co-exist in networks or have their programmes distributed by production companies (see Hickethier, 1994e).

The future of public service broadcasting

The introduction of commercial broadcasting has brought about dramatic changes in the German media scene since 1984. The initial pessimism concerning the adverse cultural effects of commercial transmissions appear in retrospect to have been unfounded because audiences in the beginning maintained an apprehensive distance from the new channels. Even today the number of households which have become cabled falls well below the number possible (see Table 4.4).

Table 4.4   Households connected to cable in Germany 1983–93

Year	Connectable[1]	Connected[1]
1983	1.8	0.6
1984	2.9	1.0
1985	4.7	2.5
1986	6.8	2.3
1987	8.9	3.2
1988	11.7	4.6
1989	14.1	6.3
1990	15.9	8.1
1991	17.5	9.8
1992	18.8	11.4
1993	19.9	12.6

Source: Deutsche Bundespost Telekom
[1] Millions of households

Of the approximately 27 million homes in former West Germany 20.1 million (74.5 per cent) were connected to cable in 1994 whereas only 26.3 per cent of all possible households in the former East Germany have cable. The Federal-backed initiative which aimed at a 100 per cent cable coverage has now been adjusted to a target of 80 per cent for 1995 (Medienbericht, 1994:220). In addition to the extension of the cable network destined for the reception of satellite transmission, some commercial operators also managed to obtain the use of terrestrial frequencies so that commercial stations can be received by a standard aerial. A further development in the eastern Länder, where only a limited cabling operation has been implemented, is the use of the private satellite dish aerial with the resulting increase in the reception of commercial television in the east of the country.

With their initial teething troubles overcome in the late 1980s, the commercial channels continued to gain ground and acquired an increasingly large share of the television market. Indeed, from 1992 the public service channels had lost their position as market leaders (although their revenue from advertising had already begun to shrink

Table 4.5 TV advertising turnover 1980–93

Channel	Net turnover in millions of DM, excluding production costs						
	1980	1985	1989	1990	1991	1992	1993
ARD	666.0	860.0	935.4	732.2	761.2	576.7	444.8
ZDF	452.7	579.8	679.1	712.8	718.8	721.0	370.5
RTL	–	153.	294.4	690.9	1,010.8	1,471.0	1,844.8
SAT 1	–	5.9	307.4	546.4	802.2	1,050.2	1,288.1
PRO7	–	–	14.5	47.0	165.1	401.6	670.0
DSF	–	–	26.0	35.7	42.4	95.0	62.3
Kabelkanal	–	–	–	–	–	12.4	31.5
RTL 2	–	–	–	–	–	–	60.5
n-tv	–	–	–	–	–	0.3	39.4
VOX	–	–	–	–	–	–	41.2
Total	1,118.7	1,461.0	2,256.8	2,765.0	3,500.5	4,328.2	4,853.1
Change compared with the previous year	+8.5	+7.7	+23.0	+22.5	+26.6	+23.6	+12.1

Source: Jürgen Heinrich in *Media Perspektiven*, 1994

anyway). Even before the viewing figures of the commercial channels had outstripped those of their public service rivals, RTL had gained the largest share of the advertising market (see Table 4.5).

One factor which explains this fall in advertising revenue for the public service channels is the stipulation under the ZDF state Treaty which only permits advertising between 6 p.m. and 8 p.m. and insists that programmes are not interrupted by commercials. The commercial operators, on the other hand, have made advertising slots available within programmes and feature films, as well as carrying them in

Table 4.6 Overall % share in the TV advertising market 1989–93

Channel	1989	1990	1991	1992	1993
ARD	41.4	26.5	21.7	13.3	9.2
ZDF	30.1	25.8	20.5	16.7	7.6
RTL	13.0	25.0	28.9	34.0	38.0
SAT 1	13.6	19.8	22.9	24.3	26.5
PRO7	0.6	1.7	4.7	9.3	13.8
DSF	1.1	1.3	1.2	2.2	1.3
Kabelkanal	–	–	–	0.3	0.6
RTL 2	–	–	–	–	1.2
n-tv	–	–	–	0.0	0.8
VOX	–	–	–	–	0.8

Source: Jürgen Heinrich in *Media Perspektiven* 1994

prime viewing time. This has given the commercial operators a distinct advantage over the public service with the result that they have won the larger share in advertising revenue. Table 4.6 indicates the dramatic shift in the advertising market which has taken place during the 1990s.

For the public service operators, the reduction in advertising revenue was just the prelude for the decrease in the viewing figures which occurred more or less at the same time. Such a decrease, however, is hardly surprising because, as the channels increased in number, so the audience was simultaneously divided between them, regardless of their public service or commercial nature.

Table 4.7   Audience share of the national TV corporations 1990–4

Channel	Share of TV audience[1]				
	1989	1990	1991	1992	1993
ARD	40.0	36.1	32.0	25.5	25.9
ZDF	28.7	25.8	24.0	18.7	18.4
RTL	11.7	14.1	15.0	18.5	17.3
SAT 1	9.1	10.3	12.4	15.1	14.8
PRO7	1.2	3.8	5.4	8.6	8.3
DSF	0.7	2.1	2.6	1.3	1.2
Kabelkanal	–	–	–	1.5	1.9
RTL 2	–	–	–	–	2.9
n-tv	–	–	–	–	0.3
VOX	–	–	–	–	1.8
Others	8.6	7.8	8.6	10.8	7.2

Source: GKF
[1] 1990–1 annual average for Western Germany; 1992–3 annual average for the Federal Republic as a whole

The reduction in advertising revenue pushed the public service operators into financial crisis which, since the Länder governments refused to raise the licence fee, the public channels tried to remedy through cuts. Whilst they were indeed able to cut costs by internal savings, the opportunities for economies in this direction remained limited due to rising costs generally and to increased production costs in particular. This crisis situation gave rise to a national debate on the future of the public service channels between 1991 and 1994. In the course of this debate, reforms were demanded which extended to a call for the dissolution of ARD and the discontinuation of the first channel altogether.

These fundamental changes in attitudes which have taken place in television since the establishment of the commercial channels are best explained within the wider context of the revolution in telecommunications in Germany as a whole. Indeed, according to Hoffman-Riem (1988), what is occurring is a paradigmatic shift of considerable importance. Up to the mid-1980s, television was regarded essentially as a cultural institution (despite the fact that, as such, it has been somewhat negatively rated by its critics). But since then, a new vocabulary has been initiated whereby people speak of 'entry into the TV market' and wherein 'market shares' are calculated. It will be noted, no doubt, that we have freely used such terms ourselves. This is because they have been manifestly accepted in the debate relating to the nature of the dual system of television. Nevertheless there is a tension between this kind of language and the one we traditionally use when speaking about broadcasting.

The cultural dimension

The need to include a cultural dimension (i.e. quality cinema, drama and music) in programming, which by no means rules out entertainment, relates directly to the mission of broadcasting in Germany as laid down in the Basic Law. The inclusion of this dimension is perceived as the guarantee of diversity of subject matter and programme styles, which, in the case of television, is accessible to millions of people, including minority audiences. Viewers still demand quality films and television drama which deal with the social and political realities of life, together with investigative documentaries and background news. The perception of television as having a cultural in-put to people's lives therefore must take cultural considerations into account in any attempt to evaluate its effectiveness. Indeed, we would argue that such considerations should take precedence over the increasing importance attached to viewing figures. This is because, within the public service sector, it is not ratings but quality which should serve as the yardstick of success. What should ideally figure in the evaluative process, in this case, are such criteria as the level of artistic creativity, and the thoroughness of research in reporting and other comparable qualities. In Chapter 1 we have already drawn a general distinction between the respective missions of the public service and the commercial broadcasters: the first is to deliver quality programmes to audiences, whereas the second is to deliver audiences to advertisers. The perception of 'quality television' therefore is attached to a concept of televisual communication which is the complete opposite of such notions as commodities and markets. In our view, the implications of these distinctions have not been fully appreciated by either media practitioners or their critics in the Federal Republic (see Hickethier 1994a). With the introduction of the concept of the market there has been an increasing tendency to elevate the importance of viewing figures as the main criteria for evaluating the performance of all channels (including public service broadcasting). It is true that the Federal Constitutional Court guarantees the continued existence of the public service television as a permanent element in the German media. This safeguard is based on the premiss that public service broadcasting best fulfils the communicative entitlement of the people to be informed, whilst, at the same time, providing access to quality programming of cultural significance. Such a guarantee from the Supreme Court only serves to highlight the dilemma in which the public service programmers now find themselves. On the one hand, they must aim at high viewing figures in order to offer some competition to the other channels but, on the other, they have to meet the quality/cultural objectives imposed upon them by their specific public service mission.

However, faced with the impending competition from the commercial operators, the public service broadcasters wasted no time in implementing a pre-emptive strike. Armed with the conviction that anything the commercial channels could do, they had already been doing for years, the public channels increased the level of entertainment programmes, put on addition serials and feature films, and removed from the schedules programmes for schools or those of a more educational content. High-quality television drama, by its nature expensive to produce, was also threatened.

In general, the changes made in the public service sector in the 1980s, and which provoked such a heated public debate, may be seen as a structural adaptation to the new situation by two major strategies: first the streamlining of its organisational structure and the standardisation of its schedules, and second, the sustaining of a core element of public service broadcasting. It was still possible to produce lavish productions such as *Heimat* (1984) and *Die Zweite Heimat* (1992) and to make films such as *Wohin und Zurück* in three parts (1982–6), as well as to continue ambitious projects into the 1990s as, for example, the forty annual productions of ZDF's short TV play series. So, notwithstanding the criticism of the political Right, which wishes to reduce the level of public service broadcasting in favour of an increase in commercial provision, the public service corporations still manage to provide a quality/cultural dimension on their channels, thereby sustaining what has already been referred to in this book as the 'communicative entitlement' of the viewing public.

On the cultural side, public service television was, and still is, centrally involved in the promotion of German films. The first film and television agreement between the public service corporations and the German film industry was signed in 1974. Since then numerous films have been co-produced and shown both in the cinema and on television. This policy of co-production has contributed to the making of films by internationally known directors such as Wim Wenders, Volker Schlöndorff, Werner Herzog, Reinhard Hauff and Rainer Werner Fassbinder.

Two further strategies have been adopted to strengthen the position of the public service channels: firstly, there has been an expansion in serial-making (*Lindenstrasse*, 1986, is a good example) because this dramatic form creates 'channel loyalty' on the part of the viewer. Secondly, news coverage has been augmented to include more up-to-the-minute reporting as well as the introduction of 'news specials' providing in-depth coverage of world events. It is then no accident that, in the area of news and information programming, the public service channels are clearly ahead of their commercial rivals. It is equally true that they cannot compete with the commercial operators in certain other areas such as the extensive programming of game-shows, serials and feature films.

Convergence?

The question has inevitably been asked since 1989 whether or not the two kinds of television broadcasting, which form the dual system, and which compete with each other, are in fact moving towards each other in their programming (Krüger, 1989). It was initially thought that the public service channels would lower their standards and move in the direction of the mass entertainment of the kind scheduled on the commercial side. However, in the 1990s there is evidence that the reverse may be the case and that, in some respects, the commercial channels are being influenced by the public service model. Initially, the commercial channels based their scheduling on programmes of mass entertainment, foreign films and repeat showings of American soaps and serials, most of which originated from the enormous reserves of the Kirch group. During the second phase, in the early 1990s, RTL and Sat 1 began to attract viewers by making large investments in the acquisition of the rights to screen sporting events (i.e. football and tennis). In consequence the familiar federal league matches were no longer shown on the public channels.[9]

Again, in the first phase in 1988, the head of RTL announced his intention to make his channel different from the rest and thereby unmistakably distinctive for its viewers. This included the strategy of the scheduling of previously 'taboo' material such as 'soft porn' films and erotic shows such as *Tutti Frutti* and much more besides. In addition to this inclusion of erotica, both commercial channels began to broaden the range of individual genres by the creation of more radical variations. Thus news and information were enriched with 'television-reality' by such programmes as *Notruf, Augenzeugenvideo, Retter* and similar programmes often depicting catastrophes filmed by chance or, as became increasingly the case, reconstructed. This kind of programme, where the boundaries between news and entertainment become blurred, has been aptly christened 'infotainment' (Bleicher, 1995).

By 1993 RTL had established itself as the market leader in German television and a new phase of consolidation began. First came the recognition that the TV-reality and soft-porn approach did not attract new viewers. Indeed, once the novelty had worn off, it was noted that viewing figures actually fell. As the result, RTL set about enticing back the viewers and adjusted the direction of the scheduling once more towards the public service model. Audience research in the late 1980s showed that public interest in American feature films was declining. This discovery prompted, for the first time in the

German-speaking world, the production of German serials and even a German soap opera – RTL's *Gute Zeiten, Schlechte Zeiten* – which was quickly followed by others in both the public and other commercial channels. In the area of TV films, for so long the exclusive domain of the public service channels, the commercial operators RTL, Sat 1 and Pro 7 also established themselves. Again they moved in response to the growing preference shown by German audiences for German actors and locations. In their news coverage, too (despite a lower level of logistical back-up than the public service channels), the commercial channels have made strenuous efforts to improve the quality of their programmes.

It can be seen therefore that there has been a tendency towards convergence within the dual German television system. But the market remains volatile and certainly may change again at any time as competition continues with increasing intensity. It looks as if, in the future, there will be ever fewer programming domains reserved for a particular channel. In this state of constant competition, the public service channels, because of their dual mission of entertainment and cultural innovation, must find the means both of holding their ground and legitimising their existence.

Change in media usage

Parallel to the far-reaching and continuous expansion of the media industry in Germany, there are other changes taking place within the context of media usage itself. The explosion of choice has resulted in new styles of media usage, particularly among young people. One such new style involves 'incidental' viewing and listening wherein in the latter takes place alongside other activities. These new viewing and listening habits can have serious consequences. Some radio programming in particular has been obliged to shift towards magazine-type programmes consisting of music and chat interspersed with short news bulletins. Here, the concept of 'format radio,' using computer-aided music selections based on a US model, is becoming established. In the case of television, younger viewers, in particular, are often skilled exponents of 'zapping' – the frequent change of channel using the hand-control – by which they escape the commercials and simultaneously look at several programmes, thus maintaining an overview of what is on offer (Wulff, 1995). The traditional form of extended, single-programme viewing is becoming less widespread. Even feature films are seldom watched in their entirety and defection from them is common – a phenomenon encouraged by the intrusion of the commercial break. In general, then, the diversification of choice has led to the diversification of usage (see Hickethier, 1994a). Various user profiles can be clearly identified. For example, brief and highly selective usage often correlates with an individual preference for news bulletins and documentaries. A more extensive, general usage, on the other hand, coincides with a preference for entertainment. Whilst there is no conclusive evidence, there appears to be a correlation between the high usage of entertainment programmes and social and political attitudes.

The frequent portrayal of violence on commercial television has re-opened the debate on the effects that such portrayals may have upon society at large. Evidence suggests that the direct transfer-effect upon children and young people in everyday situations is limited and heavily dependent on the immediate social context. Nevertheless there is considerable unease about the possible influence on social attitudes and behaviour in the longer term and there have been numerous enquiries set up by both government and the German Press Council on this issue. The commercial channels themselves have introduced self-regulatory measures on the matter of screen violence, particularly in feature films, serials, and the TV-reality programmes mentioned earlier, all of which have been strongly criticised. One solution that has been put forward, interesting only in its ingenuity at deflecting attention away from the media, is the call that has been made upon schools and parents to monitor the media consumption of children with their educational interests in mind. Thus it would seem that parents and teachers are being asked to help avoid or repair the damage caused by flawed media policies, or the lack of political initiative at an earlier stage.

Safeguarding the national media industry

For some considerable time public discussion in the Federal Republic on the subject of the safeguarding of the national media in the face of international competition has been very selective. The sort of robust and comprehensive debate of the kind that is still ongoing in France, for example, does not exist in Germany and there are various reasons which explain its absence. One is that, at the level of Federal government, and in particular during periods when it has been headed by the CDU-CSU, there has been a deliberate policy aimed at creating the strongest non-interventionist media framework possible. The experience of the 1950s and 1960s, during which the media operated in conditions of minimum constraints, demonstrated the possibility of operating within a non-protectionist media policy. Foreign programmes and, above all, those coming from the USA, were perceived favourably as providing support for the process of domestic, social and political modernisation because they opened German eyes to the American way of life and broke down traditional attitudes. The view that was repeatedly expressed at the time was that openness of this kind would strengthen the Federal Republic in the long term and, by so doing, improve its trading position.

There is a cultural-political division of responsibility in the Federal Republic which may also throw some light upon the apparent low priority that the media has in the eyes of central government. The cultural mission of the media, as far as the central government, is concerned, is the responsibility of the Länder. However, central government is perceived to be responsible, at a national level, for economic policy relating to the industry. The central government rarely saw any need to act in a protectionist manner on behalf of the national industry. From its point of view, the media are still marginal to the economy of the Federal Republic. With a turnover of DM 46,800 million in 1992, the entire media sector only amounted to 0.02 per cent of the net domestic product of the German economy (Medienbericht, 1994:64). This explains the limited interest of the Federal government in excluding the media (as a cultural asset) from the 1994 GATT agreement, and it contrasts strongly with the position of the French on this issue.

However, all the indicators show that the media sector outpaced all other service activities in the period 1982–90 and, because this increased importance was also associated with technological change extending into numerous other industrial sectors (with economic implications), the Federal government has embarked on a policy of economic support and of the expansion of the technical infrastructure. This intervention, however, has stopped short of protectionist policies.

Media concentration

The issue of media concentration, as in most other countries in Western Europe, is a problematic one, particularly so in Germany where the pluralism of journalistic opinion is guaranteed in the Basic Law. By the end of the 1980s the following groups had developed to the point where they should really be described as multi-media conglomerates due to their interests in the written press and television and film production:

- Bertelsmann, the second largest media group in the world, which began as a book club and, subsequently, with its numerous other interests, achieved a turnover of 16,000 million DM in 1991/2. Bertelsmann has a 74.9 per cent share in the Gruner + Jahr group which publishes numerous popular and specialist magazines, among them *Stern*, *Geo* and *Brigitte*, and has a share in the Spiegel publishing house and several newspapers in the former GDR. In addition Bertelsmann owns many book clubs, printers, publishing houses, record companies, regional radio stations, film production companies and television channels (Röper, 1993a).
- The Axel Springer Group remains one of the market leaders of the press and in particular of daily titles such as *Bild*, *Die Welt*, *BZ* (in Berlin), the *Berliner Morgenpost*, the *Ostsee-Zeitung* (Rostock), the *Leipziger Volkszeitung*, and the *Dresdner Neueste Nachrichten*. It also owns *Hör Zu* and *Funk Uhr*, the two TV listings magazines with the highest circulation. In addition to these important titles it also owns *Bild der Frau* and *Auto-Bild* and other popular magazines. The Springer Group also has shares in numerous film production companies, radio stations and in television channels such as Sat 1, Deutscher Sportfernsehen, Aktuel Presse-Fernsehen and

121

Deutsches Börsen Fernsehen. Closely allied to the Springer Group is the Kirch Group which has a 25 per cent share in Springer. Kirch owns numerous firms specialising in film and television production, video production and film rights. He has a share in the television channels Sat 1, DSF and Kabel Kanal and his son owns Pro 7. Many strategies for the future expansion and concentration of the media in Germany emanate from the Springer and Kirch empires.

- The Holzbrink Group. This group concentrates on the press, owning such titles as *Handelsblatt, Südkurier, Main Post, Potsdamer Neueste Nachrichten, Der Tagesspiegel* and the *Lausitzer Rundschau* among others. It also owns publishing houses, has a share three television channels and owns several magazines among which figure *TV Hören und Sehen, TV Movie, Fernsehwoche, Bravo* and *Neue Post*. Finally it has a share in RTL2 and Radio Hamburg.
- The Burda Group. This group publishes the magazines *Focus, Bunte, Bild* and *Funk*, and has shares in numerous radio stations and in the television channels Sat 1, Vox and Tele-Börse as well as in film and television production companies.
- The WAZ Group (Westdeutsche Allgemeine Zeitung) concentrates on printing and daily newspapers, in particular in Northrhine-Westphalia. However, it has a share in approximately 20 local radio stations and is becoming involved in the setting up of local television channels.

These then are the major players in the German media market but there are others such as the Gong Group, as well as the subsidiaries of *Süddeutscher Verlag* and the *Frankfurter Allgemeine Zeitung* which are also diversifying their activities by moving into television.

The hidden power of the media

It is difficult to make an overall assessment of this movement towards concentration in the areas of commercial radio and television. Although strict guidelines were established relating to ownership of channels in the state Broadcasting Agreement of 1987, the Land Media corporations were not given full regulatory powers for their monitoring and enforcement. Consequently the actual shares possessed by individual groups in television and radio are not fully known, and in any case, shares are often 'owned' by front men acting on behalf of another group. A good example of this practice is to be found in the Kirch Group. Because there is literally a nominal difference between Leo Kirch and his son Thomas Kirch, both of whom have substantial (and associated) media holdings, their share of the media market is not calculated as a single whole and thus escapes the sanction of the monopolies legislation. The business activities of Thomas Kirch are also linked with those of one of his former studio managers, Georg Kofler of Kabelkanal and Pro 7, as well as with those of several other 'silent' partners in the media market.

Group	SAT.1	PRO7	DSF	Kabel-Kanal	Pre-miere	RTL	RTL2	VOX	n-tv	VNA	ARD	ZDF	SUM
Kirch	43.0	47.5	24.5	21.4	25	–	–	–	–	–	–	–	161.4
Springer	27.0	–	24.9	–	–	–	–	–	–	–	–	–	51.9
Ackermans	–	49.5	–	22.3	–	–	–	–	–	–	–	–	71.8
Beisheim	–	–	–	45.0	–	–	–	–	–	–	–	–	45.0
Kofler	–	3.0	–	11.4	–	–	–	–	–	–	–	–	14.4
Berlusconi	–	–	33.5	–	–	–	–	–	–	–	–	–	33.3
Ringler	–	–	17.1	–	–	–	–	–	–	–	–	–	17.1
Bertelsmann	–	–	–	–	37.5	37.1	7.8	24.9	–	–	–	–	107.3
CLT	–	–	–	–	–	47.9	24.0	–	–	–	–	–	71.9
WAZ	–	–	–	–	–	10.0	–	–	–	–	–	–	10.0
Holtzbrinck	15.0	–	–	–	–	–	–	14.5	–	–	–	–	29.5
Bauer	–	–	–	–	–	–	33.1	–	–	–	–	–	37.6
Burda	–	–	–	–	–	2.0	1.0	–	–	–	–	–	3.0
FAZ	–	–	–	–	–	1.0	1.0	–	–	–	–	–	2.0
Suddeutscher Verlag	–	–	–	–	–	–	–	20.0	–	–	–	–	20.0
DCTP	–	–	–	–	–	–	–	11.0	–	–	–	–	11.0
Otto	–	–	–	–	–	–	–	–	–	19.8	–	–	19.8
Nixdorf	–	–	–	–	–	–	–	–	18.0	–	–	–	18.0
CNN	–	–	–	–	–	–	–	–	28.0	–	–	–	28.0
Time Warner	–	–	–	–	–	–	–	–	23.0	19.8	–	–	42.8
Canal Plus	–	–	–	–	37.5	–	–	–	–	–	–	–	37.5
EGIT	–	–	–	–	–	–	–	–	14.0	–	–	–	14.0
Tele München	–	–	–	–	–	–	33.1	–	–	–	–	–	28.6
Sony	–	–	–	–	–	–	–	–	–	19.8	–	–	19.8
Philips	–	–	–	–	–	–	–	–	–	19.8	–	–	19.8
Thorn/EMI	–	–	–	–	–	–	–	–	–	19.8	–	–	19.8
WMB	–	–	–	–	–	–	–	25.1	–	–	–	–	25.1
ARD	–	–	–	–	–	–	–	–	–	–	100	–	100.0
ZDF	–	–	–	–	–	–	–	–	–	–	–	100	100.0
Total	85	100	100	100	100	98	100	95.5	83.0	99	–	–	1,160.5

Source: Jürgen Heinrich in *Media Perspektiven* 1994

123

It is clear, therefore, that a closer study of the Kirch Group reveals a wider association of business interest than is at first apparent and which extends beyond the father and son relationship. As shown in Table 4.8, Heinrich (1994) has identified the following links with the Kirch Group.

It is estimated that levels of economic and editorial concentration are very high in the Kirch Group which inevitably means that economic competition as well as media pluralism are threatened in the long term. The successful entry of the Italian media mogul, Silvio Berlusconi, into the political arena has served as a timely reminder of the threat to democracy posed by the phenomenon of media concentration. One consequence has been a public debate in Germany (1993–4) concerning the dangers posed to the media by Kirch, and whether the 'Berlusconi effect' could be repeated in the German context. The results were inconclusive and an effective way has not yet been found of limiting the group's power, not least because Kirch has a close relationship with the ruling CDU/CSU parties.

As we have already suggested, whilst it is true that the social framework in which the media operate is strictly regulated by law (i.e. by state treaties and by the Constitutional Court), there are still numerous ways of avoiding the restrictions. Moreover this situation is further aggravated by the fact that there appears to be a lack of political will to oppose the process of media concentration by the major parties. To put it somewhat bluntly, the politicians avoid conflict with the media industry and by so doing allow them influence over the political mood of the country. The explanation of this reluctance to take decisive action may lie in the fact that, after all, it is the prevailing wish of all politicians to be re-elected by using the media as a means of influencing public opinion during their electoral campaigns.

The European dimension

The democratisation of the Germany in the post-1945 period led to the adoption of a principle of openness via the media to the cultures of Western Europe and North America. In the 1970s and 80s this openness was extended to other regions in the world such as Latin America and Africa. Within the European framework, linguistic barriers caused this opening to be somewhat limited. Unlike many smaller European states such as the Netherlands, Belgium, Denmark and Switzerland, long used to multi-lingualism, Germany was (and still is) predominantly monolingual. With one or two exceptions, this monolingualism is still particularly apparent in its media. There is, for example, a long tradition of 'dubbing' of imported feature films. Original-version screenings are rare and only to be found in special 'art' cinemas and film festivals. The dubbing of foreign-language films is a way in which other cultures are rendered more 'digestible for indigenous tastes' (Gentikow, 1993:312). This then is a process by which imported films undergo a form of 'Germanisation' which make them more acceptable to the receiving culture by the 'blurring of cultural differences'. The German experience seems to support Gentikow's view in so far as the acceptance of westernised cultural values and its general opening up to the West would not have occurred in the manner that it has without this means of cultural adaptation. In the past, the phenomenon of 'Germanisation' has been accorded very high, even quasi-ideological status which has been carried to wholly unacceptable extremes. In the post-war period, the influence of the media in changing attitudes and making Germany receptive to other cultures has been very considerable. Since, inevitably, the relationship between the indigenous culture and cultures external to it are always in a state of change, the extent to which German culture will reflect a greater interdependence with its European neighbours is a matter for debate.

The extent to which Germany is accessible to other cultures is linked to the recent noticeable increase in racist incidents which occurred at the end of the 1980s. It should be noted that the voices of the 'new' radical Right were given no place in the media (with the exceptions of their own publications). The attitude of the media was invariably critical of what they considered to be an over-lenient government response to the racial attacks. Nevertheless, the media themselves, in some quarters, are considered not to have covered the issue of racial tension in Germany early enough.

The language barrier

The language barrier which exists between Germany and neighbouring countries has undoubtedly resulted in the transmission of programmes in foreign languages finding scant approval among German listeners and viewers. And there is a similar attitude towards foreign-language newspapers and magazines which, for the most part, are confined to specialist users. The British, French and American radio stations, which have existed in the Federal Republic since the end of the war, have not removed these linguistic barriers. The new foreign-language channels such as CNN, Super Channel, TV 5, MTV and Eurosport do not appear to be having much impact either. Their market share in 1992 remained less than 3 per cent (Medienbericht, 1994). Even so, in the past, there have been frequent attempts to broadcast foreign television programmes in their original language on German channels, often in the context of a 'European' television drama season or the showing of old newsreels of historical interest. Such ventures, though, were limited in scope and accepted the inevitable drop in audiences which ensued.

As we have already pointed out, the preferred manner by which foreign-language material has been screened in Germany is via the dubbing process. Schneider (1994) notes two discernibly different phases in terms of the kinds of materials shown. During the 1950s and 60s, for example, the introduction of American and British films was prompted mostly by the need to fill the schedules and by the ready availability of American programmes. However, in the 1970s and 80s there has been an increasing tendency to select films on grounds of artistic merit. During the latter period the number of films of European origin has risen significantly.

In the case of radio, the proportion of foreign language productions has remained small, and this is despite the fact that in the field of drama, new developments towards bilingual (German–French) productions have emerged on Saarländischen Rundfunk and Westdeutschen Rundfunk. However, the entire area of popular music is characterised by the dominance of American and British pop music, with the result that even German groups frequently sing in English. It is true to say that the phenomenon of cultural diversity which has been emerging in Germany since the 1970s has found its voice more through the radio than through television. Such radio programmes can be received throughout the Länder and are sometimes grouped together to form a single station as is the case with SFB's Multikulti and which features the regular broadcasting of non-commercial music from the Third World. Foreign language stations can also be received by satellite, and the Turkish station TRT-International, for example, is very popular among the Turkish community in Germany. In addition to the better known foreign language newspapers, there are newspapers for minority ethnic groups; Turkish language newspapers printed in Germany enjoy a strong readership as do others aimed at the Danish and Sorb communities.

German media in the wider European context: broadcasting

During the post-war period, the West German media have integrated with external European organisations in a manner similar to that in which the Federal Republic as a whole has integrated into the developing network of European institutions. Here we are referring primarily to interest groups and umbrella organisations such as the Council of Europe and the European Broadcasting Union (EBU). Even so, for decades, the media industries in Europe have been shaped nationally and cut off from each other behind linguistic frontiers.

Recently in television, in addition to the institutional links mentioned above, there are now important initiatives being taken, at the international level, between companies in the field of co-productions. ZDF, for example, has built up close production links with Austrian and Swiss television and established a relatively stable production base, the results of which can be seen on the satellite channel 3 SAT. As an expression of the political will towards increased cooperation between Germany and France, the Franco-German cultural channel ARTE was established in 1992. Operated jointly by ARD, ZDF and the French company La Sept, ARTE is transmitted terrestrially in France and by cable in Germany, and is officially considered to be offering to both countries opportunities for improved mutual understanding (Medienbericht, 1994:324).

The European dimensions of the written press

The international influence upon the German written press is limited and exists at the superficial level of the adaptation of American and British genres and formats. This is especially true in the development of new types of newspapers and magazines, and journalistic styles. On the economic side, there has also been a tendency towards partnership arrangements with other European newspapers, but progress in this area remains limited. Of particular note in this area of activity is the cultural magazine *Lettre* produced jointly by various European papers and, in the German case by *Die Tageszeitung*. It is certainly no accident that this form of cooperation is popular with the European written press, which is generally short of capital, while in the more influential media conglomerates the European dimension has emerged through strategies of ownership.

German media and conglomerates in Europe

The tendency towards expansion and concentration in the German media market has taken place not just in the audio-visual sphere but also at a European level. The collapse of communism in Eastern Europe in the 1980s introduced a new presence there of the major German media groups. Gruner + Jahr is active on behalf of Bertelsmann especially in the popular magazine sector. To give some idea of the importance of this involvement, Gruner + Jahr had a turnover of 1.2 billion DM in 1993–4. In the same year, its turnover from its international activities amounted to 919 millions.

Expansion into Europe often occurs by successful German-language titles being copied and modified before being launched in other non-German-speaking countries. The Burda publishing group, for example, successfully introduced its fashion magazine *Burda Moden* into seventeen different countries achieving an overall circulation figure of more than 4 million copies.

The Springer group is mostly active in Eastern Europe. It had a foreign turnover of 240 million DM in 1993 which is relatively small when compared with its overall turnover. Its activities are somewhat low-profile as far as foreign ventures are concerned.

The turnover for foreign publishing activities for the Bauer group amounted to 575 million DM in 1993, a sum which represents 20 per cent of its total turnover. The Bauer Group is particularly well represented in France and in the United Kingdom.

One of the reasons for the expansion of the German media groups into other European countries is the legal restriction upon mergers and takeovers in the German market. The media groups have been particularly active in the Austrian market. The German daily, *Westdeutsche Allgemeine Zeitung* (WAZ Group), for example, has a 50 per cent share in Austria's biggest daily the *Neue Krone Zeitung* (circulation 1.1 million). The Springer Group has a 50 per cent share in the Austrian daily *Der Standard*, and the publishing group

Table 4.9 Bertelsmann/Gruner + Jahr: popular mgazines published abroad

Country	Title[1]	Circulation in thousands
France	*Femme Actuelle*	1,800
	Prima	1,175
	Télé Loisirs	1,480
	Géo	560
	Ça m'intéresse	360
	Voici	750
	Capital	335
	Cuisine Actuelle	470
	Guide Cuisine	250
	Partance (eingestelli)	130
	Gala	325
	Cuisine Gourmande	228
Spain	*Muy interesante*	290
	Mia	275
	Ser Padres Hoy	100
	Dunia	110
	Natura	70
	Géo	50
	Cosmopolitan[2]	200
	Marie Claire[3]	85
	La casa de Marie Claire	50
Italy	*Vera*[4]	350
	Focus[4]	300
Great Britain	*Prima*	610
	Best	560
	Focus	90
Czech	*(Sandra)*	?
Republic	*(Eltern)*	?
Poland	*Moje Mieszkanie*	
	(Neues Wohne)	80
	Claudi	500
	Maj (Frauenzeitschrift)	?
	Naj	?
	Tele Magazyn[5]	1,300
USA	*Parents*	1,775
	YM	1,750
	Family Circle	5,100
	McCalls	4,600
	American Home – Style	720
	Child	590
	Fitness	425

Source: Horst Röper in *Media Perspektiven* 1994
[1] Titles in brackets refer to the adapted German title
[2] 50% share: Heorst Group
[3] 50% share: Marie Claire Publishing Company
[4] 50% share: Mondadori Press
[5] Deutscher Supplement Press

Table 4.10 Burda: popular magazines published abroad

Country	Title[2]	Circulation in thousands
France	*burda moden*	100
Spain	*burda moden*	240
Italy	*burda moden*	280
Great Britain	*burda moden*	65
Netherlands	*burda moden*	115
Greece	*burda moden*	60
Czech Republic	*Verena*	40
	(*burda moden*)	?
Poland	*burda moden*	120
	Verena	80
	(*Super TV*)[3]	300
	(*Super Tele*)	950
	Supplement[3]	
Hungary	*burda moden*[4]	400
	Verena	35
Russia	*burda moden*[4]	400
USA	*burda moden*	10

Source: Horst Röper in *Media Perspektiven* 1994
[1] Aenne Burda Press
[2] Titles in brackets refer to the adapted German title
[3] Burda/Sebadlus Press – Share 50%
[4] Share 25%

Passauer Neuen Presse owns a 51 per cent share in the *Landesverlag*. Bertelsmann holds a 24 per cent share in Austria's second largest TV supplement *Tele* (circulation 1.4 million) (Pürer and Raabe, 1994). The consequence of such a strong German presence in the Austrian media market, comprising as it does only sixteen titles, is a reduction in free competition and genuine pluralism. New anti-monopoly legislation was introduced in Austria in 1993, but it was not retrospective, and hence has not broken down existing group holdings.

The large German media groups have also developed considerable holdings at the international level of a multi-media kind especially in television and other audio-visual sectors. The Kirch Group, for example, is involved with Berlusconi and Bertelsmann with Luxembourg's CLT. This kind of international collaboration, as we mentioned in Chapter 1, is prompted by the high cost of capital investment needed to set up and operate a television channel. Since the risks of failure are considerable, efforts are made to minimise them by several groups joining forces in joint ventures. What is particularly striking is the speed with which the movement towards concentration has progressed. What is also evident is that foreign companies, through this process of international collaboration, are beginning themselves to get footholds in the German market. This initially occurs through the cooperation of two (or more) consortia

Table 4.11   Springer: popular magazines published abroad

Country	Title[1]	Circulation in thousands
France	*Auto Plus*	350
	Sport Plus	85
Spain	*Nuevo Estilo*	150
	Grec 8	100
	Compile	50
	Prima	40
	Vitalidad	40
Great Britain	*Auto Express*	150
Austria	*Medical Tribune*	15
	News	?
Switzerland	*Medical Tribune*	10
Czech Republic	*Auto Tip*	35
Poland	*Pani Donn*	?
	(*Bild der Frau*)	
Hungary	*tvr-het*	700
	Lakskultura	150
	Kifkegyed	500
	(*Bild der Frau*)	340
	(*sok kônny*)	?
	(*KuB + Träne*)	
Romania	(*Auto Bild*)	40
USA	*Medical Tribune*	125
Japan	*Medical Tribune*	100

Source: Horst Röper in *Media Perspektiven* 1994
[1] Titles in brackets refer to the adapted German title

in the operation of a single channel in their mutual interests. The German partner secures not just foreign capital but also has access to the other's programme reserves. Conversely, the foreign partner gains valuable knowledge and experience for a possible later entry into the German market. This trend towards increasing collaborative activity between the big European conglomerates is expected to continue. One predicted scenario is that European television channels, associated in ever larger groups, will ultimately lose their strong national characteristics and become little more than the transmitters of internationally consumable 'televisual commodities'. An alternative scenario is that the future will see the development of a broad spectrum of regional and local broadcasting which will herald a new kind of European integration. At this stage both scenarios are matters for speculation only.

The future

Media choice has expanded over recent years at a pace which could hardly have been predicted in the 1980s. It was thought, for example,

Table 4.12 Bauer: popular magazines published abroad

Country	Title[1]	Circulation in thousands
France	*Maxi*	1,000
	Bravo Girl	350
Spain	*Tele plus*	330
Great Britain	*Bella*	990
	Take a Break	1,500
	TV Quick	700
Czech Republic	*Bravo*	300
	(Tina)	850
Slovakia	*Bravo*	?
	(tina)	?
Poland	*Bravo*	1,000
	Twoj Weekend	350
	(Wochenend)	
	(Tina)	1,600
	Tele Tydzien (TV Progr)	1,700
	Girl	600
	Swiat Koblety	?
	(Wohnen)	
Hungary	*(Sexwoche)*	?
	(Bravo)	100
	(Tina)	?
Russia	*Bravo*	?
USA	*Woman's World*	1,200
	First for Woman	1,500
	Soap Opera Update	?

Source: Horst Röper in *Media Perspektiven* 1994
[1] Titles in brackets refer to the adapted German title

that three commercial channels would be sufficient to serve national needs, whereas, in fact, no less than twelve additional channels have been provisionally approved. In the immediate future five new specialist channels – Super RTL, TM3, VIVA 2, VH-1 and FAB – have been approved by the Land corporations. RTL will be a children's channel operated by CTL and Disney, after a trial period, will be renamed Disney Channel. TM3 is conceived as a channel of family entertainment by Tele München and the Bauer Group; VH-1 will be a pop-music channel operated by MTV; VIVA 2 will also be a music channel and FAB is already operating in the Berlin area. The other seven channels proposed, but as yet unnamed, are owned by existing media groups and intended to complement their existing channel interests.

The strategy adopted by the media groups is one occupying all the available positions on the cable network before the next phase of development, the electronic superhighway, gets fully underway.

Whilst television is currently the most hotly contested field of activity, similar trends are perceivable in the written press. Five new women's magazines are planned for 1996 in Germany – *Amica* from Milchstrasse, *Allegra* from Springer, *Yoyo* from Bauer, *Joy* from Jürg Marquand and *Brigitte Young Miss* from Gruner + Jahr. The focus here is upon the young, successful career woman.

It will be increasingly the case, as we have already suggested, that trends in the written press will be dictated by the large media groups. In consequence it is likely that the current changing pattern of provision will continue, but will not extend to all social groups. Already there is a perceivable leaning in the media towards the consumerist, success-orientated, younger age groups in German society, while others are totally neglected. Similar trends exist too in the developing new television channels. There is a risk in Germany, as in other countries in Western Europe, of the emergence of social groups comprising the 'information rich' and others, less well served, comprising the 'information poor'. Such a trend could only act to accelerate the processes of social fragmentation within Germany, and in the wider context, within Western Europe, of the kind we have already noted in Chapter 1. This trend is likely to be reinforced by the envisaged new digital communications network (the so-called superhighway) towards the creation of which there are many European initiatives, although the American lead in this area is already well established (see Hickethier, 1995). Again it is the large European media groups who are making the running and demanding the total and immediate freedom of access to the market. Whether or not there is a sufficient demand for the superhighway and what form this demand will take is unclear, but five initial projects were implemented in Germany at the start of 1995. Again the main strategy on the part of the operators is to be early participants in the new digital media revolution. The speed with which operators are moving in order to keep up with the rapid pace of technological progress is in marked contrast with the more measured changes that took place in the media in the 1970s. At that time the social implications of changes in the media were thoroughly debated before action was taken. Today, it seems that media operators are throwing themselves into making changes dictated by the new technologies too quickly, and without fully examining the social consequences. One thing is already plain, the new technology will destroy far more jobs than it will create, with unforeseen social consequences, although Paul Kennedy, in his book *Preparing for the 21st Century*, has suggested one:

> Instead of the creation of the powerful masses and critical buyers of Vuitton suitcases, the telecommunications revolution could create thousands of millions of 'have nots' throughout the developing world who will develop an increasing hatred towards the 'haves', (quoted in Radtke, 1994:90).

Notes

1. Sozialistische Einheitspartei Deutschlands: the Communist Party of the former GDR.
2. The East German CDU – Christlich Demokratische Union – should not be confused with the then West German party of the same name.
3. Treuhand: the organisation set up to dismantle and sell off all state-owned industry in the GDR following unification.
4. *TV Spielfilm, Max* and *Fit for Fun*, all aimed at young adults with spending power, are good examples of the new 'lifestyle, sport and leisure' titles promoting consumerism above all else.
5. Papers from the former GDR are beginning to build a readership across the Federal Republic.
6. The so-called 'Americanisation' effect on German culture, also described in Chapter 1.
7. Peter Von Zahn, for example, was famous for his reporting on world affairs.
8. New programming was adopted for the second ARD channel based on such models as *Panorama*, and original versions of British dramas and political satire.
9. BSkyB in the UK embarked on a similar strategy by acquiring the rights for the showing of Premier League football in 1994.

CHAPTER 5

The media in Italy

Carlo Sartori

I Introduction

Since 1945 the Italian media (written press, radio and television) has developed within a legal, structural and thematic framework that is quite unique in the European context. This framework is characterised by socio-cultural, political and economic particularities which are rarely found in other European countries and which makes the Italian communication system a strikingly different model with respect to the general trend. In Italy, perhaps more than in other European countries, it is essential to understand the specific historical factors which have played their part in the development of its media from 1945. This is because these factors are still playing a decisive role in media development today.

II The development of the written press post-1945

From the post-war period to the first period of press concentration

Following the fall of the fascist regime and the Liberation (25 April 1945), and the proclamation of the Italian Republic (June 1946), a new democratic system was established in Italy. There was a widespread demand for modernisation and a greater public participation in national affairs, and a growing recognition of the socio-cultural need for the protection of freedom of expression, explicitly defended by the constitution. The first sector of the media to respond to the newly re-affirmed commitment to pluralism, and to the widespread demand for information, discussion and entertainment was the written press. Unlike the public radio broadcasting service, which, as we shall see later in this chapter, was faced with the need to rebuild its national network, newspapers were quickly able to reinstate their editorial staff and printing operations.

However, daily newspapers, although invested with a new authoritative voice, were characterised by an encoded style of reporting the ongoing lively political debate which was not entirely accessible to their readers. This task of delivering accessible information to the public was more successfully achieved by the emergence of a new popular weekly press, which captured a wide readership by its diverse response to public taste. Thus this period saw the development of the so-called sensationalist and crime weeklies, as well as of the political and cultural weekly reviews (Ajello, 1985). The growth of some of these magazines is impressive. During the mid-1950s, their total circulation amounted to 12 million copies, i.e. three weekly magazines for each daily newspaper (Ajello, 1976:191–204). In addition to this strong and rapid growth of the weekly press which, as we have noted, to some extent filled the gap left by the declining national dailies, there was also an upsurge in sports journals. This period also saw the birth of numerous daily and weekly titles devoted exclusively to sport. Some of these titles have inevitably disappeared with the passing of time, but Italy certainly still remains the only country to possess today three daily sports papers, one of which, La Gazzetta dello Sport, continues to be an absolute leader in the daily market (Ghirelli, 1976:345–9). The weekly magazine sector was further strengthened by the development of women's magazines which registered a lower but steady growth. These magazines mainly targeted middle-class readers and were characterised by a traditional content which ranged over such topics as domestic tasks, fashion, short stories and readers' letters (Lilli, 1976:284). Since the readers of the national dailies were almost exclusively male, these magazines also developed a socio-cultural role in the promotion of the image of women as being that of happy wives and mothers existing within a male-dominated family context. By so doing they naturally played a role in maintaining the social *status quo* (Buonanno, 1975:38).

The relatively weak position and function of the daily written press and the market dominance of the sports papers and other kinds of weekly and periodic titles, on the whole, reflected the inherent attitudes towards the media of the prevailing political party, the Christian Democrats, during these years (the presence of a few titles such as Pannunzio's L'Espresso, and Il Mondo were exceptions to the rule). It should be noted that it was in this context that the first television broadcasting began in Italy in 1954.

The impact of this new medium on the written press sector was certainly immediate although the effects were unevenly distributed. In fact, the distribution of income derived from advertising remained unchanged because the television was a public service and did not benefit from the proceeds of advertising until 1957. However, the arrival of television affected the circulation of the weekly magazines in two important ways; firstly, it promoted a further expansion of some titles which, aware of the changing needs of their readers, quickly adapted by regularly featuring the newly emerging television world in their publications. But, at the same time, television also contributed to the rapid decline of a number of magazines (characterised by an 'image-based' kind of journalism) which were unable to compete with the so-called 'true-life' effect of the moving picture on the small screen (Ajello, 1976:208).

The 1960s proved to be an extremely active period from both social and political points of view. The country was governed by a left-of-centre coalition, and also this was a time of a developing current of student and worker protestation. In addition, and perhaps partly in consequence, television began to develop a vast audience. Italian journalism reflected the turmoil of the country. The coming to power of the new centre-left government led to many ideological and practical changes. The Catholic daily *Avvenire* established itself as the organ of the progressive wing of the Vatican Council, another daily, *Il Giorno* of Milan, supported the presence of the Socialist Party within the government coalition. The Communist Party founded an afternoon daily, the *Paese Sera* and, most importantly of all, transformed its monthly review, *Rinascita*, into a weekly publication. At the same time it relaunched the party daily paper, *L'Unità*, to unprecedented circulation levels (Murialdi and Tranfaglia, 1976:12–115). Confronted by the student protest movement, the written press tried initially to camouflage the event by consigning coverage to the centre pages. The student protest movement only hit the headlines when the protest reached its climax during the winter of 1969. Indeed, it was the excessive restraint of the principal Italian newspapers in reporting the movement which obliged the student protesters to create alternative outlets of counter-information to the official press. This led to the publication of numerous titles such as the student magazine *15* in 1967 (which enjoyed the support of such subsequently celebrated names as Umberto Eco and Nanni Balestrini), and *Movimento Studentesco, Potere Operaio, Lotta Continua*, as well as a number of Marxist–Leninist papers and factory news-sheets which were circulating particularly during the 1970–1 workers' protest. *Il Manifesto* was founded in April 1971, initially as a periodical and later as a daily newspaper, and even today still represents, more than any other, the arguments of the Italian Left (Eco and Violi, 1976:100–32).

This upsurge in editorial activity was not, however, matched by a corresponding increase in total circulation and sales. Instead there was a kind of stand-off between the mainstream, traditional newspapers and the new rebellious press which ended in an impasse wherein the readership was slightly redistributed but did not increase. Despite a wider interest in politics (and by extension in newspapers) this impasse remained, and indeed the situation was aggravated by the economic crisis of 1963–4 which resulted in a round of price increases of the dailies, and contributed to the failure between 1967 and 1971 of three news weeklies and seven daily papers (Murialdi and Tranfaglia, 1976:20). This was also the time when the state-owned television began its drive to attract advertising, and revenue from this source, between 1962 and 1974, rose from 19.5 per cent to 28.8 per cent of the total advertising spend. At the same time, the revenue share of the written press from advertising went down from 63 per cent to 58.5 per cent (Ajello, 1976:227).

The response of the publishing sector to this crisis was to take the first determined steps in the direction of media concentration. Some of the mergers and takeovers were initiated by the press publishers themselves, but the most significant were realised by large industrial groups entering the publishing sector for the first time, or by those trying to consolidate their position within it. For example, the publishing group of the oil-magnate Attilio Monti and the Agnelli–Fiat group began taking shape at this time (Olmi, 1991:82). This period marks the beginning of the so-called 'buy and sell' phenomenon (Pansa, 1977) which thereafter has become a permanent feature of the entire Italian media system. During this time of change, the periodical press still showed signs of greater vitality, largely due to their tabloid format and to important changes in editorial policy. L'Expresso became the leading magazine of the radical and progressive, while the more popular Gente and Oggi recorded circulation records comparable to those of the period which preceded the television boom, in some instances achieving sales of over one million copies. Publishing groups such as Rizzoli and Rusconi recorded the highest profits during this period.

New developments and contradictions in the 1970s

During the 1960s journalist activity had been characterised by a general social protest movement. In the decade that followed, the dynamism of the publishing industry was more closely related to the political and institutional events occurring within Italy itself. In the space of three years, the Italians went to the polls three times: in 1974 for the referendum on divorce; in 1975 for the local elections; and in 1976 for the General Election, the latter event being marked by the success of the Italian Communist Party. The early 1970s saw the beginnings of the activity of the Italian 'new Left' which was independent of the Communist Party and, in some respects, more extremely aligned than the latter (led at that time by Enrico Berlinguer). Not surprisingly, between 1971 and 1974, a new group of newspapers emerged from this political current on the Left, appearing in reduced format and selling at lower prices. As we have already noted above, Il Manifesto was founded in 1971, Lotta Continua became a daily in 1974 and Il Quotidiano dei lavoratori was founded in 1974 (Olmi, 1991:82–3).

It was in this context, characterised by deep political and social tension, that terrorism registered a strong and widespread revival. This phenomenon was more systematic and pervasive than the one which had already left a tragic trail which began at the piazza Fontana massacre in 1969. These were the so-called anni di piombo (the years of lead) which, of all the post-war years, the Italian Republic will never be able to efface from memory. The professional role of journalists, the mission of the press and the effects of information on the public were all dramatically called into question during the tragic months of the kidnapping of Aldo Moro. There appeared to be a need, on one hand, to publish everything, from the merest rumour to the propagandist statements of the Red Brigade, or to exercise total censorship on the other (Murialdi and Tranfaglia, 1983:19). The problem turned on the need both to report the news to the Italian public while, at the same time, denying the terrorists the platform that they were seeking in the press. The government, under the leadership of Giulio Andreotti and supported by the Communist Party, did not impose media restrictions. The most difficult and liberal line prevailed, supported also by the Italian Press Association, 'to inform the citizens about everything, without, at the same time, conceding propaganda opportunities to the terrorists' (Murialdi and Tranfaglia, 1983).

From a cultural and economic point of view, in the 1970s the publication sector in Italy was faced with a somewhat contradictory situation. On the one hand, it witnessed the birth of one of the most influential Italian national dailies, La Repubblica, as well as the creation of numerous local newspapers. On the other, the financial crisis which had begun in the 1960s was deepening, and this, in some cases, such as that of the Corriere della Sera, the oldest and most authoritative national daily, led to dramatic consequences.

La Repubblica was created in 1976 on the initiative of Eugenio Scalfari, (a political progressive politician who was already the editor of L'Espresso). It was jointly managed by two large publishing groups, Caracciolo and Mondadori. Promoted as an Italian version of the Le Monde, La Repubblica introduced a number of graphic and editorial innovations which ensured its almost immediate success. These innovations included an attractive tabloid format, a new-style journalism which shunned the political jargon of the traditional papers, and a number of features which created an astute mixture of the daily paper and the weekly magazine (Murialdi, 1983:605–17). Some policy decisions, such as the exclusion of the sporting section, were subsequently revised, but the basic form of the paper remained unchanged and more progressive readers, who until then had not found a truly complete newspaper, increasingly made it their first choice, so much so that the initial run of La Repubblica of 100,000 copies rose quickly to half a million, making it the leading daily in competition with the Corriere della Sera.

· The other important phenomenon which characterised the 1970s is the growth of the local and regional press. During the 1960s local newspapers accounted for as little as 15 per cent of overall national circulation, while in France the figure was nearer 70 per cent, in Sweden and West Germany it was 80 per cent, and in the United States amounted to 95 per cent (Olmi, 1991:83–4). In about 50 Italian provinces containing 50 per cent of the entire population there were no daily or weekly papers at all in the 1960s (although there were some prestigious exceptions such as La Gazzetta di Mantova). There are a number of different factors which account for this situation, among which figure the economic backwardness of many of the

Italian regions, and the evident manipulation of the small number of local papers by various influential groups such as the politicians, local business and the Church. This kind of manipulation and control made the local press unreliable as a source of information and was the cause of their post-war decline. But there was also a problem of language and style (Olmi, 1991:84). The local newspapers tried to imitate the national ones which targeted, for the most part, a politically committed, cultured and cosmopolitan male readership. Given the difference between the latter and the average provincial paper reader, such imitation of the national model was clearly misplaced.

The factors which contributed to the development of the local press during this post-1970 period were twofold: firstly, there were the new technological conditions of newspaper production; secondly, coinciding with this technological progress, was a new social impulsion which itself created a demand for newspaper information. The introduction of the first electronic technologies, such as the new printing techniques and the integrated publishing system, reduced publishing costs, and this was an essential element in the survival of a local newspaper. We should also note that local readers were becoming increasingly interested in the affairs of their locality and region and, as such, represented ideal new markets for new publishing ventures.

These growth indicators – the creation of *La Repubblica* and the increase in the number of local titles – were not in themselves sufficient to bring about fundamental changes in the Italian publishing sector. During the 1970s, the structural weaknesses of the sector (e.g. the practice of discounting sales exclusively to news-stands while ignoring other possible sales outlets) led to the first serious financial crisis of daily newspapers. In 1975 the overall deficit for this sector exceeded 100 billion lira with only 17 newspapers out of a total of 74 balancing their books or showing a profit (Guastamacchia, 1976:609–34). This situation of financial crisis was partly alleviated by a law granting state subsidies amounting to 45 billion lira to the newspaper publishers over a two-year period. It also ushered in a new series of ownership changes which had the effect of concentrating the press into the control of certain major industrial groups, to the detriment of individual ownership. It was during this period (1974), that the Rizzoli family, with the support of the then Chairman of Montedison, Eugenio Cefis, acquired the ownership of the *Corriere della Sera* (which they had to re-sell in the early 1980s to Agnelli–Fiat, as the result of scandal). Cefis also purchased from the Perrone publishing group the influential Roman daily *Il Messaggero* and thus gave financial backing to a number of newspapers of different political persuasions (Murialdi and Tranfaglia, 1976:4). This 'buy and sell' period continued up to the beginning of the 1980s, when, as we shall see shortly below, the problems of the Italian publishing industry took on a definitive form.

New press legislation and its consequences

Two press laws, those of 1981 and 1987, are largely responsible for the current operational context of the Italian written press. The first, of 1981, had two main underlying objectives, the first of which was financial in nature and the second related to the legal status of the press. The law provided for a significant new subsidy element, abandoning the *ad hoc* 'drip-feed' subsidies which governments had distributed in the past, with the object of reviving the fortunes of some ailing publishing houses to the point where they could once again stand on their own feet. The second goal was to give the written press a legal status which took into account the special contribution of newspapers to the culture and democratic values of the country. Indeed, issues such as press pluralism, comprehensive coverage and accuracy of reporting were key concepts of special concern to both journalists and trade-unionists at this time (Murialdi and Tranfaglia, 1994:22–3). The 1981 law proved to be complicated and costly but there is no denying its innovatory nature. In summary it provided for the following:

- a guarantee of transparency in the structure of newspaper ownership;
- transparency in the funding and transfer of shares in newspaper companies;
- a 20 per cent market share limit imposed on newspaper ownership (including sporting papers);
- government subsidies for technological improvements;
- government subsidies for the purchase of newsprint;
- the extension of unemployment benefit for journalist (designed to mitigate the effects of unemployment due to the crisis in the industry);
- the freeing of price controls and the progressive increase in the number and kind of sales points (designed to rid the system of restricted practices in the distribution of papers);
- the appointment of a press Regulator (Garante per l'editoria). This was an unprecedented step for any Italian government (the importance of the role of the Regulator was to be subsequently reinforced in the 1990 law governing the radio and television).

The consequences of the 1981 press law are difficult to evaluate fully. By 1985 subsidies paid out to the written press amounted to 471 billion lira for the dailies and 114 billion lira for periodicals, many of which, in fact, did not experience a true need for the extra funding. However, by 1985 the number of publications which were in the red had fallen to twenty, and in addition the special social security measures extended to print-shop workers made it possible to introduce the new technology (reducing the labour force by 19 per cent) without creating an acute social crisis.

The second press law, passed in 1987 and intended to improve on the provisions of its forerunner, still left a number of shortcomings in the new reforms. Subsidies were extended to cover the publications of political parties (though these papers are inherently prone to recurring crises) but the periods covered by these payments were not set. Nor was any consideration given to the integration of the reforms of the written press with other media sectors (where, as we shall see in the section on broadcasting below, there was a distinct need for regulation). Finally the anti-monopoly provisions suffered from a lack of detail and effectiveness (Castronovo, 1994:68–70). A particularly telling example of their ineffectiveness was the so-called 'Gemina case' – the holding company of the Fiat group which indirectly controls two major dailies, the *Corriere della Sera* and *La Stampa*, as well as the leading sports daily, *La Gazzetta dello Sport*, and the Rizzoli publishing house. After a lengthy investigation on the part of the Regulator, which indicated that the Gemina group's holdings were in excess of the permitted limits, no further action was taken on the matter. In 1995 the Gemina case was once more referred to the Regulator when the company became involved in a new merger, the so-called 'super Gemina', which now, along with the titles already mentioned, also controls the Roman daily *Il Messaggero*.

Growth and crisis in recent years

Despite these shortcomings in the area of legislation and regulation, the 1980s saw a slow but steady growth in the written press sector at national, inter-regional, regional and provincial level (Table 5.1).

Table 5.1 Development of the Italian written press 1980–94

Year	Average circulation	Variation %	Average sales	Variation %
1980	7,427,213	–	5,341,970	–
1981	7,475,266	0.6	5,368,815	0.5
1982	7,571,807	1.3	5,409,975	0.8
1983	7,708,165	1.3	5,580,394	3.1
1984	8,135,157	5.5	5,860,691	5.0
1985	8,378,753	3.0	6,068,407	3.5
1986	8,992,407	7.3	6,365,661	4.9
1987	9,337,653	3.8	6,618,481	4.0
1988	9,562,563	2.4	6,721,098	1.5
1989	9,651,225	0.9	6,765,715	0.7
1990	9,763,197	1.1	6,808,501	0.6
1991	9,492,087	–2.8	6,505,426	–4.4
1992	9,444,954	–0.5	6,518,389	0.2
1993	9,231,694	–2.3	6,366,080	–2.3
1994	9,270,467	0.4	6,474,939	1.7

1994 data projection only
Source: FIEG based on ISTAT

Between 1980 and 1988 the circulation of daily newspapers increased by 35 per cent, and average sales by 29 per cent. The number of pages increased by 20 per cent and the number of advertising pages by 8 per cent (Garante per l'editoria, 1989). There are many reasons which explain the gradual rise in the circulation figures of the daily newspaper industry in the 1980s, and they can be briefly summarised as follows: the rising levels of *per capita* income and levels of education; the improvement in newspaper appeal through the use of more accessible language, briefer reports and more in-depth analyses of facts and issues; the introduction of new technology into the press room and the consequent fall in production costs; the more rapid relaying of information in what comes closer to real time; finally there are the professional skills of the journalists themselves and their awareness of the needs and expectations of the public (Garante per l'editoria, 1989). A major incident in the second half of the 1980s was the 'war' which broke out for the control of the principal Italian conglomerates of that period, Mondadori – publisher of one of the most widely distributed news weeklies, *Panorama* – and the Espresso corporation – whose titles included *L'Espresso, La Repubblica*, and a series of local papers. The battle which followed was directed principally by the new rising star of commercial television, Silvio Berlusconi, who became the Managing Director of Mondadori, and Carlo de Benedetti, his counterpart and adversary in the Espresso corporation. This complicated manoeuvering ended when the management of *La Repubblica* issued a statement declaring the Mondadori interest in its ownership unacceptable on grounds of professional ethics, concerns about free competition, and the potential relationships between business and politics, and between politics and publishing.

In contrast to the improving fortunes of the written press in the 1980s, the 1990s saw the beginning of a new series of difficulties for the sector. The economic recession which began in 1991 (the worst since the energy crisis of 1973) had caused a gradual reduction in the levels of newspaper circulation and a decline in the annual financial performance of the publishing houses. Apart from reduced sales, the reduction in profit margins was due to other factors such as rising labour costs, reduced levels of advertising, a reduction in investment capital, increasing dependency on the banks, and generally overall continuing uncertainty with regard to the prospect of an eventual economic recovery (FIEG, 1993). This general economic problem was exacerbated by persistent structural weaknesses in the industry, in particular the sales and distribution structure. In this vital area the press still suffers from kinds of restricted practices which prevent the development of a well structured distribution system for dailies and magazines of the kind that exist in most other countries in Western Europe. This situation is made even more difficult by the proverbial inadequacies of the Italian postal and transportation services (Megna, 1994).

The competition from television is often quoted by publishers as

Table 5.2 Development of Italian magazine circulation 1980–92

Year	Weeklies			Bi-monthlies			Monthlies		
	Titles	Circulation (000)	Variation %	Titles	Circulation (000)	Variation %	Titles (000)	Circulation	Variation %
1980	529	22,038	–	55	4,923	–	2,634	34,080	–
1985	603	21,763	-1.6	531	5,769	17.2	2,758	33,250	2.4
1986	621	19,269	-11.1	485	4,500	-22.0	2,688	29,500	-11.3
1987	602	20,151	4.6	517	2,866	-36.3	2,717	32,922	11.6
1988	627	19,884	-1.3	492	2,307	-19.5	2,571	28,166	-14.4
1989	636	20,718	4.2	478	2,500	10.5	2,848	30,250	7.4
1990	626	15,597	-5.4	290	2,308	-7.6	2,861	35,667	17.9
1991	614	19,308	-1.5	499	2,923	26.6	2,789	32,500	-8.9
1992	643	20,231	4.8	507	2,692	-7.9	2,792	35,666	9.7

Source: FIEG based on ISTAT

Table 5.3 Advertising share of daily newspapers (principal agencies) (%)

Advertising agency	1986	1987	1988	1989	1990	1991	1992	1993	1994	1995
1 Manzoni[1]	15.5	17.8	20.8	21.2	21.3	22.6	23.3	21.2	22.3	23.0
2 RCS[2]	18.3	17.0	16.4	16.5	16.8	16.4	17.3	17.3	17.6	19.1
3 Publikompass[3]	12.5	12.1	10.9	10.5	9.9	9.4	8.2	8.7	10.5	16.1
4 SPE[4]	21.2	21.4	17.4	17.4	17.4	15.6	16.5	16.7	11.3	12.8
5 24ORE System[5]	4.6	5.4	5.3	5.4	5.4	5.3	5.7	6.8	7.9	8.3
SPI	14.7	14.5	17.2	16.9	17.0	16.8	16.5	14.3	11.0	–
Others	13.2	12.1	12.0	12.1	12.2	13.9	12.5	15.0	19.4	20.7

[1] La Reppublica, with daily local inserts
[2] Corriere della Sera with Gazzetta dello Sport insert
[3] La Stampa. Tuttosport! (morning)
[4] Il Tempo, La Nazione, El resto del Carlino, Il Giorno
[5] Il Sole 24ORE
1995 data forecast

Table 5.4 Advertising share of principal agencies for magazine market (%)

Agency	1986	1987	1988	1989	1990	1991	1992	1993	1994	1995*
1 Mondadori[1]	23.9	25.0	24.7	22.0	18.9	20.2	29.0	32.1	35.4	37.0
2 RCS[2]	22.6	22.6	22.3	22.7	23.5	23.1	21.9	31.5	22.6	23.1
3 Rusconi[3]	12.0	12.0	12.0	13.0	14.0	13.2	13.3	**	8.2	8.2
4 SIPRA[4]	2.9	3.6	4.7	8.4	9.6	10.6	11.3	10.4	6.7	6.0
5 SEAT[5]	2.3	2.6	2.9	3.0	3.8	3.6	3.9	4.1	4.5	5.2
6 Publitalia[6]	4.3	4.7	4.4	4.9	5.6	5.8	0.2***	0.1	1.3	0.1
7 Manzoni[7]	6.4	6.6	6.4	5.7	4.1	4.1	4.1	3.8	4.4	4.5
8 Others	25.6	23.2	22.6	20.3	20.5	32.6	16.3	18.0	16.9	15.9

Source: Media Key no. 143/1995
1 *Panorama, Epoca, Grazia, Donna Moderna*
2 *Il Mondo, Europeo, Oggi, Amica, Anna*
3 *Gente*
4 *Famiglia Cristiana*
5 *Pagine gialle, Tuttocittà*
6 *TV sorrisi e canzoni*
7 *L'Espresso*
* 1995 figures forecast only
** 1993 data is included in RCA
*** With the exception of sporting magazines Mondadori took over management of titles in 1992

Table 5.5 Total media share of publicity revenue (%)

Year	1982	1983	1984	1985	1986	1987	1988	1989	1990	1991	1992	1993	1994
Dailies	25.8	24.2	22.9	22.2	23.4	23.5	24.0	25.2	25.7	24.8	24.1	23.8	23.6
Periodicals	26.2	21.8	20.2	20.1	20.1	20.5	19.8	19.4	18.0	17.0	17.2	16.4	15.5
Total press	52.1	46.0	43.1	42.3	43.5	44.0	43.8	44.6	43.7	41.8	41.4	40.2	39.1
TV RAI	13.5	13.3	13.5	15.3	15.0	13.0	14.2	14.2	14.3	15.0	14.4	15.3	16.3
Fininvest	9.6	17.4	26.3	28.9	28.0	29.1	27.7	26.9	27.5	29.1	31.1	32.2	32.6
Other public companies	0.0	0.0	0.0	0.0	0.0	0.3	1.2	1.1	1.5	1.2	0.6	0.5	0.3
National private companies	7.3	7.7	4.1	2.1	2.5	2.6	2.5	2.5	2.6	2.7	2.7	2.3	2.5
Local private companies	5.7	4.4	3.3	2.3	2.1	1.9	1.9	2.0	2.0	2.0	2.0	2.1	2.1
Total TV	36.2	42.8	47.2	48.7	47.6	46.9	47.5	46.8	47.9	50.0	50.6	52.4	53.7
Radio RAI	3.0	2.6	1.7	1.6	1.5	1.4	1.5	1.4	1.4	1.3	1.3	1.2	1.2
Private radio companies	2.2	2.3	2.2	2.0	2.1	2.2	2.1	2.2	2.3	2.3	2.3	2.4	2.5
Total radio	5.2	4.9	3.9	3.6	3.7	3.6	3.6	3.6	3.7	3.7	3.6	3.6	3.7
Cinema	0.8	0.5	0.2	0.2	0.3	0.4	0.3	0.3	0.3	0.3	0.3	0.3	0.3
Foreign	5.9	5.8	5.4	5.2	4.9	5.2	4.8	4.7	4.5	4.2	3.9	3.4	3.2
Total	100.0	100.0	100.0	100.0	100.0	100.0	100.0	100.0	100.0	100.0	100.0	100.0	100.0

Source: Media Key no. 143/1995

one of the principal causes of the crisis of the written press in Italy. In reality this crisis is the result of an intrinsic weakness with much deeper roots. There are a number of factors, such as the general decline in the time devoted to reading, and the indifference shown by the younger generation towards the press, which are not unique to Italy (although they may be present with particular intensity in our country). But there are other reasons which are rooted in the very cultural history of the nation. There is a marked variation between the north and south, for example: in northern Italy there are 150 daily newspapers sold for every 1,000 of the population; this figure falls to 135 in central Italy, and to 60 in the south. This situation explains the fact that the average circulation figures for the Italian written press are three to six times lower than those recorded in other countries of northern Europe (Castronovo and Tranfaglia, 1994:76). This situation cannot be remedied by changes in the press industry alone. If things are going to improve in this sector in Italy, it will be through a process which links the written press with the on-going developments in the field of integrated communications which is now gradually emerging.

III Broadcasting in Italy since 1945

The radio: from post-war emergency to the reorganisation of the RAI

The radio in Italy was initially created as public service, but was used most notoriously by the fascist regime for its own propaganda objectives (although not to the same devastating effect as the German radio under the Nazis). To the post-war ruling class, radio appeared as a powerful political and social instrument, with an enormous potential as a driving force for the task of reconstruction and modernisation of the country. The importance of the radio as formative influence upon the new Republic was clearly understood. The 'Bonomi' decree of October 1944 for the reorganisation of the state-owned radio, stressed 'the need to create within the broadcasting structure an advisory body responsible for the coordination and the monitoring of radio programming'. This clause of the decree would later be invoked as the justification of political control over the radio, and subsequently, over television broadcasting. Further light on government attitudes towards the radio is shed by the following extract from the official minutes of the Presidency of the Council of Ministers: 'The radio reflects the varied life of the nation and its voice is entrusted with responsibilities which are not to be found in other forms of media.'[1]

In practical terms, the Italian radio had to begin again from scratch in the wake of the devastation caused by the war. The network had been reduced from 46 to 14 stations. Its transmitters were mostly in the north and evidently needed extending to cover the whole country. Another urgent imperative was the financial reorganisation of the

RAI, which in 1947 was showing a severe deficit and experiencing the utmost difficulty in collecting the licence fee (which, in any case, was set at too low a level). However, these difficulties were quite outweighed by the potential political value of the radio which was well understood by the political parties of the day. The appointment in 1946 of the Christian Democrat, Guiseppe Spataro, to the post of Chairman of the RAI, signalled the first link between public service broadcasting and the new Christian Democrat government. This was a relationship which was to endure for a long time (Monteleone, 1992:208–12).

Protected by its new political allies, the RAI embarked rapidly on a process of reorganisation and, aided by a campaign of self-promotion, by 1953 increased its audience to 5 million listeners (Natale, 1990:114–18 and ISTAT, 1953). In terms of actual networks, La RETA Rossa (the Red Network) and La RETA Azzura (the Blue Network), created initially for broadcasting to northern and southern Italy respectively, were modelled on the American NBC network and were placed under a single management in 1948. A second channel, broadcasting mainly cultural programmes, was added in 1950 and in 1951 the defining features of the three RAI stations were finalised. Thus there was the National Programme, aimed at the broad category of 'average' listeners, and which offered a diversified schedule of programming comprising news, discussions and entertainment. The Second Programme offered entertainment and programming of a more popular nature, and the Third Programme specialised in programmes of a more cultural and educational kind, but was handicapped in this mission by the possibilities of only very limited reception by its potential audience (Menduni, 1994:23–4).

This distribution of radio responsibilities, which has remained largely unchanged until the present, was intended to fulfil the public service mission of the RAI and the principles of providing information, education and instruction, upon which state broadcasting was based. They took their inspiration from the BBC. In 1951 the Italian population still included 13.5 million illiterate or semi-literate citizens, 7.5 million citizens who were literate but possessed no secondary leaving certificate, 25 million who had had only an elementary education, and less than half a million university graduates (Doglio, 1959:146–7). Within this framework, and in spite of the distortions created by the close relationship between government and broadcasters, the radio undoubtedly contributed significantly to the raising of the overall cultural knowledge of the Italian population. This was achieved by the transmission of a mixture of programmes covering all the arts (particularly drama, literature and music) as well as news coverage and programmes of mass appeal.

Radio in the 1950s and 60s

In the mid-1950s, the Italian radio had to confront for the first time the implications of the dramatic entrance of television into the broadcasting scene. Both radio and television were part of the state public broadcasting services, but competition between them was inevitable, and in this television had all the advantages. The Italian preference for television immediately became evident in the purchase of the respective licences. Subscriptions to the radio licence fell progressively until 1959, whereas new subscriptions to the television licence rose, finally overtaking the radio (at 5 million compared with 4.5 million) in 1964 (Menduni, 1994:25).

The technical novelty of the new medium, in Italy as in the rest of Europe, seriously threatened the position of the radio. This threat was compounded by the introduction of light entertainment programming which traditionally had been the strength of the radio in the past. So, along with the cinema, which was also affected by the new medium, radio lost its audience in direct proportion to the rise in the number of television viewers.

The RAI's response to this challenge was a tactical one. At the end of the 1960s it implemented a plan which made a much clearer distinction between its three main networks. The first network, Il Programma Nazionale, placed more emphasis upon news coverage and increased the number and length of its news bulletins, concentrating primarily upon day-time broadcasting when the television audiences were relatively low. The second network, the Secondo Programma, which traditionally specialised in recreational programming, carried programmes dedicated to drama, light music, opera and entertainment. The third network, the Terzo Programma, relaxed its overly academic style, although it still remained committed to programming of a highly cultural nature (Monteleone, 1992:313–14). In general terms, radio attempted to counter the effects of television by reinforcing its news coverage (turning to good use its natural advantage of technical agility in covering local news), and by offering entertainment of a more cultural nature which seemed less suited to the 'mass market' mission of television. In fact radio possessed many real advantages which subsequently would allow it to respond with a more long-term strategy to the challenge of television. Despite the fact that technological developments were already well advanced (i.e. the miniaturisation of components which eventually produced the transistor), radio would have to wait for a number of underlying cultural and social phenomena to run their course before it could once again regain the dignity it had lost at the height of the crisis period. In the 1970s, due to a series of events which affected all major countries, the radio transformed itself from a housebound, communal medium to a personal possession which met the increasing demand for better sound quality (this was the time when FM transmission was introduced) in a more personalised, relaxed broadcasting environment. The cultural changes of this same period (see references to Hobsbawm's account in Chapter 1) also led to the extraordinary developments in new forms of music such as rock and roll, and country and western, which were without doubt one of the reasons for the recovery of radio at the end of this century.

1976: a landmark for Italian radio

A major landmark in the history of the development of Italian radio occurred in the mid-1970s in the form of the ruling of the Constitutional Court of July 1976. In a revolutionary judgement the Court declared that television and radio stations could operate, for the first time, outside the state-funded public service monopoly, at a local level. From that moment on, in the absence of any legislation or regulation governing the sector, private radio broadcasters began to multiply at such a rate that, by the mid-1980s, their numbers exceeded 4,000. As we have already suggested, a number of reasons account for this extraordinary growth. On the economic side, a number of record companies and manufacturers of electronic equipment, as well as local broadcasters, stood to benefit significantly from the expansion of the radio market. In social terms, the demand for independence and individuality, epitomised in the 1968 movement, favoured the radio as a means of local expression. In the political sphere, left-wing groups which had been denied access to any major media outlet viewed the new local radio stations with approval, seeing in them a potential medium for the broadcasting of an alternative political agenda[2] (Doglio and Richeri, 1980:176–8).

By the end of the 1970s it was possible to identify three categories of broadcasters in Italian local radio. The first and most widespread were the commercial radio stations, which included approximately 75 per cent of all private broadcasters. For the most part these stations were funded by local business, radio professionals and record distributing companies. They operated on advertising revenue and their programming comprised between ten and fifteen hours of music daily, designed to create a musical background to the work routines of mainly urban dwellers. The second category was 'information and news radio' which constituted between 10–15 per cent of all local broadcasting in the 1970s. These stations dedicated half their transmission time to news coverage and the rest to music of a more serious kind. They were funded either by advertising revenue, or by individuals or local institutions. The third group consisted of the politically committed stations such as the famous Radio Città Futura in Rome or Radio Alice in Bologna whose missions were overtly political and protestational in nature. They received financial backing from their respective activist groups (Doglio and Richeri, 1980:180–2).

The public service radio reacted to this invasion from the private sector with a reorganisation of its services which was sanctioned by the RAI Reform Law of 1975. The reorganisation divided the RAI's radio services into three distinct networks (Radio Uno, Radio Due and Radio Tre) and three new administrative groupings (Gr 1, Gr 2 and Gr 3). This sub-division reflects the desire to represent the balance of political power which lies at the heart of the law, especially in the area of news coverage. Gr 1 leaned towards the progressive tendencies of the non-Christian Democrat and socialist camps. Gr 2 was more moderate and fell within the Christian Democratic area of influence, whilst Gr 3 took a line which supported the parties of the centre-Left coalition. These differences, translated into the programming of the three radio networks themselves, were less marked, though the influence of the political parties was still in evidence. The most significant change occurred at Radio Tre, which after being placed under the control of a left-wing director, was to play a leading role in introducing innovatory broadcasting (phone-ins, younger audience appeal, and programmes targeting female listeners) and lead a revival of the radio in the second half of the 1970s (Monteleone, 1992:184).

Television: monopoly and political influence in the early days

Public service television was introduced in Italy in January 1954. Despite the inevitable fanfare which heralded the coming of the 'magic box', few people were willing to bet on the future success of television in Italy. The radio and the cinema seemed to offer a more than adequate supply of mass-media entertainment to what was still a fundamentally rural population (with a deep-rooted affection for circuses, travelling shows in the town square and other forms of interpersonal distractions) linked to local social structures (the parish church, local political party cronyism, trade unions and family). Indeed, the country was still poor in 1954: the gross national product was only slightly above that which it had been in 1938. The *per capita* income stood at around 250,000 lira, and more than 2 million people were unemployed. In consequence, television was an expensive proposition; a fourteen-inch screen costing a minimum of 160,000 lira (the same as a motorbike), to which had to be added the cost of installation. And yet, despite these unfavourable circumstances, and contrary to general opinion, it took the new medium only five years to be hailed as a triumph in Italy. By 1959 television was being watched on a regular basis by approximately 20 million people and had achieved almost saturation point in audience terms. The extraordinary fact was that only 5 per cent of this audience owned their own sets. Another 15 per cent watched in other people's homes, but the vast majority viewed from the TV rooms of bars and other public places in what became a collective, highly participatory and institutionalised habit in the Italy of the 1950s. Even the cinemas were obliged to hold special TV nights when the most popular programmes such as *Lascia o raddoppia* (*Double your money*) were broadcast.

These new forms of collective social and cultural activity without doubt contributed to the overwhelming and immediate success of television in Italy. As observers have noted, for the first time Italians were given a national, collective frame of reference for their private actions and daily lives. Television enlarged the horizons of the domestic community, and, at the same time, gave its members a shared sense of belonging. With extraordinary force, television opened doors which had formerly been tightly closed. It presented its audience with a new kind of language, which although it homogenised the diversity of the old, finally unified what had been until that time a country characterised by its numerous dialects. In short, within a short space of time, television introduced into Italian homes a totally new and different world ('a world in every home'), lending authority and dignity to subjects which had previously been only of secondary interest, or the prerogative of the few, while at the same time reformulating the structure of public news and information broadcasting (Sartori, 1984). This is all the more remarkable for the fact that it took place in a cultural climate which was anything but favourable towards television. Television drew to the surface of Italian life a deep-rooted ideological schism between the proponents of elitist culture and mass culture, between art (knowledge, critical awareness, quality and creativity) and escapist entertainment (mystification, lowest common denominator politics, irrationality and lower creative standards) (Abruzzese, 1986:46). Even the Catholic Church strongly condemned the new instrument of mass communication which Pope Pius XII defined as 'an evil power more traumatic than the film because it is capable of creating, inside the very walls of the home, the poisoned atmosphere of materialism, frivolity and hedonism so often to be found in the cinema' (Di Dario, 1992:9).

In fact, the powerful influence of the Christian Democratic Party upon the management of the new public service of the RAI was sufficient to exert a strict code of self-censorship over the content of words and pictures of television in its early days. Attitudes towards programming were prescriptive, aimed at creating good viewing habits which did not interfere with children's schoolwork nor disrupt the time-honoured routine of the home. Programming was organised around a three-part day beginning at 5 p.m. with children's television with an interruption from 6 to 6.30 p.m. Broadcasting resumed with the all-purpose programme *Ritorno a casa* (*Coming Home*) and ended with the main attraction *Ribalta accesa* (*Curtain Up*) which ended at 10.30 p.m. and featured entertainment of a different thematic kind on each evening of the week (i.e. films on Monday, drama on Tuesday, variety shows at the weekend and so on). But such a policy was both simple and without true rational justification, and characterised by an unquestionable lack of effectiveness in maintaining a constant audience during the week. In the second half of the 1950s it was already becoming clear that the so-called light entertainment shows were becoming the most popular in the schedule, their numbers rising from 200 in 1954 to nearly 400 by 1958. Quiz shows also proved to be particularly in the ascendant (Pinto, 1980:335).

The Golden Age of Italian television

The 1960s mark the beginning of the Golden Age of Italian television, with developments occurring that were comparable to those taking place in other Western European countries (Albert and Tudesq, 1981:8). This progress was the result of a number of factors such as a new approach to programming on the part of the RAI (with a consequent change of viewing habits) as well as the use of new television technology. It also coincided with the appointment of one of the most influential General Directors of the RAI, Ettore Bernabei, who, more than any other, was to personify the political role of the Italian television service. A trusted follower of Amintore Fanfani, one of the old 'war-horses' of the Christian Democratic Party, Bernabei, who was a courageous and bold innovator, was faced with a daunting task. On the one hand, he had to preserve the Christian Democratic hegemony over the television system (and head off the principal worries of the Catholic Church), while, on the other, he had to confront and control the increasing opposition of the Italian Communist Party. Moreover, this task had to be achieved simultaneously with providing for the cultural development of the common people, whom he did not hold in particularly high esteem (Monteleone, 1992:335). Bernabei's strategy contained two fundamental elements. The first was the rigid control maintained over programme production, and the second a new approach towards scheduling. The imposed control over production, however, did not prevent a flourishing, during this decade, of innovative and even progressive programming. This was largely due to the influx of a number of talented professionals, initiated by the Director-General, to fill key management posts.

The new scheduling policies and other changes implemented in the 1960s were of fundamental importance. Community viewing in bars and other public places became a thing of the past, and family life began to be organised around the schedule of the television. The new scheduling policy concentrated mainly upon three areas of programme content which experience showed generated the largest audiences: firstly, there was entertainment in the form of variety shows; secondly came popular music, especially that which emanated from the major 'pop' events such as the festival of San Remo; finally there were the cultural and informative programmes (documentaries and news) which achieved impressively high levels of performance in this period (Pinto, 1980:63).

As a logical consequence of this drive to capture the largest possible audience, a second channel was launched in 1963 to complement the transmissions of the first. The new scheduling across both channels was designed to combine the 'strong' popular programmes of the first channel with the 'weak', more elitist productions of the second. While it was to remain in a kind of cultural ghetto, the second channel was able to make tactical use of the schedule of its more popular companion, picking up audiences in the periods when the first channel's offering was not particularly attractive, and also collecting viewers when they became available at the close of a popular programme on the other channel.

Two further developments are noteworthy at the end of the 1960s, of a technological nature which would bring about permanent change in television broadcasting techniques. The first was the possibility of pre-recording programmes on magnetic tape, and the second the launching of the first telecommunications satellites. The introduction of video-recording (and the editing process which it offered producers) greatly extended the potential for television drama and prepared the way for the soap operas and the mini-series of the future. As far as the new satellites were concerned, they gave access to an increased flow of international information and laid the foundations for the television news programmes of the kind we know today.

Seeds of change: the coming of commercial television

From the beginning of the 1970s the stage was set for the overthrow of the RAI's public service monopoly in broadcasting. This situation came about through the coincidence of several factors, among which were:

- the imminent technological innovations (i.e. satellite and early use of cable in other countries which pointed the way towards a multi-channel system);
- the social movements of the 1970s which created a demand for more diversified programming;
- the defeat of the Christian Democrats in the 1974 election which undermined the legitimacy of the division of power in television and radio between the different political parties.

Suddenly, Bernabei's centralised and authoritarian management approach seemed no longer to relate to what was going on outside the RAI (Ortoleva, 1994:95–106). Until 1974 the argument justifying the state monopoly in broadcasting was based on the scarcity aspect of radio and television frequencies (with the implication for strict state regulation). The capacity for cable to transmit a potentially unlimited number of channels without interfering with airwave frequencies led the Constitutional Court to make an historic ruling in 1974 authorising transmission by cable by organisations other than the RAI. In 1975 the Italian parliament responded to this ruling by firstly re-affirming the right of the RAI to the exclusive responsibility of broadcasting at a national level, but at the same time entrusting the implementation of a more decentralised system, involving local public participation, to a third channel. Broadcasting by cable was also legalised but the technological specifications (narrowband cable only could be used) and limitations on audience size and on programme origins were so prescriptive that the development of cable television in Italy was effectively halted. In these controversial circumstances the Constitutional Court was again required to make a ruling, and in 1976 it declared part of the parliamentary legislation of the previous year unconstitutional and ruled that private broadcasters thenceforth should be allowed to transmit locally over the air. For various reasons (though in the main it was opposed to this ruling) the political establishment did not contest it further. 1976 therefore

Table 5.6 Total share of television advertising market (%)

Agency	1984	1985	1986	1987	1988	1989	1990	1991	1992	1993	1994	1995*
Publitalia-Fininvest	62.0	59.5	58.8	62.6	54.5	59.9	60.6	60.6	62.2	61.8	59.9	59.9
Sipra-RAI	28.5	31.4	31.4	28.6	29.8	30.4	29.8	30.0	28.4	29.6	30.7	30.6
TMC foreign	0.1	0.1	1.3	1.4	0.9	2.9	3.3	3.0	2.8	1.6	2.4	2.2
Odeon	–	–	–	1.5	2.7	1.9	0.9	0.1	0.2	0.1	0.6	0.8
Local TV	7.0	4.6	4.4	4.0	4.0	4.2	4.1	4.2	3.9	3.9	3.8	3.8
Others	2.4	4.4	4.1	1.9	8.1	0.7	1.3	6.3	2.5	3.0	2.6	2.7

Source: *Media Key* no. 143/1995
* 1995 figures forecast
** 1993 data included in RCS
*** With the exception of sporting magazines Mondadori took over management of titles in 1992

marked the beginning of a period of anarchy which led rapidly to the rowdy and hotly debated Wild West landscape through which Italian broadcasting was to travel in the following decade.

Unbounded by any rules, private television channels grew at an exponential rate and by the end of the 1970s three different organisational types could be identified:

- the independent stations – the so-called pioneers of private television which produced their own programming and sold their own advertising space;
- the so-called 'circuits' which were founded by advertising sales agencies whose role became modified to include the distribution of television programming;
- the early networks or 'super-channels' which embarked on a policy of affiliation or merger with other channels, thus centralising production activity, advertising sales and management. Though, at this time, there was no real concentration at a national level, these private broadcasters nevertheless demonstrated their enormous potential for development. Between 1977 and 1979, their audience share rose from 4 per cent to 24 per cent, with most of the increase being made at the expense of the RAI's first channel whose share fell to 52 per cent (with the second RAI channel registering 20 per cent, and foreign broadcasters 5 per cent).

During these early years of competition from the private sector, the RAI appeared not to fully appreciate the deep-rooted implications for itself contained in this new and developing situation. The widely held (but complacent) opinion within the public service sector was that the issue of the private sector would soon be settled. This complacency is perhaps understandable: after all this was the period during which the status and organisational structure of the RAI had been re-affirmed and strengthened by the law of 1975, and its channels allocated new political responsibilities.

However, the effects of the developing competition from the private sector were significant, although they occurred in imperceptible ways. Under pressure from the private sector (and despite the fact that officially it was ignored) the RAI was obliged to relinquish part of its public service mission as an educator and involve itself in the ratings battle. As a result a number of traditional programme types disappeared altogether. Early victims were the Friday night drama series, and the slots dedicated to children's programmes were sharply reduced; cultural offerings were firstly relegated to the late evening and subsequently to the late, late evening. These years have been described as a period of 'tactical degeneration' of the RAI's programme scheduling (Sartori, 1989) which nevertheless enabled it to achieve the important objective of not succumbing to the challenge of commercial television, thus preserving the future of the Italian public broadcasting system.

The creation of the third channel provided for in the law of 1975

Table 5.7 Television: prime-time audiences 1989–94*

Broadcaster	1989		1990		1991		1992		1993		1994	
	(.000)	share	(.000)	share	(.000)	share	(.000)	share	(.000)	share	(.000)	share
RAI	**10,269**	**48.4%**	**11,636**	**51.4%**	**11,181**	**48.2%**	**11,322**	**47.3%**	**11,753**	**48.0%**	**11,763**	**48.2%**
Raiuno	5,534	26.1%	5,630	24.9%	5,173	22.3%	4,959	20.7%	5,025	20.5%	5,235	21.4%
Raidue	2,902	13.7%	3,351	14.8%	3,647	15.7%	3,810	15.9%	3,853	15.7%	3,667	15.0%
Raitre	1,833	8.6%	2,655	11.7%	2,361	10.2%	2,553	10.7%	2,875	11.7%	2,861	11.7%
FININVEST	**8,061**	**38.0%**	**8,318**	**36.8%**	**9,640**	**41.5%**	**10,385**	**43.4%**	**10,737**	**43.8%**	**10,643**	**43.6%**
Channel 5	4,225	19.9%	4,271	18.9%	4,584	19.7%	4,781	20.0%	4,817	19.7%	4,993	20.4%
Italia 1	2,341	11.0%	2,402	10.6%	2,714	11.7%	2,866	12.0%	3,194	13.0%	3,267	13.4%
Rete 4	1,495	7.0%	1,645	7.3%	2,342	10.1%	2,738	11.4%	2,726	11.1%	2,383	9.8%
Others	**2,884**	**11.8%**	**2,669**	**11.8%**	**2,397**	**10.3%**	**2,234**	**9.3%**	**2,006**	**8.2%**	**2,015**	**8.3%**
Total	**21,214**	**100%**	**22,623**	**100%**	**23,218**	**100%**	**23,941**	**100%**	**24,496**	**100%**	**24,421**	**100%**

Source: Auditel
(*) Prime time refers to 8.30–10.30 pm)

occurred in 1979. The responsibility for this channel appeared to extend to the RAI a valuable opportunity to respond to the demands of the Italian regions for a regional television provision. In fact, the third channel was used for political ends in the mid-1980s to redress the balance of political influence within the television system, and in particular to extend some political media space to the Communist Party which, until then, had been excluded from the RAI's corridors of power.

A system blocked by its own development

Of all the European nations (with the exception of the United Kingdom which, as early as the mid-1950s, introduced a mixed television system), Italy was the first to be affected by the privatisation of television in the early 1970s. But the potential gains from the cable revolution were missed because they were obstructed by the RAI reform law of 1975 which relegated cable to a kind of geographical and technological ghetto that was both financially unfeasible and logistically impractical. In the opinion of the Italian legislators – an opinion shared nowhere else in the world – a separate cable would have to be used for each signal (the so-called mono-channel) thus nullifying the innovative nature of the medium which makes possible the relaying of increasingly large numbers of channels in a single cable. The response to this short-sighted legislation, and to those who thought that they had once and for all silenced the demands for privatisation, was an all-out attack against the public sector, but no longer in the field of new technology (the 'blocked' areas of cable TV). Instead the assault was made on the terrain of traditional television broadcasting (terrestrial transmission) historically occupied by the RAI. The post-1976 period, the time when allegedly 'a thousand flowers bloomed' (alluding to the exponential increase in local broadcasters) was followed by the formation of a small number of national networks capable of competing on equal terms with the RAI. At this point a mixture of contradictory factors – managerial skill and the lack of it, far-sightedness and obtuseness, active and passive political cronyism – did the rest and effectively the Italian private television industry was delivered into the hands of one man and one corporation, namely Silvio Berlusconi's Fininvest.

It is commonly accepted that the broadcasting law of 1990, known as the Mammì law after its author, does little more than legitimise the *status quo* which had come into being in various stages, untouched by any regulatory framework, in the 1980s. The law does lay down some specific obligations such as the creation of a regulatory body for broadcasting, the formulation of a plan for broadcasting frequencies and procedures for the granting of licences, and the way in which the private operators should present their annual accounts. It also imposes new programming responsibilities which include the right of private operators to broadcast live with the subsequent obligation to offer news broadcasts. But it is equally apparent that the Mammì law makes no attempt at reforming the Italian television system, and leaves intact existing patterns of ownership. In seeking apparently to avoid issues which would immediately demonstrate the fragility of the Italian 'house of cards', the Italian lawmakers simply 'overlooked' in 1990 the advances made in broadcasting technology (satellite, cable or home video), and the possibility for mixing the different broadcasting industries that these advances offered. The resulting different kinds of media outlets which emerge from these technological advances were also overlooked. It was as if in Italy there existed, and could only exist, one form of terrestrial broadcasting – the traditional, 'generalist' kind (i.e. the RAI) together with programmes put out on the commercial channels, all of which were locked in the daily dog-fights for audience ratings.

The result is the existence in Italy of a television system which differs completely from the general path of development followed by other major European countries. There is certainly no other system in Europe (and only one other in the world, Mexico) where the major players of the private sector are in the hands of a single corporation. Nor is there a situation (at least among the more advanced European broadcasters) where the entire system is reduced to a cut-throat competition for ratings.

The fact that the Italian system is structurally 'blocked' has not prevented the growth of a rich, luxuriant market, which goes a long way towards dampening any enthusiasm for change, though it also creates serious and quite risky imbalances. With a record level of growth (especially in the first half of the 1980s) television advertising pulled the entire industry up to economic levels closely resembling those of an advanced country (more than 0.5 per cent of gross national product in 1992). This development contributed, among other things, to the economic success of a large number of small and medium-size companies which in the past had not found sufficient demand for their services in either the written press or in public sector television. But in the course of its expansion television advertising overflowed into all possible programming 'niches', even to the extent of becoming an integral part of the programmes themselves, with increasingly subtle (or out-and-out brazen) forms of sponsorship and promotions. The effect often was to downgrade the content of the programmes to humiliating, secondary roles (only in 1993 was action taken by the Regulator for publishing and radio and television services to regulate the so-called 'telepromotions' of this kind). From a structural point of view, all these developments penalise in an irremedial way the resources of the other media forms. More than 50 per cent of the national total advertising spend goes to television, the rest being divided between radio, daily papers, periodicals, cinema and bill-boards. This 'perverse equilibrium' cannot be found in any other truly advanced country.

This situation naturally has consequences for the overall quality of programming. As is always the case when a new market opens up without establishing a supporting internal production capacity, the first half of the 1980s witnessed an invasion of foreign products: first American, then from Latin America, and finally from all corners of the globe, leading to the accumulation of the most extraordinary collection of international programming stock ever seen in the history of television. On the financial side the price of the most ordinary soap opera or even the most implausible Kung-fu series from Hong Kong spiralled upwards. Having fallen victims of their own greed, the Italian networks (public as well as private) eventually discovered the marginal cost-saving efficiency of domestic studio production, and this resulted in the creation of a number of innovative and noteworthy programmes (especially in the area of news coverage and in-depth analysis). The latter, however, were for the most part obscured by the majority of programme content which was as noisy as it was meaningless, obsessively copied from one programme to another and increasingly lifted from foreign originals.

These extraordinary conditions have occurred within a system which, as we have seen already, is among the least regulated in Europe (12 networks and more than 1,000 local broadcasters). But in fact it is characterised by a kind of trench warfare involving just two combatants – the RAI and Fininvest, both of which contest the same territory, the mass general audience. These two contestants are able to exclude from their territory all other competition which poses a serious threat, and ensure that between them they dispose of 90 per cent of the country's total television audience and advertising revenue. But what emerges from this ordeal is not a modern electronic media industry, but rather (and inevitably) an old, structurally repetitive television system. On the surface rich in programming (1.5 million hours of overall transmissions annually), it is actually impoverished in terms of the variety of programming which it makes available to the public in prime-time hours. By its nature, therefore, such a system discourages innovation (because it can only allocate creative television programming to low-risk marginal slots), focusing on the over-use of a small number of celebrities of proven success who in turn use a small number of tried and trusted programme formats which they churn out *ad infinitum*. It is a disposable approach to television based exclusively on tactics in the absence of any underlying strategy (Sartori, 1994:274). Such a system nevertheless manages to secure high audience ratings (and in some cases dramatic failures as well) but fails to build up any stock of its own, or win any foothold in the international market (with the exception of a small number of mini-series, TV movies and international co-productions which manage to travel across national boundaries).

In view of this situation, the Italian system is in urgent need not of modification but of thorough, radical reform of a kind that is becoming increasingly demanded in broad sectors of public opinion. The Italian government has pledged itself to take action on a number of occasions but recently such pledges have been given in the midst of a complex political situation and institutional instability. By July 1995 the reforms of the television system had not moved beyond the proposals drawn up by a special committee of the House of Deputies (the so-called 'Napolitano Committee'). It should be remembered that the RAI had already undergone a reorganisation in 1993 when a law replaced its sixteen-member board of directors – whose seats had always been distributed between the political parties – with a much streamlined body of five members comprising public figures not affiliated politically and appointed by the respective presidents of the lower and upper houses of parliament. The result of this reform was the creation within the space of two years of two successive management boards of differing views (due to a change in the political majority which occurred following the elections of 1994). In any event the two boards did manage to implement a radical reform and restructuring of the RAI with the consequence that it returned to profitable operations after years of disastrous financial results.

The current state of the radio: proliferation and confusion

The uncertainty which pervades the legislative framework relating to broadcasting is a problem which affects not only the television but the radio as well. The confused situation in which transmissions are taking place causes the much criticised 'marmalade effect' (referring to the confusion created by stations broadcasting on overlapping frequencies) and this is the direct result of the lack of political will to introduce rigorous regulation. The uncontrolled (and probably

Table 5.8 Radio: market share of principal broadcasters (%)

Year	RAI	National private	Local private	Foreign
1980	54.1	5.4	34.2	6.2
1981	53.1	4.4	35.2	7.3
1982	51.0	4.6	32.3	6.0
1983	51.9	6.7	37.3	4.1
1984	43.6	8.8	46.0	1.5
1985	44.8	8.3	45.7	1.2
1986	41.4	14.2	43.1	1.3
1987	39.1	18.4	41.1	1.4
1988	40.9	18.1	40.9	0.0
1989	39.8	21.2	39.0	0.0
1990	37.6	25.0	37.4	0.0
1991	36.6	26.4	36.9	0.0
1992	36.7	28.1	35.3	0.0
1993	34.4	31.0	34.6	0.0
1994*	34.0	33.7	32.2	0.0
1995**	35.3	33.8	30.9	0.0

* estimate
** forecast
Source: Media Key no. 143/1995

uncontrollable) jumble of radio stations should have been brought into line years ago. Regulation should have been introduced not to penalise new broadcasting enterprise but rather to sustain in an appropriate way those broadcasters best able to carry forward the ongoing development of radio and its spread throughout the country.

There still remains some room for manoeuvre, in the same way as room exists in the associated area of television, but the window of opportunity is becoming increasingly smaller as the rights of the current new broadcasters become more established and represent an element of structural disruption which even the boldest legislators would have difficulties in setting to rights.[3]

It would be a grave strategic error to fail to implement a full and radical reform of Italian radio broadcasting, particularly since this medium is currently experiencing (not just in Italy but elsewhere in Europe) an impressive recovery in terms of audience and advertising revenue. In addition radio is on the threshold of yet another technological revolution – digital audio broadcasting (DAB) – which has the potential of further improving the sound quality and resolving, once and for all, the medium's lack of total reliability in this vital area, while at the same time maximising its potential for special services and functions.

Future prospects for the regulation of the media system

This is an issue which, at the time of writing (1995), dominates the Italian political scene. Whilst the need for firm regulatory framework of communications systems generally throughout Europe has been apparent since the 1980s, it has become an issue of particularly heated debate in Italy since 1993. This was the year when Italy's most celebrated 'media man', Silvio Berlusconi, entered politics, becoming the majority party leader and then subsequently, for a few months, the Italian Prime Minister. These events brought to the issue of regulation a much wider set of implications, and gave to the task a political dimension, which in turn had ramifications for the whole political establishment and ruling coalition. An example of the seriousness which surrounded the issue is the furious controversy which broke out following the decrees on the so-called *par condicio* arrangements (the principle of equal access to news reporting and party political broadcasting during electoral campaigns).

The situation therefore is highly charged politically which, while it serves to concentrate attention on the issue, also creates a climate of antagonism between the different parties with the real risk that the outcome will be yet another compromise. There can be no denying that just such an attitude resulted in the Mammì law of 1990. This was a law born of a clash of views between the parties which were either for or against Fininvest, for or against the RAI, or for or against the written press, in such a way that the result was a hodgepodge of compromises which, as we have said already, completely failed to meet the goal of creating a new structure for the industry (it is noteworthy that no fewer than five ministers resigned in protest over the Mammì law).

Though the current political outlook offers little cause for optimism the new communications scenarios are developing, and it is here that the future rationality of the system will be measured. We would propose three possible areas where progress could and should be made. They are as follows:

Firstly, the establishment of a new anti-monopoly legislation which takes into account the overall development of the communications sector and which sets out both clear and flexible reference points permitting a pluralistic multi-media development. The main issues upon which the legislation should turn relate principally to the following: the number of media holdings legally allowed for any individual or group; the inter-relationship between management and the ownership of different kinds of media outlets; the financial resources which can be accumulated within any one sector, or within the system as a whole, by a single corporate group.

Such measures as these should facilitate a more balanced and varied distribution of media 'presence' among the major players in the new multi-media communications system. In addition steps could be taken to promote a more open attitude towards the internationalisation of the system which favours a more widespread participation of international corporations (especially European ones), in the Italian system. On this issue, an initiative of special significance is the 'Operation Wave' policy of Fininvest, which in response to political pressure and debt announced the sale of an initial share of its capital to foreign investors – the German group Kirch, the South African Rupert Corporation and the Arab company Al Waleed – in 1995.

A second area of legislation should concern the establishment of a new regulatory body for the radio and television sectors of the communications system. There is an irrefutable need for a new body with statutory power to direct the system, particularly in the light of the new and rapidly developing tendency of media globalisation. At present the numerous responsibilities for regulation are divided between the Regulator of Broadcasting and Publishing, the Minister of Posts and Telecommunications, and the Parliamentary Monitoring Committee. This distribution of responsibilities, as well as creating an extensive area of overlap, has also produced ominous vacuums of power in the administration of the system, especially in the drafting of guidelines for the management of the process of convergence towards the 'information society'. Italy is one of the few major European countries which has still to establish a coordinating body at government level for the so-called 'electronic superhighway', despite repeated invitations to do so from the European Union and the Senate. A foreseeable possibility here, based on the proposals forthcoming from various political groupings, is the eventual formation of an independent, highly specialised authority, with an excellent knowledge of the relationship between telecommunications, the media, financial resources and public needs, which will be capable of taking rapid action in the swiftly changing media landscape.

The third area of necessary legislation would relate to the growth and spread of new communications technology and new media. This is a key element, not only because it introduces new rules on cable and satellite TV, but also because it would promote a fruitful integration of the new forms of communications and telecommunications (digital transmission, broad-band networks, cabling, satellite equipment, integration strategies with informatics and electronic publishing) with the current media (television, radio and written press).

This whole process of which these three areas of possible future legislation are a part must promote an integrated global communications system in which the barriers between the respective media sectors disappear. To put it slightly differently: there must be a global system of networks created which serves as a vehicle for the provision of products and services which are currently offered separately.

Technological developments: beyond the closed system

The true frontier of the Italian communications system, as indeed it is for other countries as well, is that of technological innovation, and the process of integration between media, informatics and telecommunications. This is where the building of the information superhighways of the future will take place. But it is a frontier which, given the current state of things, appears a long way off in Italy. The Italian communications system in fact leans heavily in the direction of retaining its existing features with little apparent desire for change. This explains why few steps have been taken to introduce cable, and why the number of dish aerials can be counted only in tens of thousands and not in millions as elsewhere in Europe. It also explains why there are few Italian-language programmes broadcast in Europe via satellite (except two RAI channels and a version of Euronews). The single experiment of pay-TV undertaken by Telepiù which began in 1991 has struggled to get off the ground with currently 700,000 subscribers and a break-even point (still a long way off) set at 1 million. This shortfall exists despite high-quality offerings such as films seen for the first time on TV, and exclusive live broadcasts of big-league soccer. The reasons may be attributed to the ample provision of the traditionally 'free' television to which the Italian public has become accustomed. Despite this sluggishness, there are some signs of activity, albeit still disjointed in nature. Some of the most significant instances of movement in the direction of change include:

- the government decree issued to regulate cable TV and the initiatives taken in anticipation of the definitive liberalisation of the telecommunications sector;
- the reservation made by Italy on the 'Hot Bird' European satellite

for eleven transponders (the equivalent of more than forty channels using digital standard);
- the formulation of a project by Telecom Italia to cable 10 million homes by 1998;
- the interest shown by the RAI in the new thematic programming offered in part by special agreements with major international broadcasters such as Time Warner, Sony, France Television and CNN.

Generally speaking the current technological weakness of the Italian system can be transformed – assuming that urgent, all-encompassing strategic policies are adopted – into a point of positive strength. Indeed the fact that cable has not yet been installed means that Italy can introduce modern, wide-band networks from the outset (unlike Germany, which now is obliged to transform its widespread co-axial cable to fibre-optic). Similarly Italy's initial failure to promote the new media could be turned to advantage since it can now select (with the benefit of the latest technological advances) the media outlets best suited to carry a particular service (unlike France, for example, which is now having to reconvert its Minitel services).

Bearing in mind the overall outlook described above, we can offer a brief analysis of the three main elements around which the development of the Italian telecommunications system will evolve. They are as follows.

The first element is the process of liberalising of television transmission and services which are still managed on an almost exclusive monopoly basis by the collossus Telecom Italia. Only recently after considerable pressure from the European Union has a partial breach been made in the sector through the assignment of responsibilities of cellular phone services to the Omnitel consortium.[4] These services should begin operations in the beginning of 1996. This move towards liberalisation is a key element for all countries in the Union but is particularly important in the Italian context. No major system of technological innovation can succeed unless the major players of the Italian private sector, as well as the European corporations, are allowed to participate on an equal footing (but in a regulated environment which favours competition). In the building and the management of the new networks, they must be allowed to participate either in association or in competition with the large state organisations (principally Telecom Italia but also the RAI). In the light of impending European legislation relating to the telecommunications sector due to be implemented in 1996, this is an imperative which cannot be postponed.

Closely linked to the objective of liberalisation is the process of privatisation of public bodies and state holdings which in recent years has found general support with government. In the communications sector, for example, it is clear that the partial privatisation of STET, the holding company with the majority share in Telecom Italia, will be the catalyst which sets in train the participation of the private sector. Within this same movement towards liberalisation, the outcomes of recent referendums supporting the opening up of the public radio and television services to private capital (despite the legal and operational problems that this raises) are very important.

The second element relates to the need for the simultaneous diversification of the roles played by each of the participants within the new system. Until now, Italian television has been characterised by a strong form of what we have referred to in Chapter 1 as vertical integration, a model which has encouraged a single organisation to assume all the principal functions – management, production, programming, transmission and so on – of broadcasting. Once again this model bears little resemblance to developments in the rest of Europe, where at least a partial distinction is made between these roles. This vertical model has led to a weakening of the potential of Italian television, resulting in a situation characterised by a small number of independent producers, standardised marketing and transmissions policies, and a low level of technological experimentation. For this reason the gradual diversification of broadcasting activities away from the vertical model, together with the controlled integration of the new participants into the communications system, will be a key element in its future development.

Such an opening up of the system would allow broadcasters and publishers to concentrate on the content aspect of communication rather than its management, with the result that the old prescriptive views relating to the content or function of a given medium (print, radio, television and even the new electronic media) would be replaced by new, fresh and innovative approaches to programme-making and service provision. It would be possible through this approach to find new roles for the weakest media forms by their identification with new specific roles[5] and the abandoning of any legacy of inferiority *vis-à-vis* the others (Menduni, 1994). Radio is particularly well placed, in a new media order, to offer a wide collection of special services to its audience ranging across such diverse activities as 'real time' news to chat programmes and traffic information. At the same time the traditional broadcasters will have to interact with the new participants – network managers, software designers, hardware manufacturers – with the aim of establishing a totally new dialogue which will serve as the foundation for a newly integrated communications system.

The logic of this kind of thinking raises some intriguing questions relating to key areas of any future government policy of integration. For example, will Telecom Italia be allowed to produce television programmes? Will Fininvest be allowed to operate telephone networks? Apart from the rough-edged nature of these questions, they do in fact encapsulate some of the primary issues which stand at the centre of the future development of the entire communications system. If significant opportunities are not offered to private-sector players to share in the operation of Telecom Italia's telephone network, then private sector participation in the running of the future cable system will hold little appeal. Equally, a complete unregulated opening of the cable market may well favour not only the continuing domination of Telecom Italia, but the actual strengthening of its hold over the market.

The final element relates to the role to be played by the state in the construction of the information superhighway, and in particular the nature of the safeguards which need to be created for the protection of the public interest. The launch of the information society can no longer be approached along the old economic route of using financial incentives and public resources in the form of subsidies. Instead the government and public agencies must demonstrate a will to participate actively in the revolution. To this end it must allocate both funding and human resources in order to give the information society a significant public aspect which stands alongside the obvious interest which will come from the private sector. Indeed a true multi-media system will only become a reality if it is taken up and used by the country's schools, hospitals, ministries and other public agencies, with a public dimension which ultimately permeates the entire communications system. In reality, Italy still lags behind the other countries of Europe. Though it has one of the highest figures for the daily viewing of television (208 minutes according to Eurodata research), it is also a country that invests the least in information technology research. In fact in 1993 the state actually allocated 7.1 per cent less funding to information technology research than in the previous year (Tasca, 1995:75).

It follows from this that a determining factor will be the state's capacity for redressing the issue of the so-called 'telematic illiteracy' in Italy. Computerised systems can only succeed if Italian citizens view the service as a practical response to their need for rapid communication and services, unobstructed by bureaucratic red tape. Similarly, consumers of commercial services must also be led to appreciate the benefits offered by telematics for the equally rapid and efficient extension of sales networks and distribution systems which are accessible long after traditional retail selling points and service agencies have closed. In our view, only the state and not private operators will be able to undertake the educative measures necessary, acting as a catalyst for the creation of the new communications system.

With regard to the safeguarding of the public interest, clearly consideration will need to be given to the quality of content which characterises the new system. The role of public service radio and television will need to be reappraised (and in particular that of the RAI). The latter, if it wishes to survive, will have to transform itself into what amounts to a public communications service. Indeed the increase in programme types and services will give the system an almost exclusive commercial character, no longer dependent on either taxes or advertising revenue, but deriving its income instead directly from the citizen's use of the varied programming and services on offer. In these circumstances, it may be the case that the principle of public service may well be sacrificed on the altar of economic convenience (Richeri, 1993:49).

The future market and the growth needed for survival

A single figure can give a clear picture of the current situation of the communications market in Italy. The ratio between gross national product and advertising investments forecast for 1995 was 0.51 per cent. This figure certainly compares unfavourably with those found in other advanced countries, but nevertheless places Italy back on the same levels reached in the boom years of the mid-1980s. However, the saturation point has clearly been reached for this model of growth and the figure strongly suggests that the expansion of the advertising market, stimulated by commercial television, has come to a close. Today the entire Italian market is in search of new formulas and solutions capable of reversing what is now considered to be a recessionary phase in advertising. The future of the Italian communications market will be determined on the basis of three fundamental conditions.

The first is the need to identify new communication techniques which make advertising investments in the traditional media more effective. This will involve a move away from generalist scheduling to more distinctive fare, with advances being made into fully-fledged 'narrow-casting', networks or channels resulting in what could be termed the 'selective pulverisation' of audiences. This approach, though it targets audiences which are smaller than the tens of millions of Italians who watch international football or the San Remo song festival (an audience which is becoming increasingly reluctant to sit through hundreds of commercial breaks), would lay the foundation for effectively reaching the tens of thousands who are seriously interested in a certain kind of programming. In short, viewers will be more receptive to commercials which, far from being undifferentiated, will be designed as services linked to the kind of content that characterises the programming on a particular channel. This revolution in approach will also have implications for the quality of the advertising message. The effectiveness of a commercial will no longer depend so much upon the slick packaging of the image, currently designed to grab the attention of the viewer, as it will upon its capacity to convey maximum information about the product and its uses. Such a trend will also inevitably influence distribution systems which will increasingly direct their efforts towards interactive channels. Successful products will be those which, following an effective promotional campaign, can be purchased through the medium of television at the touch of a remote-control button.

The second condition regards the need to find an alternative system of funding for the radio and television public services. Revenue from the licence fees and advertising are already insufficient to maintain growth, and this inadequacy will become more pronounced over time. There is an increasing worldwide tendency in television

Table 5.9 Revenue derived from advertising, licence fees and direct sales (written press only) of the principal media organisations (in billion lira) 1993

	Fininvest/Mondadori		RAI		RCS		L'Espresso	
	Resources	% of total	Resources	% of total	Resources	% of total	Resources	% of total
Advertising[1]	3,340	39	1,431	17	653	8	572	7
TV	2,843	61	1,321	29			512	24
Dailies	19	1	–	–	378	18	60	4
Periodicals	478	33	–	–	275	19	–	–
Radio	–	–	110	35	–	–	–	–
Sales (press or licence fee)	1,838	–	2,069	–	2,269	–	440	–
Total[2]	4,681	29	3,500	22	2,922	18	1,016	6

Source: Media Key no. 132, February 1994
[1] This line includes the advertising revenue from TV, Dailies, Periodicals and Radio which are detailed below.
[2] This includes the total advertising revenue from Advertising, Sales and licence fees.

away from broadcasting towards narrowcasting (Richeri, 1993:110). Although this is the general trend, the Italian industry lags far behind developments in other countries. In 1994 the total income forthcoming from pay-TV amounted to no more than 5 per cent of the total generated in the television sector. As mentioned earlier, the sole pay-TV initiative is still struggling to get off the ground, having attracted so far only 700,000 viewers. This figure represents 3 per cent of the potential family audience which, compared with 20 per cent in France and 17 per cent in Britain, is an extremely modest share.

Research indicates that if the television and radio systems remain unchanged, by 1998 their growth rates will be zero (taking the inflation rate into account). If, on the other hand, the foundations are laid for significant growth in pay-TV, then the Italian television system could attract new finance of more than 1.6 trillion lira, with an annual forecast growth rate of 7 per cent.

The third and final condition for market growth relates to the arrival on the scene of new entrepreneurs with roles to play in the Italian communications industry. There is a need, on the one hand, to introduce new blood into the traditional media system (a recent example is the purchase by the businessman Cecchi Gori of Telemontecarlo and Videomusic), and, on the other, for publishing houses to enter the field of multi-media activities along similar lines, for example, to those taken by the Sardinian publisher Nicki Grauso with Video On Line, a company active in the distribution of telematic/information services.

The European dimension

If a date had to be put on the first perceptible changes in the Italian communications sector then it could be placed no earlier than 1998. By that time full implementation will have been made of the legislative changes which have been referred to earlier relating to the limits on media holdings, as well as to the conversion of national networks towards thematic narrowcasting schedules. At the same time the new regulatory body for the media will be assuming its functions. By 1998 it will also have been possible to assess fully the effects of the ending of the state monopoly in the field of telecommunications, thus reinforcing the prospect of real competition in the process of multi-media convergence by the entry of new national and international players. By the same date there should be unmistakable evidence of the trends mentioned above which will favour the more sharply focused use of traditional media. It should by that time be possible to identify new media outlets and new kinds of scheduling and services (distinct from the current generalist fare) in order to harness them for the economic development of Italian communications.

In these circumstances of change, to what extent will the Italian system be susceptible to any wider process of Europeanisation? In the first place it should be stressed that the general Italian attitude towards the wider European community is one which still prioritises

Italian problems and their solutions. There is of course an obligation to tie in national legislation to conform with the requirements of various Community directives, as well as with the broader based values linked to cultural, social and political integration.

However, there are numerous underlying conditions which make it seem likely that some form of Europeanisation of the Italian media will become a key element in its development. This is mainly because the impact of the Community should prove decisive from a legal point of view, especially if the Commission decides to issue a forceful directive of its own relating to levels of media concentration to stand alongside the other directives on television and telecommunications. In this case, Italy will be forced to comply with a system extending beyond its national frontiers whether it wishes to or not.

Secondly, the influence of Europe will have a significant effect in the technological field, especially with regard to advances which can no longer be contained within national boundaries (such as standards for decoders and procedures for limited access). Within this context, representative bodies such as the EBU and other bodies with extra-national functions, including Eutelsat, will play increasingly important roles in facilitating the success of Italian media policy.

Finally, a key element in the Europeanisation of the Italian system will be the gradual integration and collaboration on an international level of the various public and private protagonists. There has already been a partial opening up to other players of Fininvest capital; the RAI is currently entering into discussion with virtually all the world's leading companies in the telecommunications field including Time Warner, Sony, CNN, Walt Disney, the BBC and France Television for the purpose of arriving at a common strategy for thematic programme scheduling via satellite. In anticipation of the liberalisation of the sector, other European groups are already looking at the possibilities of entering the Italian telecommunications market and the Kirch group is now counted among the shareholders of the Telepiù pay-TV channel. All these are the signs of a gradual European 'cross-breeding' present in the Italian media which extend beyond single corporation boundaries and national frontiers.

But there is a further unique role for Italy to play on the international media stage: no process of internationalisation can be complete without the active participation of a country which numerically represents a key market of 57 million people (the fourth largest population in the Union following Germany, France and Britain). Secondly, it should be remembered that Italy possesses 60 per cent of all the artistic and cultural wealth of the entire continent (Migli and Protettí, 1995:223). In the creation of a continent-wide information society, there can be no ignoring the European storehouse of historical identity and memory that exists in this country.

It is within this context of reciprocal influences and exchanges that any process of the Europeanisation of Italy's media should be viewed. There are, in the final analysis, three paths which Italy must follow quickly if it is to take decisive steps in the direction of Europe. The first is to ensure that its legislation is in step with that of the rest of the continent, rather than persisting in maintaining the particularities of its own national system. The second is the move towards the convergence of telecommunications, information technology and media systems, creating a new system which integrates current diversified and separate outlets. The third is an advance in the globalisation of markets and companies rather than the maintenance of the current sectoral parochialism and weakness within the international economic framework.

These three options will determine the future progress of the emergence of a European dimension in the Italian communications system. They will create a route which, given the inevitable nature of the processes already under way, coincides not only with opportunities for the growth and development of the Italian media, but with their very survival.

Notes

1. This *dirigiste* line is echoed in Chapter 3 in Lamizet's account of French government's attitudes towards the broadcasting media.
2. Again Lamizet makes a similar point regarding a similarly perceived role for French local radio in Chapter 3.
3. In the post-Mammí period no less than 2,000 radio and 700 television broadcasting licences have been granted.
4. Olivetti and Bell Atlantic are major shareholders.
5. Lamizet describes telematic links to data bases already established by some French newspapers in Chapter 3.

CHAPTER 6

The media in Spain
Lorenzo Vilches

I Introduction

The history of the media in Spain should be viewed as falling into two distinct phases of development and interpretation. These historical phases distinguish between that of the dictatorship, 1939–76, and that of the transition to democracy, 1976 to the present. The dictatorship phase was characterised by the dependence of the mass media on the political, ideological and cultural hegemony created by the nationalist movement which emerged victorious after the Civil War. It was the state which explicitly organised the media, whilst, at the same time, deciding on the manner in which information was mediated by means of laws, propaganda and repression. This policy had as its objective the specific aim of guaranteeing the dissemination and acceptance of the government's values and view of Spain as 'the guardian of the West', and whose national unity also invoked 'a universal mission.'

Thus it follows that, during this period, concepts such as Gramsci's 'hegemony' and Althusser's 'ideological state apparatus' were popular instruments for the analysis of that initial, historic, phase. Arguments for the reform of the Spanish media during the dictatorship centre around the need for an ideological and cultural shift in order to effect changes in the power relationships between government and the governed. However, in the second phase, post-1976, a new mode of analysis has been proposed which focuses particularly on the development and structure of the media in terms of the economic and commercial processes of international marketing. Spanish media analysts fall into three broad categories. Some of them still uphold a mainly Marxist tradition; others adopt a stance which is a mixture of North American liberalism and European Marxism, focusing on imperialism and transnationalisation; a third group, based specifically on a liberal position, are interested only in economic market-type analysis and the globalisation of communication.

The end of the dictatorship and the establishment of democracy coincided with the start of important changes both in industry as well

173

as in the world and European economies which necessarily influence any analysis of the Spanish media in the last two decades of the twentieth century. In Spain, these changes are particularly evident in the field of ownership and management of the media, as well as in the field of advertising revenues. But in addition, the tremendous impact of the media in cultural and political life has had consequences for Spanish society in the 1990s that have not yet been adequately evaluated by communication theorists. We shall deal with this period later in this chapter. For the moment, to begin at the beginning.

II The written press: from dictatorship to transition

The Franco legacy

The Spanish Journalists' Union in the last half century boasts an exceptional founder member in the person of the dictator Francisco Franco, who on 20 July 1949 installed himself as 'Number One' on the Official Register of Journalists. The dictatorial regime which arose out of the defeat of the Republic marks the precise point at which the Spanish media got off the ground in the 1940s. Communications in Spain during that period have been compared with the dominant totalitarian Italian and German models. The pyramid structure of organised information that was set up in Germany by Dr Goebbels in 1938 was chosen as the cohesive mechanism which would symbolise the new Spain, and be the new source of Catholic culture for the nation (Timoteo Alvarez, 1989:221). At the bottom of the pyramid were the newspapers, radio, cinema, theatre and publishing houses. The National Press and Information Office controlled the press, and the Information Service controlled the radio. At the apex, exercising supreme control, was the Ministry of Information. In this way information had a function, and a medium to enable it to fulfil its pedagogic mission: to educate the population and to guarantee state security by means of pre-publication censorship. This centralised, totalitarian structure survived until the 1960s when Spain opened up to Europe through some minimal reforms which gave rise to the first legalised media of opposition. But during the worst of the repression – the so-called hunger years of the 1940s and 1950s – there was a resistance press, associated with socialist, communist and anarchist organisations which succeeded in the publication of underground titles sometimes reaching circulation levels of 20,000, often in heroic circumstances.

Following a Bill in 1936 which outlawed all 'socialist, communist, libertarian, and in general, subversive' newspapers, journals and literary publications, a large state media conglomerate was set up. Called variously the Prensa del Movimiento or the Cadena del Movimiento, this organisation was to survive until the 1980s.

The beginning of the dictatorship, which included the New Right inspired by Opus Dei, brought with it a new press and printing law. This law transformed pre-publication censorship into a censorship carried out implacably against anyone who contravened the ideological principles of the regime, or the needs of state security or national defence. Despite this tight form of censorship, there nevertheless developed a kind of tolerance in the regime with regard to the private press. The official vigilance under which journalists operated led them to use a special kind of implicitness of style designed to cheat the censor. This policy was rewarded by the growing public support for the private press, particularly in the case of such newspapers as Barcelona's *La Vanguardia* and Madrid's *ABC* and *YA*. In terms of readership, for example, from 1945 onwards, the state-owned press trailed far behind the private sector which, by 1970, had gained 74 per cent of the market share (Nieto, 1973).

After Franco's death, Juan Carlos I was crowned King of Spain and Adolfo Suárez became head of government. The days of the state media conglomerate, La Cadena del Movimiento, were now numbered. Shortly afterwards, the remains of the state information empire were sold off at private auction and passed into private hands. In 1976 Spain initiated a news media climate which was very different from the previous one, with the appearance of the first newspapers directly associated with the new democracy, *El País* and *Diario 16*.

The written press post-1976

The pattern of journalism in Spain has changed radically from 1976. Sixty newspapers disappeared in the first few years, to be replaced by an equal number of new titles. This was an unparalleled development in ownership patterns, and the consequence was an increase in interest on the part of the people which was subsequently translated into increased readership and sales. Despite the loss of some of its leading titles, the written press sector grew continuously so that by 1992 the publication of daily newspapers had increased by 27.9 per cent, moving from 3.05 million copies to 4.5 million in 1994 (*Comunicación Social Tendencias*, 1993). However, despite this substantial growth rate in this sector, there are no grounds for complacency. As may be noted in Figure 6.1, only in 1992 did Spain manage to achieve a ratio of 100 copies per 1,000 inhabitants – the threshold figure set by UNESCO as an index of development in the domain of newspaper readership.

When Spanish newspaper figures are compared with the rest of the other member states of the European Union, which account for almost 80 million copies daily, Spain is positioned in penultimate place before Portugal (see Figure 6.2).

According to these figures, for Spain to reach the European average circulation figure, it would need to go from the present figure of 3.9 million copies to 9.1 million copies (Diaz Nosty, 1993:44–5) as shown in Figure 6.2. But in spite of this position, Spanish dailies have moved up the international league table, especially *El País* which is ahead of several European titles such as *The Times* and *Le Monde*.

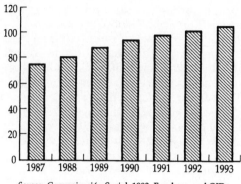

Source: Comunicación Social, 1993, Fundesco and OJD

Figure 6.1 The development of the daily written press in Spain (readers per 1000 inhabitants)

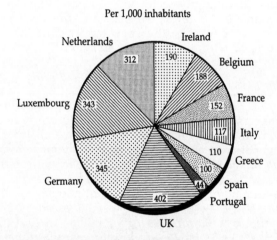

Source: Comunicación Social 1993, Fundesco

Figure 6.2 Index of press distribution in the European Community

In Table 6.1 the position of Spain's two most important papers can be compared in the context of the 50 leading European dailies for 1991–2. *El País* maintains its leading position in the Spanish press with over 1.5 million readers (EGM,[1] 1994–5). The average national level of daily readership in Spain, 36 per cent, is well below the 61 per cent which is the average for the rest of Western Europe. Nevertheless, in the quality press sector at least, Spanish titles compare favourably with their French and British counterparts: the first seven Spanish newspapers[2] represent a circulation of 37 editions per thousand

Table 6.1   The 50 most important daily newspapers in the EC (1991–2)

Daily	Sales	Publishers	Country	Year
1 *Bild Zeitung*	4,485,874	Axel Springer	D	1992
2 *The Sun*	3,567,863	News Inter	GB	1992
3 *Daily Mirror*	2,859,240	MGN	GB	1992
4 *Daily Mail*	1,693,000	Asociados	GB	92
5 *Daily Express*	1,542,693	United	GB	92
6 *WAZ (group)*	1,173,890	WAZ	D	91
7 *Daily Telegraph*	1,038,336	Hollinger	GB	92
8 *Daily Star*	809,253	United	GB	92
9 *Ouest France*	749,058	O.F.	F	91
10 *De Telegraaf*	725,000	De Telegraaf	NL	91
11 *La Repubblica*	691,840	La Repubb	I	91
12 *Corriere della Sera*	674,344	RCS Rizzoli	I	91
13 *Evening Standard*	520,457	Asociados	GB	92
14 *Today*	509,457	News Inter	GB	92
15 *Sachsische Zeitung*	479,616	G+J	D	92
16 *Mitteldeutsche Zeitung*	456,903	DuMont Sch	D	92
17 *Köln Express*	424,902	DuMont Sch	D	92
18 *The Guardian*	416,923	GMEN	GB	92
19 *Algemeen Dagblad*	413,900	Elsevier	NL	91
20 *Le Figaro*	407,427	R. Hersant	F	91
21 *El País*	407,379	Prisa	E	92
22 *Suddeutscher Zeitung*	389,202	SZ	D	91
23 *The Times*	389,202	News International	GB	92
24 *Frankfurter Allgemeine*	383,398	FAZ	D	92
25 *De Standaard*	383,000	VUM	B	92
26 *Le Parisien*	380,468	Amaury	F	91
27 *The Independent*	377,300	Newspaper I	GB	92
28 *Le Progrès*	375,878	Progres	F	91
29 *Le Monde*	368,970	Le Monde	F	91
30 *Augsburger Allgemeine*	364,579	Holland	D	92
31 *Sud Ouest*	351,885	Atlantpresse	F	91
32 *La Voix du Nord*	347,230	LVN	F	91
33 *Leipziger Volkszeitung*	344,556	Madsak	D	92
34 *Volkstimme*	344,279	Bauer	D	92
35 *Rheineische Post*	342,572	RP	D	92
36 *De Volkskrant*	342,100	Prescom	NL	91
37 *BZ*	322,201	Axel Springer	D	92
38 *Het Laatste Nieuws*	317,000	VUM	B	92
39 *ABC*	304,098	P. Española	E	92
40 *Hamburger Abendblatt*	299,758	Axel Springer	D	92
41 *Branbant Pers Dagblad*	295,250	Elsevier	NL	91
42 *Financial Times*	291,782	Pearson	GB	92
43 *Il Messaggero*	286,645	Il Messaggero	I	91
44 *Le Dauphine Libéré*	286,145	R. Hersant	F	91
45 *Kolner Stand Anzaiger*	284,930	DuMont Sch	D	92
46 *Berliner Zeitung*	271,689	G+J	D	92
47 *Il Sole 24 Ore*	270,177	Confindustria	I	91
48 *Nouvelle Republicain*	261,616	NRCO	F	91
49 *Nice Matin*	244,448	Nice Matin	F	91
50 *Die Rheinpfalz*	244,095	Rheinpfalz	D	91

Source: Jürgen Heinrich in *Media Perspektiven* 1994

inhabitants, a figure which is superior to French and slightly lower than British levels (*Comunicación Social*, 1994:63).

The 1990s have been characterised by an uneven expansion in media use. The daily press has experienced the largest growth, although it still manages to reach 36 per cent of the total population of people over fourteen years old. However, in the last few years there has been a 25 per cent increase in readership which clearly outperforms those of the radio (10 per cent) and of television (3 per cent), despite the marked increase in programme supply in the latter two areas. The reader of a Spanish newspaper is by and large male (63 per cent) whilst women, on the other hand, generally prefer magazines (55 per cent). Nevertheless, female readership of the daily press continues to rise and has now reached 37 per cent (source *EGM*).

It would seem an appropriate point, at the end of the section on the written press, to examine the phenomenon of women's magazines and other periodicals. Conspicuous in this sector is *Hola*, established in 1944 with an initial circulation of 175,000, and published now in English under the title *Hello!*. This magazine, together with *Lecturas* (established 1921), constituted the kind of press which for many women was the source of an emotional escapism particularly fashionable during the dictatorship. Today, the first place in this category is occupied by *Pronto* (established in 1972) with a circulation of 697,000 compared with that of *Hola* of 660,000. Later arrivals to the market place such as *Elle*, *Marie-Claire* and *Vogue*, have further invigorated the women's magazine sector and altogether the market serves a global readership of around three million.

The general magazine sector is also experiencing a healthy growth. There are currently 400 different titles published in Spain with an average circulation of over 16 million in 1995 (*Anuario El País*, 1995) which is double the total for the beginning of the 1980s, the decade which saw the appearance of massive international capital in this sector.

Legislation and regulation

Despite the impact of the profound political changes of attitude relating to press freedom in post-Franco Spain, they have not found expression in any specific statutory regulation of the press. The Spanish Constitution of 1978 is the only one in Europe, apart from that of Switzerland, that includes a professional secrecy and conscience clause as a full right for journalists. Nevertheless, it has not been possible to introduce more detailed press legislation. This is principally due to a lack of agreement between parliamentarians, press owners and journalists themselves concerning the nature and purpose of such laws. Taking their cue from the perceived spirit of the Constitution, the opponents of specific legislation claim that 'the best press law is no press law at all', and that any further legislation would, *de facto*, limit rights and access to information. This view is opposed by other professional associations who see in the text of the Constitution a vagueness surrounding professional secrecy *vis-à-vis* the courts. Hence, in professional journalistic circles, there is a general desire for the implementation of a more specific legal framework relating to the conduct of the written press. As things stand, the professional operations of the press are managed on a self-regulatory, *ad hoc* basis through private agreements and editorial statutes between the interested parties.

The absence of further detailed legislation (not necessarily a full press law) manifests itself in Spain in the weakness of editorial boards to resist the influence of the newspaper proprietors, as well as in the weakened position of journalists caught up in the processes of multi-media concentration. This absence of legislation also raises concerns relating to rights of freedom of expression of journalists, as was illustrated recently by a court intervention which publicly criticised a news item on public television.

III The development of the broadcasting media

From dictatorship to transition: the state radio

Spanish radio, just like the written press, was set up as a post-war organisation powerfully controlled by the state. The dictatorship's propagandist and pedagogic perception of the role of the media led it to place the radio under the control of the Ministry of Education. In 1951 it came under the control of the Ministry of Information and Tourism where it remained until after 1976. The legal framework for radio broadcasting goes back to a law of 1934, passed during the dictatorship of General Primo de Rivera. This law established a national broadcasting network which included the state's transmitters as well as those belonging to the private sector which had been granted broadcasting licences (franchises). Radio Nacional de España was set up in this way and financed by the state with a programming structure similar to the present one: a mixed range of programming broadcast nationally on medium wave, and relayed by regional transmitters. In addition today, there is a classical music station, as well as a third educational and cultural station both broadcast on FM. At the end of the 1960s radio broadcasting by cable was set up involving the participation of the National Telephone Company, which also includes a foreign languages teaching station. In 1953, a Concordat was signed with the Vatican which provided for the creation of the Cadena de Ondas Populares Españolas (COPE), a Spanish popular radio network controlled by the Catholic Church (for further discussion see below).

Private radio

Private radio broadcasting, especially after the arrival of the Sociedad Española de Radiofusión (SER), the first national radio network before the Civil War,[3] continued its expansion until it finally linked up with

179

the majority of the country's commercial radio stations. Nevertheless, this amalgamation revealed a significant structural weakness in the Spanish radio system in general. Towards the end of the dictatorship, the number of radio sets per thousand citizens was only 230, far below the average for the rest of the European Community countries (Gorostiaga, 1976:153). In fact the first audience survey carried out in the 1970s shows that the daily audience amounted to only 20 per cent of the national population (Franquet and Martí, 1985:153). Many Spaniards were resistant to receiving the regime's propagandist information and instead tuned in to the foreign transmissions aimed at Spain from outside its frontiers. After the Civil War the heart of the resistance centred upon 'information wars' conducted across the airwaves and in the clandestine written press. But unlike the latter, clandestine radio came entirely from abroad: Radio España Independiente (from Moscow) later renamed Radio Pirenaica, the BBC, Radio París, Radio Moscow, and Radio Euzkadi (French Basque country) (Plans, 1981; Mendezona, 1979). There were, in addition, other international transmissions from Radio Peking and Radio Tirana which, along with Radio Moscow, also served the Chilean resistance which grew up after the 1973 coup in that country. Finally, and rather late on the scene (1975), came the Voz de Canarias, representing the independence movement, MPAIAC, transmitting from Algiers.

The post-1980s expansion of the radio

At 5 p.m. on 23 February 1981 thousands of Spaniards were listening to Cadena SER and Radio Nacional de España following the events surrounding the election of Calvo Sotelo as head of government, when the proceedings were interrupted by the sound of shots being fired accompanied by shouts of military commands inside the Parliament building. It marked the beginning of a short-lived but dramatic attempted 'coup d'état' which was to last until the following morning. Throughout those hours radio was the only medium by which the country was able to follow the events as they happened. Spanish Television (Radio Television Española, RTVE), in accordance with the censorship tradition, inherited from the dictatorship, of avoiding live broadcasts,[4] maintained its policy of covering parliamentary proceedings in the evening only. Thus it was left to the radio, which paradoxically had been marginalised by the state, to assume the role of a powerful news broadcaster capable of acting in the service of liberty and the emergent process of Spanish democracy.

The process by which radio news broadcasts became a credible force began formally in 1977 with the abolition of the monopoly of Radio Nacional de España. This process of democratisation was strengthened in 1980 with the creation of a legal framework, the Spanish Radio and Television Statute, which defined radio and television as essential public services to be managed by the state corporation RTVE (Radio Televisión Española). The state retained control over the use of long and short waves for overseas broadcasts, two thirds of the medium wave were reserved for the RTVE, and the remainder given to the private sector. The 1980s saw the rapid increase in radio audiences with an increase of 8 million listeners between 1976 and 1982, the time of the coming to power of the first socialist government. We can summarise this general trend by describing radio broadcasting in Spain at the end of the so-called 'boom' decade of the 1980s as being one of a highly centralised structure at the national level, with the main axis based upon the transmission of networked programmes both in the public and the private sectors.

The current public radio service

The new public radio service currently comprises the following three systems:

- National Radio: Radio Nacional de España (RNE) which has 84 stations and belongs to the public organisation Radio Televisión Española (RTVE). It has four state-wide networks: Radio 1 on medium wave, which broadcasts programmes of general interest; Radio 2 which is devoted to classical music; Radio 3 which covers pop music and distance learning; Radio 5 which is a non-stop news station.
- Regional Radio: regional radios serve each autonomous region which have broadcasting responsibilities – Catalonia, the Basque Region and Galicia.
- Municipal Radio: these are local radios subsidised by local organ-isations.

Regional radio deserves special mention here because of its completely unique features within both the Spanish and the European context. The constitution of 1978 which defined Spain as a state made up of seventeen 'Autonomous Communities' made possible the setting up of radio and television networks in four of the 'Communities' which would be joined eventually by those of Madrid, Murcia and Valencia. Although the autonomous system of decentralisation in Spain marks a victory for the democratisation of the state from the media point of view, no one is happy with the way the system has turned out, either from a social or from an economic viewpoint. The cost of maintaining these networks, compared with audience size, is high and frequently involves the particular Autonomous Community in huge annual deficits. For some people, regional radio of this kind is a heterogeneous model with no clear-cut local identity. In the eyes of its critics it has failed in its aim of defending its own culture and language because it is more concerned with competing for funds and influence at the national rather than the regional level (Diaz Mancisidor, 1995).

The new private radio sector

The main commercial radio stations of the 1990s constitute a radical readjustment of the national broadcasting scene. The main features of this new radio landscape are the concentration of the radio companies and the simultaneous diversification of systems (i.e. conventional, formula and thematic programming). They fall into four principal networks:

- the Sociedad Española de Radiofusión (SER): this network is the oldest and the largest network in Spain. It was taken over in 1986 by PRISA, the company which publishes *El País*.
- Antena 3 Radio (no connection with Antena 3 Televisión). This station began broadcasting in 1981; its main shareholders are the Godó and PRISA groups.
- Cadena de Ondas Populares de España (COPE): this network is now owned by the Episcopal Conference of the Catholic Church in Spain. It has 73 transmitters.
- Onda Cero: this station is owned by the powerful group Organización de Ciegos de España (ONCE) which is also a shareholder in TELE 5.

Local radio

The local radio phenomenon is to some extent the indirect result of the historical marginalisation and centralising policy of the Spanish state, as well as the result of developments of a wider significance in Western Europe. In the mid-1970s popular music and the teenage demand for a more independent social involvement found a powerful and skilful form of expression in local radio. There were democratic winds blowing in Spain already in the 1970s and these, combined with the currents of the new Left emanating from the student revolts of 1968, helped to create a new form of radio communication. This trend gave rise to the establishment of independently financed free radio stations, private radios and unauthorised stations. But the most important aspect of this general broadcasting trend were the municipal radio stations mostly concentrated in Catalonia (130 in 1988). There are currently 500 stations broadcasting in small and medium-sized towns throughout Spain.

Radio in the 1990s

There is a decisive preference first of all among Spanish listeners for the FM wavelength (70 per cent) over the medium wave (30 per cent). This confirms the pattern that first became pronounced in the late 1980s, the great decade of expansion of radio broadcasting. The dramatic pace of modernisation during this period brought about a rapid middle-class conversion to FM while the traditional 'die hard' Spaniards have stuck with the poorer sound-quality medium wave.

In 1992 the SER/Antena 3 networks, with their 425 stations, accounted for 58.44 per cent of the total audience share. The public service (state) sector came a poor second with 18.8 per cent. COPE took third place with 12.7 per cent, with Onda Cero last with 10 per cent. In terms of quality and performance, conventional radio is superior to the formula variety. As regards regional distribution, Andalucía is the community with the smallest audience for conventional radio, whilst the Basque Region occupies first place for all types of radio audiences (*Tendencias*, 1993:78).

The total radio audience in April 1995 in Spain just exceeded 20 million listeners which represents 52 per cent of the total available audience over the age of fourteen (*EGM*, 1995). This figure amounts to a significant increase in the radio audience, and it is interpreted as one of the consequences of the social unrest caused by a series of political and financial scandals in 1994–5. The commercial radio stations are attracting 80 per cent of the audience to the detriment of the national public service stations (Radio Nacional de España) which so far has failed to put together radio schedules culturally attractive to the majority of Spanish listeners. This fall in audience is in spite of the initial advantage gained by the creation of a continuous news station (*Todo Noticias* on Radio 5).

Age and gender are the most significant variables for the determining of listening habits. However, there is growing evidence to suggest that 'conventional' radio is attracting younger listeners from the music and formula stations. The number of young people, for example, who tune in to sports programmes is continuing to expand. The mix between male and female listeners is fairly evenly balanced. According to recent statistics, the Spanish radio audience is weighted increasingly towards the middle-class socio-economic category, with a corresponding decline among lower-middle and working-class groups.

One of the features of Spanish radio is to be found, surprisingly, not so much in its content or its form, but in the celebrity status of its presenters who have become the 'radio stars' identified with their particular stations. Thus, for example, there are sports commentators who give a particular station its distinctive masculine stamp, and female presenters who are identified with older women listeners. There are radio journalists, too, with declared political leanings, who have their own audience following, even when they move to another station. In the field of European radio, Spain ranks second among the other sixteen existing and future members of the Union in terms of the number of stations currently operating: 1,700 in Spain, compared with 2,500 in Italy, 1,400 in France, 169 in Germany and 161 in the United Kingdom. The Spanish 'market', however, is over-supplied when compared to actual demand, and falls into thirteenth position in the context of other comparable national radio audiences in Western Europe.

In conclusion, the position of the Spanish radio, both in terms of its historical and its present development, is markedly different from that of other countries in Western Europe. Combining a particularly strong form of the European 'dirigiste' model and the North American liberal one, it has been able to develop a modern form of its own in spite of the political difficulties of its history, and the comparative lateness in the development of its economy. On the one hand, there is a rigid centralist structure, while on the other there can be few countries more liberal than Spain in protecting private enterprise. There is both a high degree of concentration in the private sector, heightened in recent years by the appearance of the multi-media groups, as well as extreme fragmentation (in 1987 there were 900 recognised private and public stations). Paradoxically, one of the consequences of this fragmentation on scheduling is the lack of variety of genres and formats, though there is a considerable national output. Finally, in concept public service radio (and television) is one of the most decentralised in Europe. This situation is explained only partly on linguistic grounds; it also derives from the historical recognition that Spain is a pluralistic and culturally distinctive society in other ways too.

Television: the early days

On 28 October 1956, while the Soviet tanks were entering Hungary and the youth of the capitalist West were descending into the streets to dance to the first rock and roll music to enter the hit parade, the first Spanish television channel, TVE 1, was being launched with a Catholic Mass (Baget, 1975:50). Until 1962 Spanish television lived through a period characterised by autarchy and centralism of a kind no other Western European system has had to endure. From the early 1960s there followed a mild opening up of the television system to a wider European market as well as the creation of a second channel, TVE 2. This brief period of modernisation came to an abrupt end with the assassination of Franco's chosen successor, Admiral Carrero Blanco, and the triggering of a serious political crisis. It was this incident which caused the door to be slammed once again on any kind of cultural tolerance and gradual modernisation, and created a situation which endured until Franco's death in 1975. Financed exclusively by advertising and sponsorship, programming policy meandered on in contexts dominated either by indirect political control, or the grossest manipulation of information content. Although there were some early attempts at decentralising television during the Franco regime – with transmissions, for example, in Catalan from Barcelona in the early 1960s – regional programming did not begin in earnest until 1973 in the Basque Region, Galicia and the Canaries (Baget, 1981; Costa, 1986). The 1970s began with a gamble in television which was only partly successful so, for example, an attempt to set up a cable network beyond Barcelona and Madrid was suspended. In 1972 colour television was widely introduced. Economic considerations resulted in the PAL system being adopted instead of the first choice of SECAM. In this way Spain joined the developing 'European village' of the moving image.

Television in the post-1980s

Television, more than any other medium, reflects the recent changes in economic and political power in communications. The end of the 1970s found European television in deep crisis for which there were various explanations but which fundamentally affected the very principles upon which public sector broadcasting was based. By 1975, for example, the BBC had lost 50 per cent of its audience to commercial television, in Italy hundreds of private television stations emerged which were to become the prelude to a later process of concentration in the hands of Berlusconi. In France the financial reforms introduced by Valéry Giscard d'Estaing relating to advertising revenue resulted in the public service sector being led by audience ratings. For Spain the 1980s were a giddy decade of audio-visual expansion and frequent crisis. No sooner had the country emerged from the tunnel of dictatorship than television found itself having to respond simultaneously to three ongoing processes. Firstly, there was the democratisation that was taking place in radio broadcasting which had implications for television; secondly, there was the pressure for the liberalisation of the medium coming from economic groups who, in a Europe with new and changing information priorities, were seeing a new role for the private sector; finally, there was the demand for greater decentralisation coming from the 'Autonomous Communities'. The end of the single state system was marked by the law regulating the 'Third Channel' in 1983, almost a year after broadcasting had started on Euskal Telebista, in the Basque region and on TV 3 in Catalonia. Broadcasting on these two autonomous channels was followed by the creation of a third major community channel with the setting up of Televisión de Galicia. In 1988 the Spanish government passed legislation providing for the creation of three national private channels, grouped under an administrative authority, RETEVISION, and broadcasting under the auspices of the RTVE. The conditions for the granting of licences followed the French regulatory model (also adopted by Portugal): a contract of ten years' duration, with the concessionary firms only holding 25 per cent of the shares, and foreign capital being restricted to 25 per cent. The first licences were awarded to Antena 3, Tele 5 and Canal Plus. The impact of private television was such that by 1990 a crisis was already in the making. This crisis came in the shape of a serious shortage of programming which threw the television industry – programmers, advertisers and viewers – into a state of great uncertainty and loss of direction. The autonomous television companies which, for example, had begun, true to their linguistic mission, by translating *Dallas* into the vernacular, ended up by becoming much more generalist in nature, hardly distinguishable from the national television channels. The public service sector, formerly proud of the quality of its news coverage and cultural programming, fell into such political and programming disorder that it experienced one of its worst financial crises. The central driving force in television now centred on advertising. The traditional prestige enjoyed by the public service channels was seriously damaged, and an urgent need for managerial reforms and a review of its public service mission were called for on all sides. In short, the situation of Spanish television in the beginning of the 1990s was ripe for the application of what Raymond Williams proposed in the context of the changes in the newspaper industry a decade or so previously: 'What was once a medium for carrying out a broader kind of political activity, has become, in many cases, politics itself' (Williams, 1995:32).

The delay in the introduction of cable television and services in favour of satellite transmission brings down the curtain on the first phase of development of Spanish television within the wider European context.

Television in Spain has not yet, by any means, overcome the problems confronting it in the new context in which it finds itself. The private sector, with the exception of Canal Plus, appears not to have successfully established itself, either from a financial or from an organisational point of view. To some extent the explanation lies in the lack of clear guidance and initiative on the part of the government, and its unwillingness to confront the administrative and financial problems which have arisen in both public and private sectors. In the meantime, public criticism of the poor quality of programming in both sectors is met with wholly inadequate statements of intent, which are too general in nature and, in any case, not universally applicable to all channels. As far as television is concerned in Spain, there is no moral or legal authority sufficiently empowered to ensure either diversity of scheduling or minimum standards of quality of programme content. This has resulted in the proliferation of conservative voices and moralising groups demanding greater censorship, particularly in the portrayal of sex and violence, as a remedy for the ailments, not just of television, but of western society as a whole. Whilst there are moves in Parliament to set up a watch-dog body to oversee television standards, this is more of a reactive response to the situation than a serious attempt to set up an independent sanctioning power of the kind, for example, found in Britain (i.e. the Broadcasting Standards Council). There is no investigative tradition in Spanish television of the kind to be found in other European countries. It would seem that Spanish politicians place too much emphasis upon the politico-economic significance of television as a medium and are quite unable to understand the importance of the wider socio-cultural dimension. It is only an understanding of the interplay between these four variables, and the establishment of policies which maintain a balance between them, which will provide the plurality and diversity of expression that is vital to a democracy.

Television reaches 90 per cent of the Spanish population, and the latter's viewing time has increased over the last six years from 174 minutes to 202 minutes daily. However, the number of programmed hours has increased dramatically from 35,570 hours annually in 1989 to a disproportionate 85,854 hours in 1995. This extraordinary increase in programming in television (it is the same pattern for radio, too) is a typical feature of broadcasting development in Spain, and one which is likely to become even more pronounced with the introduction of cable and satellite systems. Younger people (14–24 years) tend to watch more television than the older age groups and there is a clear imbalance between the viewing habits of men and women. Women over 16 years spend some 223 minutes per day watching TV whereas men watch it for only 173 minutes. As regards channel viewing preferences, the most important development has been the sharp downward turn in the fortunes of the state service as the result of competition from the commercial channels. TVE has declined from an 82 per cent share in 1990 to 28 per cent in 1995. In terms of subject matter, all channels, public, private and autonomous (regional), display a distinct tendency towards an output dominated by fiction, films and TV drama series which together account for 43 per cent of all programming, and stand well above the 14 per cent figure for quiz shows and light entertainment. This preference for fictional programmes may ultimately augur well for the production industry, in Spain as well as in Europe, although at the moment the demand is met by American imports, particularly in films. Finally, the news on the public channel still retains high ratings and large audiences, explained no doubt by the continuing 'credibility' factor of the public service sector, and a traditional channel loyalty in the domain of news.

The television–cinema relationship

The Spanish cinema industry has been recently re-regulated (1994) with the overall effect of reducing state subsidies, thus obliging the industry to reorganise and seek financial aid elsewhere. Part of this reorganisation has led to an improved framework for cooperation between the Spanish film and television industries, which in the past took little notice of each other. The strength of this relationship may be judged by the fact that 77 per cent of all Spanish films made in 1994 received aid in some form from either the public service channels, TVE or Autonoma, or from one of the private channels. Such cooperation is evidently mutually beneficial for both sectors since it provides the film industry with its much needed financial resources for production purposes, and offers the television channels the possibility of adding new films to their catalogues for future transmission.

Unfortunately the Spanish cinema is losing ground both in terms of its artistic merits and in the popularity it enjoys with the public, who increasingly prefer American imports (in the first eight months of 1994 alone, it lost 500,000 cinemagoers). However, on a more optimistic note, the Spanish cinema still fosters the talents of directors of international reputation such as Saura, Almodovar, Luna, Trueba and others, with other up-and-coming younger people still making highly original films. Nevertheless, the comparative importance of the film industry within the context of the rest of the Spanish mass media may be judged by Table 6.2, where it can be seen that the share of national audience is now in single figures.

Table 6.2 Spanish media usage
1994 (% of population)

Newspapers	36.8
Magazines	54.0
Radio	55.4
Television	90.4
Video	5.0
Cinema	7.8

If we had to sum up the most important aspects of Spanish television in the 1990s, we would have to acknowledge that this is a period characterised by the deterioration in the quality of its broadcasting, together with a deterioration of the financial situation of the public service sector which is more serious than it appears on the surface. The current annual expenditure of the TVE amounts to 300,000 million pesetas, whereas its revenue is only 200,000. The deficit of 100,000 million has to be met by the public purse. From 1990 onwards the TVE opted to take the commercial path, increasing its purchase of films in order to compete with its rivals in the private sector and reducing its creative production activity to practically nothing. Despite this regression, in 1994 TVE began to re-invest in production although it was still lagging behind the private sector (Antena 3, for example, invested twice as much in fiction production as TVE in the same period). In general terms, as we have already noted above, part of the cost of production has been met by an increasing trend in television to consolidate an alliance with the cinema via co-productions.

The Spanish television experience is fairly consistent with what is happening elsewhere in Europe, where the viewing trends outlined above – preference for films, TV dramas and light entertainment – are developing into a common pattern. Moreover, there is often little to distinguish public from private channel in terms of programme content. Under pressure to retain their audience share of the market, the so-called 'first' public service channels across Western Europe appear to be adopting scheduling policies which promote a kind of 'convergence' with the private sector in relation to genre and content of programming (this trend is less pronounced on the 'second' public channel, which retains much of its distinctive quality). In Spain this convergence phenomenon[5] is certainly a characteristic feature of the two sectors, and can also be perceived in the so-called regional programming of the Autonomous Communities. From the wider perspective of European production, again Spain is no exception to the general trend: it is the public service sector which is the predominant importer of European products. Sport, and football in particular, would appear to be the only real signs so far of a European broadcasting identity.

Media concentration

The European movement towards closer union and the rapid growth of global communication has coincided in Spain with the process of modernisation, and the acceptance of a 'market logic' extending above and beyond the political-economic 'dirigisme' which characterised the old regime's attitude to the mass media.

The process of press and radio concentration in Spain is a typical example of horizontal integration (see Chapter 1) by which one company combines with another operating in the same media sector but in a different market. On the other hand, public service television offers a good example of vertical integration because the same company controls most of the levels of production within a specific market (Bustamante and Zallo, 1978). It has been pointed out (Flichy, 1990) that this kind of television is unique in the way in which it constitutes a 'cultural industry' in the strictest sense of the term. If we compare television financing within an overall context, it will be noted that in the early 1980s Spanish television received 94 per cent of the total advertising spend, whereas during this time in France, for example, the share amounted to 34 per cent, and in the United Kingdom up to 55 per cent (Annual Statistics, Unesco, 1982). These figures were updated in the European Community's Green Book, 1984, which indicates that TVE still had a high percentage (78 per cent) of its budget derived from advertising compared, for example, with 61 per cent in the case of the French channel TF1. On the other hand, state subsidies to television fell dramatically in the 1980s from around 18.7 per cent to less than 2 per cent by 1986. This situation raised problems of both a legal as well as a political nature: legal because the law of 1980 had established the state's role in the funding of TVE; political because, in reality, the socialist government handed over the public service sector to the financial mercies of the market. The result has been an economic and cultural fiasco for the media and has led to the near bankruptcy of TVE, on one hand, and to its being attacked from the private sector for unfair advertising advantage, on the other. Today the parliamentary Right speaks openly about the privatisation of the public service television system. The effects of liberalisation upon TVE have also been detrimental both to the quality of programming where the levels have fallen, and to the associated area of the programme production industry as a whole.

The situation is hardly more encouraging when we turn to examine the state of regional television. Here the problems and their consequences which we have already mentioned as existing at the national level are repeated. The regional television channels in public ownership follow the TVE model of commercialisation, and compete directly with the private sector with a similar kind of scheduling (sport, films, light entertainment, soaps and American imports). In this way they find themselves confronting apparently irreconcilable objectives. On the one hand, they are obliged to create the kinds of schedules that will expand their audience, generate increasing advertising revenue, and by so doing consolidate their political presence, whilst at the same time fulfilling their regional/cultural mission on the other. However, unlike what is happening at national level with the TVE, the regional television companies benefit from greater financial support with which to offset their deficits, as well as from a greater political support from the regional authorities which stands above electoral or party politics.

International concentration

The process of international penetration and concentration of the Spanish media market stems from the early 1990s (Canal Plus, Fininvest, News Corporation, Kirch) although other big corporations were already present before this period (Bertelsmann, Hachette and Axel Springer). The reason for this concentration in Spain and, indeed, for the similar concentration in other European countries, can be explained by the weak state of the national industry which encourages this kind of outside intervention from international conglomerates, and the prospect of a quick return on investment (Sánchez-Tabernero, 1993:97). It is also partly due to the reluctance of Spanish investors to risk capital in this field, and in part, too, to a lack of dynamism and creativity in the production/software industry (Bustamante, 1994:19). However, this downward trend may be reversed over the next few years through new alliances between film and television companies. For example, in 1995 Canal Plus and TVE began collaborating in the co-production of films. Similarly, Antena 3 Televisión are also embarking on a programme of film and TV movie productions.

Multi-media groups

A third type of media concentration in Spain takes the form of multi-media groups or conglomerates through which the written press and the broadcasting media combine in strategies of vertical concentration. As in most countries in Western Europe the written press, the radio and the television are all closely linked commercially. The most representative of all these groups is PRISA which publishes *El País* and is a majority shareholder in the SER network which has the only pay-TV concession through its alliance with the French-owned channel Canal Plus (currently with a million subscribers). The PRISA group's natural area of expansion is in satellite broadcasting, and it currently has three channels on Astra and one on Hispasat serving America. This group, together with Spain's public service radio and television corporation, RTVE, are the only two groups which compare with the largest European multi-media giants such as Hachette and Havas in France, News International in Britain, Fininvest and RAI in Italy, and Bertelsmann, Springer and Kirch in Germany.[6] PRISA is also involved in international expansion and 1995 witnessed its significant involvement in Newspaper Publishing plc in the UK (publishers of the *Independent* and the *Independent on Sunday*). PRISA also has substantial shareholdings in the Mexican media, and a substantial share in Antena 3 Radio.

Under this heading of multi-media trends, mention must also be made of the special case, in the Spanish context, of the powerful Organización Nacional de Ciegos (ONCE). This is a public corporation with interests in the private television channel Tele 5, the private radio station Onda Cero, which it owns, and it also has shares in several newspapers. Various broadcasting and written press owners have accused ONCE of unfair competition in its private-sector activities (see above under 'Private radio' section).

From the perspective of trends towards increasing European concentration, the Spanish example emerges as one of the least regulated markets (either vertically or horizontally). In spite of the legal provisions contained in the 1987 law (LOT) which forbids the presence of two broadcasters within the same broadcasting zone, the involvement of PRISA in Antena 3 Radio has caused a serious convergence of networks in the country's main cities. Moreover, the restrictions placed on private television have been sidestepped in the case of Fininvest's share of Tele 5 in such a way that it has been possible for the Italian corporation to own 80 per cent of the shares. In other words, the former (and possible future) head of state of another European country may end up owning a Spanish television company! These are but two examples of the crises which have resulted from the re-alignment of Spain's broadcasting media towards a more deregulated interactivity with Europe. As is the case in other countries of Western Europe, the future of their television systems depend on factors which are often beyond their control.

From the perspective of its communication policy, Spain is in line with trends in other European countries which tend to privilege, for reasons of economic viability and political expediency, the transfer of broadcasting power into the hands of a few owners. Curiously, everything seems to indicate that, in practice, the socialist government has favoured this trend towards concentration by the granting of television franchises to the private sector for both terrestrial and satellite broadcasting. The effect has often been the displacement of existing communication systems such as regional broadcasters and newspaper distributors. Paradoxically, despite the predominant spirit of deregulation which prevails in Spain, some analysts still perceive in government policy a strong 'dirigiste' strategy wherein 'state initiative is more of a determinant of media outcomes than market forces when it comes to the process of concentration' (Bustamante, 1994:21). This view of the state as the arbiter of the media's fate is not confined to academics alone, and oddly finds expression among such leading conglomerates as the PRISA group in the context of its efforts to gain greater access to the telecommunications sector.[7]

This process of concentration is sometimes accompanied by what can best be described as 'ideological manoeuvering', particularly in some parts of the national written press aimed at consolidating public opinion behind what is in practice a fact. A good example is the case of

El País which has succeeded in creating an image for itself as a national source of reference, and has developed a discourse (i.e. mediation) which simultaneously justifies pro-Spanish/pro-European and other liberal positions. In this manner, a nationalist style of discourse is generated (to prevent the Berlusconis and the Hersants of Europe from becoming *de facto* owners of the Spanish media). Similarly, a pro-European-culture style of discourse is also developing, in order to demonstrate, among other things, that Spanish multi-media groups are working within the European market (and thus avoiding cultural colonisation).

The state of communications in Spain today is characterised by a combination of factors which include a modern economy and a concentration of media groups existing alongside a proliferation of small and medium-sized firms, mostly subsidiaries of the large companies. The overall impression is of an apparently decentralised system, with an equally decentralised distribution of media influence. At first glance this appears to be the case, for example, with radio broadcasting in Spain. Closer examination reveals, however, that the network structure concentrates power in the hands of four or five large companies. In reality, therefore, the impression of decentralisation is misleading; moreover, the situation of concentrated power is unlikely to change in the foreseeable future. Also, the inter-relationship between political power and the power of the communications industry has been consolidated in the belief, encouraged by the media, that the guarantee of independence and freedom of information is linked to the survival and well being of the national media conglomerates. This view, which is fostered in some areas of the media, ignores the effects that the influence of such outside players as the national banks, foreign investors or the government itself may have upon the formation of public opinion and socio-cultural allegiances, on one hand, and national policy-making relating to the media, on the other. Thus, for example, the mutual affinities of interest existing between the PRISA group and the socialist government have been determining factors in relation to the development of media policy in Spain, both in terms of the former benefiting from television concessions, and in terms of influencing policy which bears upon the broadcasting and the telecommunications industries. For its part the González government intervened to allow Group Z to gain shares in the Antena 3 television channel, and the PRISA group entry into Antena 3 radio in order to neutralise the anti-government stances of those media.

Spain, like the rest of Europe, is embarking upon a technological transformation of its telecommunications system into what will ultimately constitute an information highway. Nevertheless it should be noted that the current modernisation of its media has been carried out mostly in a domain still dominated by traditional technology. The process of concentration and deregulation has occurred in the press, radio and terrestrial television, and not in the new telematic/telecommunications sectors. At the end of the 1980s the telecommunications companies launched a huge publicity campaign around the miracles of videotext, which was presented as the new information and education technology of the future. In the mid-1990s no one could recall or explain what had happened to this great promise of technological innovation. On the other hand, the innovation of financing private television by operating a traditional (terrestrial) pay-TV system (Canal Plus) is progressing well in Spain, whilst the pay-TV channel beamed from the Hispasat satellite has turned out to be an expensive disaster due in large part to high operational costs.

The advertising sector

The re-industrialisation of the advertising sector in Spain has been exclusively international (and transnational) in a country where the world's top twenty advertising companies are to be found. The degree of concentration of the advertising companies in Spain is less pronounced than that which exists in the communications sectors, but the transnational element of advertising is considerably more developed. The advertising industry is the one area which had the earliest experience of transnationalisation dating back to the 1960s. However, the expectations emanating from Spain's entry into the then EEC relaunched the establishment of big international companies in this sector. Even in the 1980s the impact of the advertising industry on the Spanish economy amounted to 1.1 per cent of Gross Domestic Product, below that of the United Kingdom (1.39 per cent) but above that of France (0.7 per cent) and Italy (0.5 per cent) (Zallo and Bustamante, 1988:282–91). The reasons for this intensifying process of transnationalisation were essentially due to Spain's serious economic crisis, and to the organisational weaknesses in existing advertising companies at the time, to which must be added the profound transformation which took place at the centre of European advertising activity itself. Spain was a beneficiary of the speed by which European markets consolidated, and from the economic and advertising booms which occurred simultaneously in Southern Europe in the 1980s. Even in 1993, in the midst of an economic down-turn, when advertising investment reached a low point unknown in the previous 15 years, the total investment in advertising still amounted to 593 million pesetas (see Figure 6.3 below for the distribution among the media). In 1995 the advertising industry recovered, although the figures were similar to those of 1993, and the television market still showed signs of instability (Infoadex, *El País*, 3.2.1995).

In 1992, Spain was rated third in the world (after the USA and Japan) for the quality of its advertising and took its place among the six major European countries (the UK, France, Germany, Italy and Scandinavia) which together accounted for 82 per cent of the advertising spend in Western Europe (Sánchez-Tabernero, 1993:149). If we compare the advertising market – television, radio, newspapers, magazines – in some of these countries, we note that the dominant areas of advertising are similar in each case, with the exception

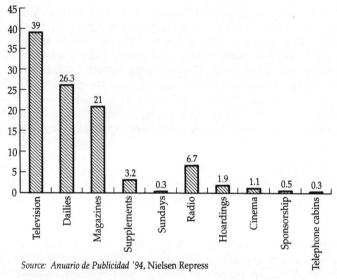

Source: *Anuario de Publicidad '94*, Nielsen Repress

Figure 6.3   Advertising investment in media in 1993

of Italy which has the highest percentage in television. As Figure 6.3 illustrates, in Spain, advertising investment in the press (i.e. newspapers and magazines) represents 47.3 per cent, which is higher than the television sector's total of 39 per cent (although television with 207,000 million pesetas is the medium which attracts the greatest level of advertising). The ten leading advertising agencies increased

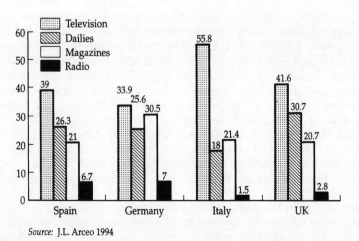

Source: J.L. Arceo 1994

Figure 6.4   European advertising investment in 1994 (%)

194

their income in 1994 by 6.5 per cent compared with that of the previous year. This increase has caused observers to be optimistic about the sector's future and to believe that Spain has emerged from the crisis of the early 1990s in order to better face up to the challenge of the last years of the century and the beginning of the next.

The socio-cultural influence of the Spanish media

In the second half of this century, the relationship between the media and Spanish society has passed through two historical phases particular to Spain: first the dictatorship, and second, the subsequent transition to democracy. To these two phases, we could justifiably add a third, which Spain has latterly experienced in common with the rest of Europe: a period of Europeanisation which had already begun elsewhere with the original Rome Treaty of 1957 and culminated with the Maastricht Treaty in 1993. The rapid changes which have taken place since 1976 in Spain, transforming it into a society based on democratic ideals with a modernised national structure and economy, have coincided with the development of a communications model based on a market philosophy. The advertising sector has developed into a huge communications industry at a time when the globalisation of the economy and the deregulation of European communications markets were paving the way for the end-of-the-century technological revolution. As in the rest of Europe, the media in Spain underwent a transformation away from the state-sponsored 'Big Brother' model towards one which encouraged the media to become social players in their own right, capable of imposing themselves upon the government and, at the same time, claiming a socio-cultural role based on the traditional mission of providing their audiences with information, education and entertainment. In the 1980s, the loosening up of the money markets, the international economic crisis, and the prospect of the Single Market caused the concept of deregulation to be extended and applied to other areas (such as the media), which had been formerly subject to public control. One of the consequences – media concentration – not only threatens the diversity and independence of information and sources of opinion, but it also gives rise to a conservative-orientated innovation: by reifying technology and the globalisation process, all the means by which these ends are achieved are deemed to be both sound and necessary. This argument is promoted by the leading media groups themselves. Having gained a legal basis for operating within the Single Market, the next step, they argue, is for the Spanish media to expand and consolidate themselves economically within Europe. However, in the broadcasting field the fall in investment forthcoming from advertising, the economic crisis, the irrevocable destabilisation of the concept of public service television, and the fragmentation of channels, have had an influence not only on broadcasting policy but also on the finances of the broadcasters, with dire results. The first victim of this situation has been the Spanish public. The latter has been obliged to receive a poorer quality of mediated information, as the consequence of commercial interests prevailing over others of a more social or cultural nature.

The socio-cultural role of the media has undergone a radical change over the last fifty years. During the dictatorship both press and radio were regarded with deep distrust for the evident way in which they served the political, economic and legal power of the state. As McQuail says, 'the power of the media presents itself in the form of a non-commercial authority, but the people perceive it in the form of authority at the service of propaganda and ideology' (McQuail, 1991:60). The phase of democratic transition from 1976 onwards also coincided with change in the concept of communications generally throughout Western Europe. The idea of the broadcasting media, in particular, being linked to state power has been challenged; similarly, the concept of a 'mass audience' has given way to that of audiences of a more fragmented nature. As has already been pointed out in Chapter 1 and elsewhere in this book, the phenomenon of social fragmentation experienced all over Europe, was reflected in the media industry by a radical reorganisation in both its structure and its mission. It could be argued that this change, for reasons of its recent history, is more marked in Spain than elsewhere in Europe.

Political mediation and the crisis of democracy

The transition from a state-dominated monopoly to the loosely regulated mercantile model that has been adopted today is clearly one of the most noteworthy features of the contemporary Spanish media. The formal relationship between state power and the media has been replaced by one of a different order (i.e. liberal, deregulated) which we have briefly outlined in the previous section. A key question to which, despite a mass of empirical evidence, we have no clear-cut answers, relates to the manner and extent to which the new media have exerted an influence upon public political opinion in the post-1976 period. We would propose at least two examples of the role played by the media in influencing the political climate in Spain over the last decade. The first concerns the manner in which the media represented the referendum on Spain joining NATO. The second relates to the recent coverage by the media of the cases of alleged corruption in high office and the implication of the government in alleged criminal acts in its anti-separatist activities.

On 12 March 1986 the referendum on Spain's joining NATO took place and ratified its entry into the Atlantic Alliance. Curiously, the Spanish Socialist Party (PSOE), before taking office in 1982, had committed itself to taking Spain out of the Alliance by a simple vote of Parliament, without resorting to a referendum. Once in power, however, as the party of government, the PSOE changed its mind completely in favour of a referendum. The referendum was taken up by the media who turned it into a key political issue of the moment. Media influence also became a major catalyst for changing the government's mind in favour of NATO. The political parties decided to use the media exclusively to explain their position, thus inhibiting the mobilisation of popular action. Furthermore, the referendum was presented by the media as an exercise in democracy, above and beyond the political parties, despite the existence of radically opposed ideological positions occupied by the Right and the socialists, on one hand, and the Communists and the radical Left, on the other. Information was expressed within a higher order context of foreign policy, wherein the attitudes of the media professionals was allowed to have a bearing upon the issue in the guise of a moral stand for the good of the country. The influence of the media was particularly strong in the case of television for several reasons, among which were: the sheer size of the TVE audience, the disarray of the main political parties, the credibility enjoyed by television as a source of information, the use of techniques of persuasion derived from advertising, and finally, a certain degree of complicity between political leaders, particularly those of the PSOE, and the media controlling information.

The second example of the increasing political power of the media as social players in their own right occurred in 1995, when the media became involved in a controversy concerning government power not seen since the times of the opposition to Franco. As has happened in many parts of democratic Europe, the process of 'media logic' by which the mass media divides up consumers of information into listeners, users and spectators, has intensified in Spain in the period of deregulation. The rise of a television magnate, Berlusconi, to the rank of prime minister of the Italian government, and the frustrated attempt of a banker (later imprisoned on charges of alleged corruption) to follow suit in Spain appropriately demonstrate the nature of the media industry as an instrument of power. The European elites have manipulated public opinion as a rhetorical weapon in the political debate with the same intensity as they have criticised the pernicious effects of television.

However, in Spain the 'annus terribilis' must be located between 1994 and 1995, a period in which bankers, financiers, the head of the Civil Guard and some of the chief figures in the fight against terrorism were convicted and sent to prison. As the result, the government finds itself discredited in the eyes of the public, and the situation generally prevailing throughout Spain is one of political volatility. The democratic 'game' between government and opposition has become, as never before, the object of mediation, but by a media with potentially important commercial prizes at stake in some cases. *El Mundo*, the daily paper with right-wing leanings, has seen its circulation and readership rise steeply as the result of its charges of alleged scandals and corruption implicating government figures. The private television stations actively seek to improve their prime-time ratings in the news bulletins on the principle that viewing figures alone have total sovereignty over the quality of content. The politicisation of the judicial power has also led to the practice of the leaking of information to the sensationalist press, which then reconstructs in Orwellian style the lives of ex-cabinet ministers and clamours openly, alongside the serious press, for the dismissal of the Prime Minister. Even the moderate newspaper *El País*, in an editorial, abandoned its moderateness of tone and implicit support for the government to announce 'the end of the socialist era'. Indeed, it would not be an exaggeration to say that Spanish society, the market, the peseta, as well as socialist politicians are staggering in the face of the treatment they have received in the media. The credibility of the Prime Minister, Felipe González, has been compromised as the result of being allegedly involved in state terrorism against ETA. Perhaps such consequences were to be expected. It would seem a truism (albeit a cynical one) to suggest that there is a direct correlation between the level of discredit of political office, on the one hand, and the level of intensity in the coverage by the media of political issues, on the other. Some newspapers recall that this loss of prestige among the political classes is not restricted to Spain alone but is a general condition throughout Western Europe, which is currently littered with the political casualties of alleged misdemeanours of all kinds. At the back of the minds of some journalists, however, is the fear that such discrediting of the political classes may tempt some elements to seek non-democratic solutions, outside the parliamentary framework, to which all democratic systems are prone. The responsible press is now beginning to react, realising perhaps that a parliamentary system must be protected from the dangers of blackmail from whatever source it may come, even if it appears in the guise of appeals to patriotism, as has been the case in some of the media.

The media in the face of terrorism

The manner in which the Spanish media have responded to the activities of the Basque separatist movement, ETA, deserves special mention here in so far as, to our knowledge, no media in Western Europe have had to contend with external threats to their independence of the kind experienced in Spain. Since 1973, when ETA assassinated Franco's heir apparent, Carrero Blanco, there has been a long line of political assassinations which, among others, include five mayors, two provincial council leaders, councillors and political leaders of both the Upper and Lower Houses of Parliament. ETA's assassination activities are always accompanied with information drives aimed at explaining and justifying their criminal acts within a political context. ETA can depend upon the daily paper *Egin*, which is sympathetic to their ideological objectives, for full coverage of their campaigns. But they also inevitably achieve further coverage in the rest of the media with each new political or civil attack which they undertake. The Spanish media have almost unanimously condemned the furtherance of political objectives by violent means, not just on the part of ETA, but also of other separatist movements in Catalonia and Galicia. ETA is committed to a policy of attacking the independence (or the alleged lack of it) of the media with regard to the coverage of campaigns of violence. In January 1995 Gregorio Ordóñez, leader of the Popular Party and candidate for the post of mayor of San Sebastian, was assassinated. Such was the outcry of public opinion and media condemnation that ETA produced a document which was published in *El Correo*, setting out the most effective ways in which journalists might be physically attacked and intimidated. Media professionals, trade unionists and politicians were quick to condemn the threats contained in this separatist document and their reaction well illustrates the widespread view in support of the rights of journalists to the independent, free expression of opinion. This issue relating to the threatening and intimidation of journalists is a particularly sensitive one in the Basque Country, where the identity and location of individual journalists is common knowledge within the area. Despite these real physical dangers, there is a general refusal on the part of media professionals to heed the warnings issued by ETA on matters which compromise their professional rights and obligations.

The European dimension

There is not yet a common identity within the European Press, and cultural and other particular idiomatic differences are obstacles to all kind of integration other than the economic.

This was the summary printed in *El País* on 15 January 1995 of a debate which took place in Paris between representatives of *Le Monde*, *Il Manifesto*, the *New York Times*, *Die Zeit* and *El País*. Also mentioned in the same article were the problems encountered by such transnational ventures as the *European* (established by Robert Maxwell in 1988) and the television news channel *Euronews*. Notwithstanding this pessimistic conclusion, we should note that there are some newspapers – *Le Monde*, *El País*, the *Guardian*, *La Repubblica*, *Frankfurter Allgemeine*, among others – with similar formats and similar readership profiles. But it would be premature, on the basis of this surface resemblance, to perceive in this any real beginnings of a common European media identity. Nevertheless it is a fact that several newspapers are making efforts to strengthen the European dimension in their activities. The *Guardian*, for example, prints an international edition in London, Frankfurt and Marseilles, and *El País* has a national edition printed in Roubaix (France) which is transmitted through Eutelsat. On the other hand, attempts to publish foreign titles on Spanish soil as in the case of *Bild Zeitung* and *Libération* have failed completely. However, internally, the Spanish media devote a significant amount of news coverage to the representation of the European Union. Of all the media, the sharpest focus tends to be found in the written press with a tendency for the radio and television to pick up a European theme only after it has been given prominence in the newspapers. Borrat, in a study of the coverage by topic of the leading European titles, has pointed out that Europe is most newsworthy in the context of obvious conflicts of interest. Even though these conflicts are of a multilateral nature, involving several European member states, they are invariably presented by the media as if they were bilateral. Furthermore, the level at which the information is pitched, in terms of the interested parties, is more relevant to the interests of the politician, the financier and other professionals than it is to those of the average reader. The two principal elements of European activity which are most frequently represented by the media are restricted to the realms of economics and political debate. Germany, France, Italy and the United Kingdom are more or less represented as the permanent players, and political motives are often explained by resorting to national stereotyping. Thus, for example, Chancellor Kohl's ambitions may be likened to those of Bismarck, and the policies of Felipe González described by the non-Spanish press as resembling those of Mrs Thatcher. In Spain, as elsewhere, the 'pro-European political argument' is poorly understood and there is no mention at all in the media of any alternative European discourse (Borrat, 1994:149–59).

Borrat's findings, and those of the European Union for the Media[8] stand in sharp contrast to the conclusions of another study supervised by Willy de Clerq for the Commission, *Reflections on the Information and Communications Policy of the European Community* (1993). This report stresses the economic/commercial shortcomings of European mediation, but ignores the under-representation in the media of social, political and cultural issues. These early findings suggest that there is no, or very little, common discourse within the media of the European Union because there is no common and effective policy relating to communications.

The transition to the multi-media European 'highway'

The word 'audiovisual', apart from having a very restricted, technical meaning in the English language, is also, probably, one of the most indefinable and ambiguous in other languages too (i.e. the French term, 'l'audiovisuel'), for it is used to define both cinema and television, as well as video, both as an industry and a technology. In the 1980s another term appeared, 'multi-media', which embraced the meaning of audio-visual, but also added to it a sense of futurity, and an integrating and inter-relationship between the old systems, including telecommunications, and the new satellite technology with its associated support technologies. Most analyses of the so-called multi-media revolution still tend to examine it in the context of its technological and macroeconomic ramifications. There is a danger when evaluating the present or future performance of the Spanish audio-visual sector (it has not yet wholly achieved multi-media status) in this way. No matter how important the technological and economic aspects are, the activities of the sector must be seen against a background which promotes the democratic qualities of social equality, equal opportunities, linguistic pluralism and cultural identity. Several things follow on from this in the context of a multi-media Europe. One important lesson must be that the economic arguments which favour the movement towards multi-media concentration, and which appear to be promoted in the European Green Paper *Television Without Frontiers* must not allow the such cultural imperatives as diversity and pluralism to be overlooked. In the specific case of Spain and the new unfolding audio-visual/multi-media landscape, two facts should be borne in mind. The first is Spain's comparative structural weaknesses within the European Union, and the second is the current crisis of the television sector itself, already described above. It is clear that the Spanish audio-visual industry cannot be separated out in future from the macroeconomic patterns of the European and the international market. It is equally clear that the audio-visual market, for better or worse, is one of the most globalised of media sectors. The problem, as far as Spain is concerned, is that the neo-liberal philosophy which dominates the thinking centred on the Spanish economy has been unable to conceive of an audio-visual policy which embraces all the relevant areas: economic, technological, socio-cultural, as well as the safeguarding of pluralism. Even so, the factors which have brought about the deterioration of the Spanish programme production are neither exclusively creative nor economic in nature. They are, in fact, mostly political. The ineptitude of policy-making has created even greater structural and financial havoc in the cinema and television sectors, as well as in the new telecommunication services, so that the very social and cultural bases of information themselves appear to be under threat.

Notes

1. Estudio General de Medios: the principal audience research body in Spain.
2. *El País, ABC, El Mundo, La Vanguardia, El Periódico de Cataluña,* and *Diario 16.*
3. It adopted this name in 1941.
4. This policy even extended to sport and included a two-minute delay between real-time action and transmission.
5. Hickethier describes a similar, but more evolved process of convergence between public and private channels. See Chapter 4.
6. According to the report published by ZENIT and quoted by Sánchez-Tabernero (1993:126) RTVE and PRISA figure among the fifty foremost European media companies in terms of their dominance within a single country.
7. See Lamizet's forceful argument for this situation also existing in France in Chapter 3.
8. Borrat's findings have been confirmed by a second report, commissioned in Spain (*The European Union of the Media,* Fundesco, 1994).

CHAPTER 7

Conclusions

Anthony Weymouth and Bernard Lamizet

In this, the concluding chapter, we intend to pull together some of the major threads which run, implicitly and explicitly, through the text of this study of the media in Western Europe. Part I addresses the issue of mediation, and the manner in which the supra-national state of the European Union will be represented by the media in the next decade and beyond. Its findings suggest that the concept of Europe as a political and socio-cultural entity will be much less defined than might have been expected in the context of the vastly increased number of media outlets created at the end of the twentieth century. Part II examines the nature of future influences upon the media. In particular it reappraises the (underestimated) potential of the public service sector for making its presence felt in the new European audio-visual landscape in the next century. Part III looks at the complex problems facing the media policy makers, and anticipates a new cycle of legislation which will be imposed upon the de-regulation of the last two decades.

I The Europeanisation of the media?

In Chapter 1 we suggested that there was a theoretical possibility, at least, of Western Europe being represented (mediated) as a socio-cultural community in the second phase (post-1980) of media development, in a manner comparable to that of the nation-state in the post-1945 period. We also cautioned the reader that such a repetition of media function was unlikely given the extraordinary socio-economic, political and technological changes which characterise the second phase. In this chapter we intend to re-examine the original proposal, as well as to elaborate upon the theoretical arguments which might support it. We shall then re-examine the reality, that is to say the dominant themes which emerge from the national chapters in order to gauge the extent to which a European dimension exists in the media, as well as to identify its principal elements.

Let us look again, then, at the predominantly theoretical context within which a wider European concept of socio-cultural identity could emerge as a consequence of media activity. The argument runs something like the following.

The European dimension

The European media have achieved levels of distribution and new modes of delivery in all sectors which not only give them an increased critical mass as an economic force, but also change their nature. In order to appreciate any ongoing or future process of mediation, which may contribute to the establishing of a European sphere of communication, it is necessary to consider the media in their entirety within the European context. Until recently the process of mediation has been limited to the national context wherein an important outcome was the structuring and the ordering of national identity. During the period when the media were dominated by the radio and the written press, their function was to offer their listeners/readers both an accessible and an intelligible interpretation of events, which reinforced national identity and, with it, their sense of belonging. However, the emergence and development of new technology in the fields of fibre optics, satellites and computing has influenced the old scheme of things by offering the media potential new roles within the public sphere. It is no longer merely a question of the establishing of citizenship through the sharing of information, and the development of socio-cultural awareness at the national level. The possibility exists, in the new context of the increased availability of information and new modes of delivery, for the development of a new kind of European awareness capable of extending beyond national frontiers. This potential for the development of a wider sense of 'Europeanness' will depend upon three principal factors. These are firstly, the new conditions in which information relating to European issues is disseminated; secondly, the extent to which governments need to operate and coordinate policy at a European level; and finally, the conditions in which information on European culture is produced and exchanged. To take each of these factors in turn.

The new conditions for the dissemination of European information

Until the concept of a more unified Europe began to emerge after 1945, the public sphere was perceived by the peoples of Europe as existing at a national level. However, from the time when western politicians committed themselves to the construction of a closer European union, the public sphere has ceased to be as concrete a reality as it has in the past. In its European aspect, the sheer scale of the latter has meant that the public sphere has, of necessity, been constructed on the basis of *information* about Europe rather than experience of it. This is an important point because it suggests that the future representation of Europe will be mostly symbolic: an 'imagined community' unattached to precise geographical frontiers or to a common cultural history (see Axford and Huggins, 1995:1413). If it is to develop in the public sphere, the European dimension will rest upon three elements: firstly, an increase in the volume of information about European issues; secondly, the development of European information networks; thirdly, in consequence of the two previous elements, the creation of a demand for information relating to Europe.

To take the volume issue first: the development of a European dimension in the public sphere will be determined, in part, by the volume of information presented in the media on European affairs. For some considerable time now, the written press, the radio and the television have significantly increased their output of European news coverage. This increased coverage has been given further nourishment by the existence of a new, enlarged single market which has attracted to the media a massive investment from the private sector. This investment has resulted in the setting up of new media forms (cable, satellite and teletext) and new forms of output (programmes and services) financed in the long term on a subscription or advertising basis.

The second element, closely associated with the increase in the volume of information relating to European issues, is the manner in which it is delivered or networked (i.e. radio station, cable operator or specialised newspapers such as the *European*). The development of a European dimension in the public sphere will be determined, again in part, by the manner in which information is relayed or distributed to the public. There is a link between the way information is gathered by an identifiable group of journalists, and its dissemination to the reader, listener, viewer or user of a particular service. The preference for using one network over another is a recognised form of establishing social group membership. The extraordinary development in communications technology, and its industrial application, have combined with the emergence of a new European political initiative for closer union to create the possibility of adding a European dimension to information networks as described above (the Euronews Channel is a good example of this phenomenon). At the European level, there are two specific contexts which can provide for the development of a European dimension within networks. The first is the link-up between cable networks and satellites, and the second is the legislative framework which underpins transnational broadcasting, in this case, the European Directive of 1989, widely mentioned throughout this book.

The final element in the process of 'Europeanisation' relates to the general function of mediated information. By presenting European affairs to the public, the media will generate future obligations for itself and corresponding expectations and rights on the part of the citizen-user. The development of this potential element of growing European awareness (it would be both optimistic and premature to use the term 'European citizenship') could proceed on two levels, the first of which is the increasing political commitment on the part of the media to the concept of a more unified Europe, the second being the emergence of editorial policies designed expressly to promote coverage of European issues. The French national daily *Le Monde* is a good example of both these kinds of developments. A regular sampling of its pages reveals an impressive dedication of its column space to the coverage of European issues.

Strictly from a media perspective, the foundations for a more widespread sense of Europeanness could be constructed on the basis of three media-related innovations: the first is a common legislation relating to European communications; the second is mediation of common political and economic policies (i.e. European elections, debates on the future enlargement of the Union); the third is the circulation of information on cultural models resulting from the improved conditions for the exchange of both picture and sound (images and discourse) between the various member states.

The European dimension in government

There is an undisputed need for governments within the European Union to operate at a European as well as a national level. The European dimension in the political domain has created the need for supranational procedures and, in consequence, a need also for a new approach to the mediation of political activity by the media. We can begin here to identify certain of these new kinds of approaches by the media in the context of their wider European activities. The first new trend which may be perceived, for example, is the extension of media coverage to other countries of the Union. In this manner, it could be argued that the media are beginning to construct a kind of symbolic proximity of Western Europe by a process of mediation. The extension of information coverage to the political systems of other member states enhances and reinforces the role played by the provision of information about Europe, not least in the expectations it creates concerning the rights of citizens to receive it. The media, by the act of disseminating information relating to European issues, will begin to create a European dimension within the public sphere.

A second manifestation of the European presence is the growing importance given by the media to the role and activities of such European institutions as the European Commission, the Parliament, the European Court and the Council of Ministers. At the same time, the decision-making procedures and the institutional organisation of individual member states are also becoming the object of media coverage. The principal players in the political life of the Union are also becoming household words across Western Europe. This development can be explained as the consequence of the increasing impact of European policies and legislation upon national governments and, through them, upon the respective peoples of the Union.

The third trend relates to the modification of political commentary in the media which takes account of the new political structures operating at supranational level of the Union. Political power, like all other kinds of social phenomena, has its own operational realm or space. The latter have existed for centuries at the level of the state, but the operational space of European politics has yet to be established. It is and will be the role of the media to represent to their public the operational space of the politics of the European Union. In this respect, a significant change may be observed in media behaviour over the course of the last twenty years. Media representation of conflicting national and Community interests has already given way in some member states to one of partial complementarity, cooperation and compromise. This trend, for example, is particularly observable in the media of France and Germany. Whereas in the past the interests of the then European Community were frequently presented as conflicting with those of national governments, they are now increasingly presented as complementary, possessing their own operational realms which are characterised by the specific requirements of a European, as opposed to a national, order.

By way of conclusion to this section, it could be argued that the European dimension will figure increasingly in the daily routines of selection and prioritisation of information practised by the European media. Editors and programme makers will no longer be able to ignore information relating to European issues for the simple reason that the public will expect to find it. In this event, a new democratic imperative – access to a meaningful concept of Europe – would become established.

The cultural factor

The third factor which will contribute to the foundation of a wider, more consolidated European awareness is without doubt the cultural one. The media contain a whole range of coverage relating to cultural and social issues which affect the lives of the peoples of the European Union. By so doing, they create an intelligible socio-cultural dimension, albeit slowly – the language barrier is still the greatest obstacle to the exchange of cultural information – which will form the basis not of a common culture (such a concept in the light of the current cultural diversity in Europe is neither feasible nor to be wished), but an *extended cultural knowledge* against which background a new kind of identity extending beyond national frontiers can emerge.

The representation in the media of socio-cultural issues of Western Europe, rather than those entirely related to the indigenous culture of the particular newspaper, radio station or television channel, may only ever appeal to a minority audience. A more widespread and popular vehicle for the mediation of socio-cultural issues at the European level may be located in the commercial activities of the media, and in advertising in particular. Advertising is not just a textual and visual incitement to consumerism. It is also a representation of a way of life, of social behaviour, and of attitudes. To some extent today we are witnessing a distinct trend to what may be termed the Europeanisation of advertising. The tendency towards the internationalisation of production in Europe manifests itself in the media in the form of identical products (i.e. cars, perfume, alcohol, soft drinks, confectionery) being represented by identical or similar advertising. The degree to which aspects of Western European culture are mediated by common approaches to advertising should not be overstated. Nevertheless, the role of this commercial representation of lifestyles, commodities and social attitudes is, and will continue to be, significant and should not be overlooked.

So far in this chapter we have outlined a theoretical framework within which the mediation of a wider European awareness could occur. We have mentioned the fact that there still exists today a tension between political power centred on the state, and power which is currently developing within a wider European framework. In order for the latter to be successfully mediated and defined for the citizens of the Union, there is still one final condition, briefly mentioned above but in need of reiteration here. It is imperative at the level of European government to establish an overall European policy for communications (i.e. which goes considerably beyond all current legislation). In the absence of a single, homogeneous group of European citizenry, the development of a sense of political proximity to European government will be an essential function of the media. At the European level, the exercise of political power and the significance of the actions of the major players in public life are much less intelligible than comparable events at a national level. In consequence, the European dimension of political power can only be rendered meaningful on the condition that a strong, effective and coherent communications policy is developed. Without such a policy, guaranteeing pluralism and a strong, dynamic media, European political power becomes invisible.

In conclusion, we need to point out that the (mostly) theoretical conditions which we have set out above are projected into a particular set of circumstances and trends, many of which we have mentioned and discussed at length in Chapter 1 and which have recurred in the national chapters. The movement, enshrined in the Maastricht Treaty, towards ever closer union of the states of Western Europe, is characterised by a paradox. 'Project Europe' is taking place at a time when the traditional components of the state – social class, political parties, trade unions, the Church, the Welfare State – are passing through a period of identity crisis and fragmentation. Traditional political power within each member country is having to take account of new, non-traditional sources of influence assailing it from many and often conflicting directions. These non-traditional sources of influence are disparate in nature, ranging from the growing economic power of globalised foreign capital in the form of the multi-national conglomerates, on one hand, to single-issue pressure groups such as animal rights, environmentalists, gender liberationists and regional separatists, on the other. Such influences are relatively new to our experience in Europe, and render the task of crystal ball gazing more complicated. For this reason, our attempts to outline a framework for the development of a European dimension in the media must remain extremely tentative. They must also take into account the specific themes which emerge from the five national chapters. At this point, then, we turn from the speculation of the kind we have initiated above in this chapter to a more empirical examination of the dominant trends of media development emerging from the national chapters.

The reality: the elusive Union

These dominant trends can be initially classified under three headings:

- Firstly, there is a predictable inconsistency in the development in the principal media sectors examined across the five countries concerned.
- Secondly, there are strong disparities in the particular performance of comparable sectors of the media across Europe.
- Thirdly, there is also a strong commonality of trends of a commercial/economic nature affecting all sectors of the media, particularly in the post-1980s phase.

We propose below to take each of these factors and relate them briefly to the specific countries.

The inconsistency in the development of the European media

Given the pronounced socio-cultural differences between the five countries (not the least of which is their linguistic diversity), as well as the historical contexts of their respective post-1945 experiences, the unevenness of their development is hardly surprising, and manifests itself in several sectors, of which some examples are:

- The disparities in the current state of development of the written press in the five countries. There is a sharp difference between the circulation figures of the northern member states – Britain and Germany – and those of the south – Italy and Spain – with France occupying a mid-way position, which is itself characterised by an imbalance between the national and the regional press. The German magazine sector is particularly strongly developed both nationally and on an international scale compared with the other four countries.
- A similar imbalance in the development in the broadcasting sector. In television, for example, there has been a comparatively harmonious existence between the BBC and ITV in the UK (although this situation is set to change) which contrasts with the hostile, competitive contexts in which the public service channels have had to endure in the other countries (particularly in Italy and Spain). There are also striking differences between the growth of local radio

networks – slow and controlled in Germany and Britain, and much more rapid and deregulated in the case of France, Spain and Italy.

• There is an inconsistency in the nature of policy-making and legislation relating to the regulation and industrial organisation of the media, particularly in the broadcasting sector – strong in Germany (a constitutional issue), Britain and France, and the less pronounced in Italy and Spain. A good example, in the case of France, of state interventionism is the selling off of its 'flagship' public channel TF1 to the private sector in 1986. On the other hand, in Italy, an almost total lack of media policy relating to television led to Berlusconi acquiring a virtual monopoly over private sector television in the 1980s. Vilches concludes that the absence of a properly conceived communications/media policy is the cause of many of the acute problems facing television broadcasting in Spain.

• There are sharp differences in national policy relating to developmental initiatives in the field of communications generally. Italy is still in the process of developing a policy for cable and satellite whereas in Germany the policy is already paying impressive dividends. In France the move to create a dynamic, widespread teletext service (Minitel) was state-initiated (but according to Sartori, premature – see Chapter 5). The cooperation between France and Germany in the developing of a transnational, public service channel, ARTE, is a unique example of transnational policy making.

• Associated with differences in national policy making, there is a particularly uneven rate of technological adaptation (i.e. cable and satellite penetration). Again this is highest in Germany (43 per cent for cable, and 8 million dish aerials) and lowest in Italy (negligible for cable and 110,000 dish aerials), with a slower than anticipated progress in the UK and France.

This general unevenness in media development may be attributed to many factors relating to a country's historical experience, its economic growth, or its socio-cultural attitudes towards the media themselves. Thus, the *laissez-faire* policies of the post-war British government promoted a fruitful partnership between the BBC and the private sector. On the other hand, the French *dirigiste* tradition mostly accounts for the state initiative in the telecommunications sector, mentioned above, as well as for the creation of ARTE. It also accounts for the prescriptive legal framework under which the written press has operated in France in the post-1945 period, as well as for the interventionist policy adopted by the state towards broadcasting. In Germany a combination of economic dynamism and the recent collapse of the Eastern Bloc largely explains the rapid expansion and internationalisation of the German media conglomerates. In Spain, the abrupt departure of the dictatorship in 1976 has meant that its media has had to adapt simultaneously to the dual process of transition to democracy as well as to the post-1980s audio-visual and neo-libertarian revolution. This dual adaptation process largely explains the weaknesses in broadcasting policy making mentioned by Vilches in Chapter 6. Finally, in Italy a policy vacuum in the mid-1970s and some extraordinary subsequent decisions by both parliament and the Constitutional Court opened the flood-gates of commercial competition which cannot now be closed.

Performance variation in the European media

An associated phenomenon to the unevenness in the development of the Western European media is that of variation of role and of performance. Thus, for example, whilst the written press in the UK is one of the strongest markets in Europe, in terms of economic performance, a large part of this sector may fail even to qualify for the title of 'newspaper' as described in Chapter 1. The British mass tabloids stand at the most extreme and most doubtful end of any continuum of definition into which the semantic item 'newspaper' can be placed. However, if, as we have claimed, a large part of the British press is unruly and unregulated, then this situation is in marked contrast to the one existing in France, where the state, by regular modifications of the statutes governing the media, occupies a central role in their affairs. In France it would appear too that state-nurtured attitudes towards the written press have excluded from it the extremes of low journalistic standards of the kind exemplified by the tabloids in the United Kingdom. However, in Germany, according to Hickethier, the influence of the sensationalist press is in decline, and that of the 'serious' press in the ascendant. Vilches, on the other hand, on the subject of the role of the newly democratised press in Spain, suggests that its power, in recent times, is so strong that it has come near to destabilising the González government.

This variation in the performance in the written press is mirrored by a similar trend in the broadcasting and telecommunications sector. British broadcasting channels and stations (BBC radio and television, and ITV) still provide information services of quality which stand high in public esteem, and provide an effective complementary antidote to the tabloid press agenda. The relative stability of the British broadcasting services still stands in marked contrast to the volatility of regulation and the fluctuating quality of the Italian and Spanish systems. In France the privatisation of the principal PSB channel TF1 has resulted in the decline in programme quality of a significant part of the terrestrial system. In Germany, too, it is claimed that the arrival of the private commercial broadcasters has adversely affected the quality of available television programmes overall.

Many of these disparities of performance have been the result of sudden upheavals in the operation of a particular system due to the rapid process of change in the post-1980 period (referred to under 'Common features' below).

So much then for some of the more evident disparities between the various states of development, and the respective differences in performance, of the media sectors in the five countries examined in this book. We shall turn next to some of the features they all hold in common.

Common features

The features which the Western European media have in common, for the most part, have developed in the post-1980 period and are linked to accelerated socio-economic, political and technological development. These common features, mentioned in all the national chapters, include, among others:

- the emergence of the communications/media sector as a dynamic industry in its own right;
- the trend towards the concentration of media groups and the establishing of multi-media conglomerates;
- the increasing availability of new services through public access to cable and satellite;
- the reorganisation of the broadcasting/communications sectors through deregulation and privatisation;
- the weakening of the former public service concept of broadcasting;
- the fragmentation and differentiation of media markets;
- a common European legislation to facilitate a single communications market;
- a general shortage of programmes and a significant increase in production costs.

Whilst the impact of these common factors is different in each national case, it is the technological/commercial influence which represents the most tangible common European experience. In short, Europeanisation, in its most identifiable form, designates a technological/commercial process which has determined the organisation and mission of the new media, as well as the remodelling of the old. The effects on media performance resulting from the impact of the technological/commercial revolution have been considerable. The private sector challenge to the existing public service order has been very effective, certainly by its own standards, in offering a greater choice of channels, stations and other media outlets to the public. In broadcasting, however, greater choice of channel or station has not been matched by a corresponding increase in choice of content. The explosion in the number of broadcasters has dramatically increased the demand for, and the price of programmes. This surge in demand has been mostly met by low-cost productions, many of which are imported from the American market. Thus, as several of the contributors to the national chapters have pointed out, more media outlets simply means more of the same low-quality productions being put out by broadcasters desperately short of both money and material.

The public service broadcasters have inevitably been affected by the arrival and the activities of the new private-sector media. Furthermore, the arrival of the latter came at a time when the licence fee, or state aid for supporting PSB, was either being reduced or withdrawn altogether (a trend common to all the countries examined in this study) forcing them to shed personnel and reduce spending on programming.

Indeed, in some cases, they all but collapsed in the face of the aggressive competitive onslaught from their new commercial rivals. Berlusconi almost dealt a fatal blow to the RAI in Italy. In Spain TVE was abandoned to the mercy of the market by a socialist government, and is still staggering from a ratings war which it appears to be losing. Only one in three people now watch public service television in France. In contrast, the public service broadcasting services in Britain and Germany appear, for the moment at least, to be holding their own (and the fortunes of the RAI also seem to be improving).

Evidently, in itself, the defection of audiences from one broadcaster to another is not necessarily a cause for concern. Pluralism is, after all, a cornerstone of a democratic media. However, a problem arises if the net effect of such migrations is the lowering of the information threshold beyond the minimum levels tolerable within a democratic society. In the past these threshold levels were maintained by the public service broadcasters by a principle of diversity in scheduling which astutely mixed entertainment with other educational and informational objectives. The shift away from the informational, axis towards entertainment, if it carries with it the majority of the potential Western European audience, will have the effect of lowering the information threshold (the communicative entitlement of every citizen) to unacceptable levels.

An inconsistent mediation

We have identified the three major factors which emerge from and characterise the situation of the media in Western Europe as presented in the five national chapters. These factors are: firstly, the marked differences in the current state of development of the respective media; secondly, an equally marked difference in the performance between comparable sectors; thirdly, the commonality of the experience of the post-1980 media revolution. In the light of these factors we must go back to, and considerably modify, the theoretical assumptions made earlier in this chapter relating to the creation of a European dimension in the public sphere.

The events and processes which we have outlined in the first part of this chapter, which could form the basis for a more clearly defined concept of Europe, are undoubtedly both present and operative, but they will be obliged to pass through the filters of the respective national media, as characterised above, with varying degrees of effectiveness in each case. The likelihood is that the progress towards the building of a European dimension in the public sphere will reflect the inconsistency of performance and the fragmentation of the media themselves: at best it will be uneven, clearer in some national sectors than in others; at worst it will be misleading, confused, or even non-existent, depending on the choice of medium. In these circumstances, it may well be that the best opportunities for the representation of Europe to its diverse citizenry still reside in the public service sector since, for the most part, they still retain their commitments to universal access, education and information. This speculative comment invites a further important question relating to the survival or the demise of public service broadcasting in Western Europe, to which we shall now turn.

II The future of the public service sector

A doomsday scenario?

We began this book by predicting that the media in the next century would be more varied, more economically powerful and more used by the citizenry of Europe than ever before. This forecast has been amply reinforced by the information and the analyses provided by the five national contributors in the foregoing chapters. However, our evaluation of the potential role of the media for representing a consistent image of Europe within a common socio-cultural context is much less positive, for the reasons we have explained above. In the light of our findings relating to the situation of the media in the five countries that we have examined, the question that now needs to be answered relates to the nature of the influences that will shape and determine the organisation and role of the media in the twenty-first century.

From the commentaries and analyses offered in the national chapters, the apparent self-evident answer to this question is that the most forceful players in the next decade will emerge from the private sector. Whilst there is a lot of evidence to support this view, it may not be the whole story (see below). The private sector will be instrumental in exploiting the newly emerging 'niche' markets that have been created by the socio-economic changes, as well as by the technological advances in electronics over the last twenty years. This exploitation will be manifest firstly in the form of more private operators entering the broadcasting/communications arena in competition with each other, and the existing public services. Secondly, this private sector intervention will manifest itself in the 'new media' activities of personalised, interactive services using cable, satellite and information technology (pay-per-view TV, teleshopping, Internet, and so on). The dangers for the public sector broadcasters confronted by competition from private operators are, firstly, that they are likely to suffer a further loss of audience share, and secondly, at the same time, be drawn into competition in key areas of scheduling (i.e. popular entertainment) from which they may emerge the losers.

The impact of private-sector activity in the already privatised sector of the written press will, if current trends continue, result in a greater concentration of press titles with the inevitable reduction in pluralism. The effects of this kind of concentration of ownership of the daily press appear to be potentially more serious for some countries (France and Britain) than it does for others for reasons already discussed.

Finally, superimposed upon all the commercial activity briefly mentioned above (which essentially is a quantitative phenomenon involving an increase in media outlets) will be a general reorganisation of the European communications industry into multi-media conglomerates with transnational interests. In short, what we are facing in the next decade is a further period of change in which market forces and economic criteria will continue to determine the nature and role of a significant part of the media, instead of those derived from a mission of social responsibility and implemented by the public service broadcasters. The overall, compounded effects of the extension and reinforcement of market forces in all European communications sectors will be felt firstly at a national level. Future examples of these effects could be, for example:

- A further reduction in the number of titles in the written press in France and Britain.
- The privatisation of the TVE in Spain.
- A dramatic move towards the provision of commercially motivated thematic networks and services on the part of the RAI.
- A significant reduction in ARD's audience share as the result of future competition from a strong and consolidating cable and satellite sector.

In the domain of broadcasting, the implication is that we are witnessing the terminal decline of the public service sector as we know it. Such a prognosis, if it were true, would give rise to well-founded concerns across a whole range of issues which risk being overwhelmed by the two-dimensional imperatives of the market: efficiency and profit. A possible and ironic danger for the receivers and users of information in Western Europe is that, in spite of the massive increase of capital investment, and the equally extraordinary multiplication of media outlets, they may well end up with a reduced choice of programme type, as well as with a lower quality of information.[1] In short, the 'communicative entitlement', referred to in Chapter 1, which arguably has been provided throughout Western Europe by the public service broadcasters, giving its citizens access to the public sphere, will be significantly reduced. However, such a doomsday scenario, while possible, is not wholly inevitable. Its avoidance will depend finally on the capacity of the public services to re-assert and consolidate their position within the new communications landscape, and secondly upon the willingness of governments actively to pursue regulatory policies which promote quality, diversity and social responsibility as concomitants of pluralism.

We do not accept as inevitable either the prevailing (post-modernist) or the pragmatic (economic) 'terminal decline' accounts of the future of public service broadcasting. Evidence supporting this prognosis may well indeed be present in the countries we have examined, but there are other features which point to less terminal outcomes. Our reasons for taking this view can be summarised under the three following headings of perceived trends:

The market factor. Market forces need not necessarily spell the end of the public service sector. The process of audience fragmentation, whilst it has occurred at the expense of the public sector broadcasters, still leaves a significant share remaining in their hands. This base may yet decline further but can (and should) be defended to constitute a solid, if reduced, presence in the European media landscape. Secondly, in terms of market cycles themselves, the process of fragmentation could presage the creation of a market niche for a 'common rallying point' medium (which evidently still exists in the form of public service television and radio). If they didn't exist, then presumably they would be re-invented, at some future point, by the entrepreneurial initiative coming from the private sector.

The quality factor. At the outset, it should be acknowledged that it is no longer a wholly true account to characterise the manner in which the private sector broadcasters are filling their schedules by accusing them of resorting to the use of cheap American imports or equally cheap low-quality quizzes and tele-reality shows. Major private broadcasters such as Fininvest, Bertelsmann, News Corporation, Antena 3 and Canal Plus are all setting up as producers in their own right. By so doing they avoid paying the spiralling costs of external programme purchase, and control more tightly the quality and the planning of their schedules. Nevertheless, as we have noted already, they are not primarily motivated by concerns of either social responsibility or artistic excellence. The likelihood is that the new production emerging from the private sector studios will continue to have an eye for what the market will bear in terms of cost/quality ratios, rather than what the public need, want or deserve. This means that the experience of public service broadcasters in the field of creative, innovative production, and the professional treatment of information, may yet still have the edge on the private sector. Far from joining the private sector in low-cost, low-quality scheduling, the public sector may well yet press home to good effect its unrivalled advantage in creativity, professionalism, and its wealth of experience in the processing of information.

The combative factor. Under 'quality' above, we suggested that public service broadcasters may have underestimated their assets in the face of competition from the private sector. Any reappraisal of the way in which the social, aesthetic and democratic values which the public services broadcasters bring to European society can be preserved must include a willingness on their part to protect them, both inside as well as outside the market. From the evidence available it could be argued that this has already been successfully implemented by the RAI, the ARD and the BBC. Translated into action, this means the literal selling of the public services to the public in ways which were never countenanced prior to 1980 in the days of monopoly status. It means engaging in a high degree of public accountability aimed at persuading the people of the public sector's cost-effectiveness and value for money (i.e. the licence fee). It also commits the public service sector to the public promotion of its own values and self-proclaimed advantages over its competitors, namely impartiality, high standards of performance, social responsibility (i.e. educational role) and universal access.

All of these qualities, which in the past were assumed, but largely unsung, will need to be continually brought to the attention of national audiences, which, as the competition increases, will be tempted to desert the public service broadcasters for new pleasures in the private sector. As we have noted, the combative factor has been in evidence in the activities of at least three national public service broadcasters, those of Italy, Germany and United Kingdom. In Italy, the RAI is contemplating a much more combative, commercial approach than either the BBC or the ARD, involving the possible introduction of thematic networks, and the possible introduction of private capital to its funding. In contrast to this commercial approach, the ARD has streamlined its organisational structure and maintained a substantial investment in the production of quality drama, TV films and documentaries. The BBC, too, has embarked upon a controversial but seemingly effective path of internal reorganisation, a new, if controversial, production policy ('Producer's Choice'), and a confident, assertive and professionally directed public relations exercise of self-promotion.

These three factors all lend themselves to an overall market strategy for defending public service values. They make economic sense, and create the context in which the public services compete with the private sector, not in obscurantist word-play (imposed by their opponents) about the meaning of press or media freedom, but in crucial areas which directly relate their activities and strengths to the market, and to points of comparison from which they could emerge superior to the competition. There is an in-built assumption here that the public service broadcasters should not follow the private sector down the path of commercialisation, with all the implications that route has for the future of programming. Convergence will inevitably call into question (and justifiably so) the public funding of public service broadcasting. It follows that such funding can only be justified in return for services which by their creativity, intrinsic interest and distinct nature are perceived to be value for money. It is extraordinary, therefore, if the public service sector can deliver programmes of this kind, that it should countenance doing anything else.

These perceived trends in what could be the beginnings of a revival in the fortunes of the public sector should be tempered by the point that was made earlier in this chapter about the varied conditions of health in which particular PSB services currently find themselves. Despite the pessimism expressed at a national level about the capacity of the BBC to survive in its current form, in a European context its position would appear to be a strong one. However, at the other extreme, the position of TVE in Spain looks poised to plunge it into the abyss.

PSB: a political argument

The trends which we have mentioned above are noteworthy because they appear to point to a possible revival in the fortunes of the PSB sector which has taken account of and responded to the new realities of the market. There are, of course, other non-market-orientated arguments which we have already discussed in some detail in Chapter 1. We will not repeat them here except to make one general point of a political nature. The maintenance of PSB within western democracies was justified historically because it was commonly perceived as a socially cohesive force, universally accessible regardless of social class or wealth. As Hickethier points out, in the rapidly changing European communications landscape, there is a risk of a division occurring, not between groups of equal status satisfying their individual communication needs, but between the 'information rich' and the 'information poor'. It cannot be in any national interest for any divisions between the new social groupings currently emerging in Western Europe, one of which is beginning increasingly to look like an underclass (Hobsbawm, 1994:308), to be reinforced by expensive media outlets on the one hand, and the disappearance of PSB on the other. There is, in other words, a strong political argument which in the name of equal opportunity, but more effectively in the interests of social stability, supports the continuing existence of PSB, not as a cultural or social ghetto, but as an essential democratic provision in its own right.

The future role of the European Broadcasting Union

This discussion has so far been limited to the possibility of the return of a revitalised public sector initiative to the European communications arena at a national level. It is at this level, after all, that the future of PSB will be determined. However, it should be remembered that, at a European level, public service broadcasting has a powerful ally in the European Broadcasting Union (mentioned already in Chapter 1) which represents the interests of the entire European PSB sector.

The EBU is already successfully representing these interests in the production markets of Europe and the world in the capacity of programme purchasing, particularly in the area of sporting events. It is also increasingly making its voice heard as a lobbyist in the domain of policy making. Recent reorganisation at the EBU under its new Secretary-General, Jean-Bernard Munch, suggests that it is taking a new, hard-headed view of the future of PSB. It appears to have taken stock of the irreversible and increasing presence of the commercial sector, and to be seeking a route for PSB which safeguards its special values and mission, while exploiting the potential opportunities for new activities made possible by the upsurge of market interest and activity in the field of communications. The EBU of course has no powers either of coercion or legislation; nevertheless its potential role as a rallying point and pressure group could be of considerable assistance to any recovery of PSB in the coming years.

III Future policy making

Camouflaged issues

Policy making for a democratically based communications industry within the European Union, in the context of the rapid transition that is taking place, is clearly an area fraught with difficulties. These problems are the reflection of national differences of approach to media policy making. The most evident of these differences are those espoused by France and known as *dirigiste*, designating government interventionist initiatives (as described by Lamizet in Chapter 3), and the libertarian approach favoured by Britain (but historically best captured by the French expression *laissez-faire*!). This cleavage of opinion goes to the heart of European approaches to policy making in the field of communications. If, for example, the European Directive of 1989 may be used as a gauge of the success of one faction or the other, it would seem that the neo-libertarians are in the ascendant since the major preoccupations of the Directive are economic rather than socio-cultural. In addition to this major difference in attitude in approach to policy making at the European level, there exist a multitude of other conflicting interests at a national level, too, which render Euro-policy making a problematic undertaking. An historical example of such differences is the French government's extraordinary decision to privatise the main public service television channel TF1 in 1986. A current example is the Spanish government's apparent willingness to contemplate the loss of the public service channels in Spain altogether.

At the same time, throughout Europe (and independent of government policy), new alliances are being struck in the private sector between media conglomerates both at national and international levels which may be difficult to undo should ever they be deemed to be against the public interest. Berlusconi's Fininvest and the German giants Kirch/Springer are actively cooperating to their mutual benefit in both Spain and France. In the United Kingdom, the BBC has entered into partnership with the Pearson group, and through the latter, comes into contact (technically at least) with Murdoch's News International (see Humphreys, 1995:1408).

Effective legislation at a European level reflecting the *dirigiste* and neo-libertarian divide, and which also embraces national political and socio-cultural differences towards the media, is therefore difficult to contemplate. On the issue of multi-media concentration the prospects for pan-European legislation are equally problematic. Firstly, there is an implicit difference of opinion between the member states (contained in national legislation) over acceptable limits of multi-media ownership. Secondly, the shifting sands of corporate diversification and transnational alliances make the task of data collection extremely difficult for the purpose of maintaining an up-to-date global picture of the European situation.

Hickethier in Chapter 4, commenting on the practice of 'camouflaged' ownership, draws attention to the manoeuverings of the Kirch group in Germany. Kirch spreads its holdings between members of the family (which are then calculated separately), has close business alliances with former media associates, as well as links with Berlusconi's Fininvest, inside and outside Germany. Kirch also has a close relationship with the CDU/CSU political parties. The German groups are by no means alone in cultivating links with political parties. In the United Kingdom it is widely held that the domination of News International in the British newspaper sector is due to the consistent support offered by Murdoch to the Thatcher government in the 1980s. But the most audacious of all media-political party partnerships was forged in Italy between Berlusconi's Fininvest and Forza, Berlusconi's political party. When he assumed the premiership of Italy in 1994 Berlusconi was in the unique position of owning half of the Italian television system.

The whole issue of multi-media ownership is currently caught between the protracted and inconclusive deliberations of the European Commission (there have been several consultative papers[2] circulating in the 1990s), and the inability or unwillingness of national governments to act decisively in this field. It is clear that eventually there will be a need for action on the part of the Commission in the form of a new Directive setting out a regulatory framework to deal with multi-media activities. The drafting of such a framework, however, is still some way off. In these circumstances, there appears to be no option, in the medium term, but to leave the task of regulation to national governments and not to the Commission. Such arguments are supported by developments in the United Kingdom in 1995, where government proposals on media ownership[3] effectively excluded media conglomerates such as Murdoch's News International and the Mirror Group from owning further significant shares in private-sector television, on the basis of a calculation of their existing market holdings. The British government's proposals did not find favour in all media circles in the United Kingdom for the simple reason that they constituted a relaxation in the existing legislation relating to television and press holdings. However, relatively speaking, their virtue in the wider European context lies in the fact that they do set out firm proposals for limits on multi-media ownership. If similar guidelines were adopted as the basis for policy making elsewhere in the Union, then current levels of media concentration would undoubtedly fall. We should make it clear, perhaps, that the point of offering this example is not so much to commend the detail of the British government's proposals to the rest of Europe as it is to underline the fact that action on multi-media ownership is feasible at a national level.

The argument in favour of delegating responsibility for controlling the multi-media conglomerates to national governments derives from the reasonable assumption that they have a clearer view of the manoeuvring of the private-sector operators, as well as of the likely impact of their activities upon media pluralism in their own countries. It also assumes (and here's the rub) that national governments have the political will to act in the public interest against media concentration when necessary. In the light of the evidence offered and the observations made in earlier chapters on this issue, there must be real doubts as to whether such determination exists.

Post-script

The socio-cultural changes which have occurred over the last quarter of a century, the trends towards global economies, the weakening of the powers of national governments, and the revolution in audio-visual technology have all combined to send a shock-wave through the media of Western Europe. New kinds of media outlets have been created which at the present time have not been matched by a corresponding increase in real choice nor by improved quality in media performance. The first phase of deregulation of the European communications market has not delivered the promised new media landscape, rich in imaginative productions and myriad in programme choice. Perhaps these are early days, and this kind of criticism is overly harsh, given the stage of development of the new media. Certainly one important factor, partly explaining their failure to deliver, is the rapid growth of media outlets which has significantly outstripped programme production. The nature of the development of the European production industry will therefore play a crucial role in the future fortunes of the private-sector broadcasters.

As far as the mediation of Europe is concerned, the exponential increase in media outlets has coincided with the powerful political impulsion within the European community towards ever closer union. Ironically, we conclude from our studies that the representation of 'Project Europe' by its own media, to its diverse citizenry, risks being a fragmented and inconsistent process.

The upsurge in private-sector capital in the European communications market has been accompanied by a process of media concentration and cross-media ownership in all the countries examined in this study. In other industrial sectors, such concentration might be acceptable market behaviour. However, in the politically charged arena of communications, where the nature of the product permeates our consciousness and affects attitudes in such fundamental ways, the phenomenon of concentration is undesirable and the motives of its exponents suspect.

The future course of events is uncertain. It is to be hoped (we put it no more positively than this) that the first cycle of deregulation will be followed by a second of re-regulation in which some of the errors of its antecedent will be corrected. To succeed, the next stage of policy making will need to integrate, more effectively than the last, the requirements of the market with the needs of the citizens, and their rights to media systems of the highest order rather than of the lowest common denominators.

Notes

1. This view, however, is not necessarily shared by all the contributors – see Sartori in Chapter 5.
2. See Bibliography for details.
3. See Bibliography for details.

Bibliography

Chapter 1 Introduction: the role of the media in Western Europe

References

Boyer, J. H. (1981) 'How editors view objectivity', *Journalism Quarterly* 58:24–8, cited in McQuail (1992).

Blumler, J. G. (1992) *Television and the Public Interest*, London: Sage Publications.

Chomsky, N. (1989) *Necessary Illusions: Thought Control in Democratic Societies*, London: Pluto.

Collins, R. (1992) *Satellite Television in Western Europe* (Revised Edition), London: John Libbey.

Collins, R. (1994) *Broadcasting and Audio-Visual Policy in the European Single Market*, London: John Libbey.

Commission of the European Communities (1983) Interim Report *Realities and Tendencies in European Television: Perspectives and Options*, COM(83) final, Brussels.

Commission of the European Communities (1984a) *Television Without Frontiers*, Green Paper on the establishment of the Common Market for broadcasting, especially by satellite and cable. COM(84) 300 final, Luxembourg.

Council of the European Communities (1989), Directive on the coordination of certain provisions laid down by law, regulation or administrative action in the Member States, concerning the pursuit of television broadcasting activities. 89/552/EEC OJ L298. 17.10.1989.

Dawson, C. (1994) 'Television in Europe: Into the Third Dimension', paper presented at *European Television Marketing* Conference, London: ADMAP.

EBU (1995) *The EBU sets out the Strategy Options: A Consultation Document prepared by the EBU on Broadcast Systems Strategy (BSS)*, Geneva: EBU.

Fairclough, N. (1989) *Language and Power*, Harlow: Longman.

Foucault, M. (1971) *L'Ordre du discours*, Paris: Gallimard.

Habermas, J. (1989) *The Structural Transformation of the Public Sphere*, Cambridge: Polity Press.

Hahn, W. (1982) Report on radio and television broadcasting in the European Community (Rapporteur W. Hahn), European Parliament: Committee on Youth, Culture, Education, Information and Sport, Luxembourg: EP 1013.

Hall, S. (1980) 'Coding and encoding television reality' in S. Hall, D. Hodson, A. Lowe and P. Willis (eds), *Culture, Media, Language*, London: Hutchinson.

Hobsbawm, E. (1994) *Age of Extremes*, London: Michael Joseph.

Keane, J. (1993), *The Media and Democracy*, Cambridge: Polity Press.

Lamizet, B. (1992) *Les lieux de la communication*, Liège: Mardaga.

Lichtenberg, J. (1990) *Democracy and the Mass Media*, New York: Cambridge University Press.

McQuail, D. (1992) *Media Performance*, London: Sage Publications.

Pilati, A. (1993) *Mind–Media Industry in Europe*, London: John Libbey.

Sánchez-Tabernero, A. (1993) *Media Concentration in Europe*, Dusseldorf: The European Institute for the Media.

Scannell, P. (1989) 'Public service broadcasting and modern public life', *Media, Culture and Society*, II: 135–66.

Silj, A. (1993) *The New Television in Europe*, London: John Libbey.

Tester, K. (1994) *The Life and Times of Post-Modernity*, London: Routledge.

Weaver, D. and Mullins, L. (1975) 'Content and format characteristics of competing daily newspapers', *Journalism Quarterly*, 52:257–64, cited in McQuail (1992).

Winnington-Ingram, R. (1994) 'The Economics of Television in Europe', paper presented at the *European Television Marketing Conference*, London: ADMAP.

Further reading

Journals

Cable and Satellite Europe (monthly), London: Headley.

Media, Culture, and Society (quarterly) London: Sage Publications.

New Media, Technology, Society and Culture (six editions per annum) London: Sage Publications (from 1996).

European Journal of Communications (quarterly), London: Sage Publications.

The Bulletin (quarterly), Dusseldorf: European Institute for the Media.

Other

Luyken, G.-M. *et al* (1991) *Overcoming Language Barriers in Television*, Manchester: European Institute for the Media.

Nowell-Smith, G. (ed.) (1989) *The European Experience*, London: BFI Publishing.

Sepstrup, P. (1990) *Transnationalization of Television in Western Europe*, London: John Libbey.
Weddell, G. (1991) *Towards a European Common Market for Television*, Manchester: European Institute for the Media.

Chapter 2 The media in Britain

References

Alvarado, M. *et al.* (1992) in Silj, A. (1992) (ed.), *The New Television in Europe*, London: John Libbey.
BBC (1994) *BBC Reports and Accounts 1993/4*, London: BBC.
Bell, E. (1994), 'Has Sky got the clout to dish it out?', *Observer*, 20.11.94.
Bell, E. (1994) 'Tunnelling into the 21st century', *Observer*, 27.11.94.
Cable and Satellite Europe (1995) 'DTH Survey', *Cable and Satellite Europe*, 1.95.
Calcutt Report (1993) *Review of the Press: Self Regulation*, Cmnd 2135, London: HMSO.
Curran, J. and Seaton, J. (1988) *Power without Responsibility: The Press and Broadcasting in Britain*, London: Fontana.
Daily Mirror (1942) 'Editorial', 26.8.1942.
Department of National Heritage, (1995) *Media Ownership: The Government's Proposals* Cm 2872, London: HMSO.
Dyke, G. (1994) *McTaggart Lecture*, Edinburgh.
Ecclestone, J. in Franklin, R. (1995) 'Taming the unruly Leviathan', conference paper presented to *The Press in Europe – Past, Present and Future*, City University 4.2.95.
Franklin, R. (1995) 'Taming the unruly Leviathan', conference paper presented to *The Press in Europe – Past, Present and Future*, City University 4.2.95.
Green, A. and Steedman, H. (1993) *Educational Provision, Educational Attainment and the Needs of Industry: A Review of Research for Germany, France, Japan, the USA and Britain*, National Institute of Economic and Social Research, London: St George's Press.
PCC (1994) Press Complaints Commission, Press release, London: PCC (November).
Peacock Report (1986) *Committee on Financing the BBC, Report*, Cmnd 9824, London: HMSO.
Peake, S. (1993) *The Media Guide*, London: Fourth Estate.
Royal Commission on the Press (1949) *Report*, Cmnd 7700, London: HMSO.
Royal Commission on the Press (1962) *Report*, Cmnd 1811, London: HMSO.
Royal Commission on the Press (1977) *Final Report*, Cmnd 6810, London: HMSO.
Seymour-Ure, C. (1992) *The British Press and Broadcasting since 1945*, Oxford: Blackwell.

Short, D. (1995) 'Battle for big business', *European*, 2.3.1995.
Smith, A. (1991) 'Public service broadcasting meets the social market', in Miller, N. and Allen, R. (eds) (1991) *And now for the BBC*, London: John Libbey.
Tunstall, J. (1992) 'The United Kingdom', in Ostergaard, B. (ed.) *The Media in Western Europe*, London: Sage Publications.
Williams, G. (1995) 'New Times', *New Statesman*, 24.3.1995.

Further reading

See under 'Further Reading' in Bibliography for Chapter 1 for previously mentioned general references.
BBC (1992) *Extending Choice: The BBC's Role in the Future Broadcasting Age*, London: BBC.
BBC (1995) *People and Programmes: BBC Radio and Television for an Age of Choice*, London: BBC.
Briggs, A. (1961–95) *History of Broadcasting in the United Kingdom* (in 5 vols), Oxford: Oxford University Press.
Miller, N. and Allen, R. (1994) *Broadcasting Enters the Market Place*, London: John Libbey.
Sampson, A. (1992) *The Essential Anatomy of Britain: Democracy in Crisis*, London: Hodder & Stoughton.

Chapter 3 The media in France

References and further reading

Albert, P. (1988) *La Presse*, Paris: PUF, Collection 'Que sais-je?'
Albert, P. (1993) *Histoire de la Presse*, Paris: PUF, Collection 'Que sais-je?'
Albert, P. (1990) 'La Presse Française', in *Notes et Etudes Documentaires*, No. 4901, Paris: La Documentation Française.
Albert, P. and Tudesq, A.-J. (1986) *Histoire de la radio-télévision*, Paris: PUF, Collection 'Que sais-je?'
Balle, F. and Eymery, G. (1987) *Les Nouveaux Médias*, Paris: PUF, Collection 'Que sais-je?'
Bellanger, C. et al. (eds) (1969–76) *Histoire Générale de la presse française*, 5 vols, Paris: PUF.
Charon, J.-M. (1991) *La presse française de 1945 à nos jours*, Paris: Seuil.
Charon, J.-M. (ed.) (1993) *L'Etat des Médias*, Paris: La Découverte, Collection 'L'Etat du Monde'.
Cayrol, R. (1991) *Les médias: Presse écrite, radio, télévision*, Paris: PUF.
Collins, R. (1990), *Satellite Television in Western Europe*, London: John Libbey.
Cook, M. (1993) (ed.) *On y va: French Culture since 1945*, Harlow: Longman.
CFPJ (1989) *La presse audiovisuelle*, Paris: CFPJ.
CFPJ (1989) *La presse écrite*, Paris: CFPJ.

Flower, J. E. (1993) (7th edition) *France Today*, London: Hodder & Stoughton.

Gayan, L.-G. (1990) *La presse régionale en France. Le premier média de France*, Toulouse: Milan Media.

Guehenno, J.-M. (1987) 'France and the electronic media', in Ross, G., Hoffman, S. and Malzacher (eds), *The Mitterrand Experiment*, Cambridge: Polity Press.

Guillauma, Y. (1989) *La Presse en France*, Paris: La Découverte, Collection 'Repères'.

Hamelin, D. (1990) 'Decentralisation de Radio France' in *Mediapouvoirs*, Paris: No. 18.

INA (1985) Dossiers de l'Audiovisuel No. 3: *Trois plans pour le câble*, Paris: La documentation française.

Kuhn, R. (1988a) 'The modernisation of the media' in J. Gaffney (ed.), *France and Modernisation*, Aldershot: Gower.

Kuhn, R. (1988b) 'Satellite broadcasting in France' in Negrine, R. (ed.), *Satellite Broadcasting: The Politics and Implications of the New Media*, London: Routledge.

Le Diberder, A. and Coste-Cerdan, N. (1991) *La Télévision*, Paris: La Découverte, Collection 'Repères'.

Lussato, B. and France-Lanord, B. (1990) *La Vidéomatique: De Gutenberg aux nouvelles technologies de la communication*, Paris: Edition de l'organisation.

Mermet, G. (1987) *Démocratura: comment les médias transforment la démocratie*, Paris: Aubier.

Weddell, G. *et al.* (1990) *Radio 2000*, Manchester: European Institute for the Media.

Wolton, D. (1990) *Eloge du grand public. Une théorie critique de la télévision,* Paris: Flammarion.

Wright, V. *The Government and Politics of France*, London: Unwin Hyman.

See under 'Further Reading' for Chapter 1 for previously mentioned general references.

Chapter 4 The media in Germany

References

Bausch, H. (1980) *Rundfunk in Deutschland*, Munich (5 vols).

Bleicher, J. (1995) *Chronik zur Programmageschichte des deutschen Fernsehen*, Berlin: Edition Sigma, Rainer Bohn Verlag.

Geissler, R. (1993) 'Medien im vereinten Deutschland. Fortschreibung bestehender Strukturen', *Medium 1993*.

Gentikow, B. (1993) *Aneignungen. Ausländisches Fernsehen und nationale Kultur*, Arhus: Universitäts Verlag.

Heinrich J. (1994) 'Keine Entwarnung bei Mediakonzentration. Ökonomische und publizistische Konzentration im deutschen Fernsehsektor 1993/4', in *Media Perspektiven 1994*, pp. 297–310.

Hickethier, K. (1980) *Das Fernsehspiel der Bundesrepublik, Themen, Form, Struktur, Theorie und Geschichte, 1951–1977*, Stuttgart: Metzler.

Hickethier, K. (1994a) *Geschichte der Fernsehkritik*, Berlin: Edition Sigma.

Hickethier, K. (1994b) *Aspekte der Fernsehanalyse, Methoden und Modelle*, Hamburg: Lit Verlag.

Hickethier, K. (1994d) 'Krisensymptome. 'Kapitalistische' versus 'Sozialistische' Öffentlichkeit', in Wolfgang Wunden (ed.), *Öffentlichkeit und Kommunikationskultur. Beitrage zur Medienethik*, Hamburg/Stuttgart: J. F. Steinkopf, 1994, pp. 113–24.

Hickethier, K. (1994e) 'Rundfunkprogramme in Deutschland', in Hans Bredow-Institut (eds), *Internationales Handbuch und Fernsehen 1994/95*, Hamburg: Hans Bredow-Institut, pp. 106–16.

Hickethier, K. (1995) 'Online mit der Zukunft, Zum Diskurs über die neuen Medien', in *Ästhetik und Kommunikation* yr. 24, 1995, Vol. 88, pp. 9–15.

Hoff, P. (1993) 'Organisation und Programmentwicklung des DDR-Fernsehen', in Hickethier, K. (ed.) (1993) *Institution, Technik, und Programm. Rahmenaspekte der Programmgeschichte des Fernsehens*, Munich: Fink Verlag, pp. 245–86.

Hoffman-Riem, W. (1988) *Rundfunk in Wettbewersrecht*, Hamburg.

Holzer, H. (1993) 'Rollkommando – Kapitalismus. Zur Blitz-Kobnisierung einer Medienlandschaft', *Medium*, Vol. 1, pp. 27–30.

Jarren, O. (1994) *Medien und Journalismus 1*, Opladen: Westdeutscher Verlag.

Krüger, U. M. (1989) Konvergenz in dualen Fernsehsystem?', *Media Perspektiven*, Vol. 12, pp. 776–806.

McQuail, D. (1983) *Mass Communication Theory. An Introduction*, London: Sage Publications.

Medienbericht (1994) 'Bundesregierung über die Lage der Medien in der Bundesrepublik Deutschland, 1994', Bonn: Drucksache, 12/8587 des Deutschen Bundestages v.20.10.1994.

Pürer, H. and Raabe, J. (1994) *Medien in Deutschland*, Munich, Ölschlager.

Radtke, M. (1994) 'Zuschlagen, tauschen, verduften. Kleine Sittengeschichte der Medien-Mogule', in Monkenbusch, H. (ed.) *Fernsehen, Medien, Macht, Markte*, Reinbek: Rowohlt, pp. 85–100.

Röper, H. (1993a) 'Formationen deutscher Medienmultis 1992', in *Media Perspektiven 1993*, Vol. 2, pp. 56–74.

Röper, H. (1993b) 'Konzentrationswerte im Zeitungsmarkt wieder gestiegen. Daten zur Konzentration der Tagespresse in der Bundesrepublik Deutschland im 1. Quartal 1993', in *Media Perspektiven 1993*, Vol. 9, pp. 402–9.

Ross, D. (1967) *Die Dritten Fernsehprogramme in Deutschland*, Hamburg: Hans Bredow-Institut.

Schneider, I. (1994) 'Ein Weg der Alltaglichkeit. Spielfilm im Fernsehprogramm', in Schanze, H. and Zimmermann, B. (eds), *Das Fernsehen und die Künste*, Munich: Fink Verlag, pp. 227–301

(Geschichte des Fernsehens in der Bundesrepublik Deutschland, Vol. 2).

Schütz, W. (1994) 'Deutsche Tagespresse, 1993. Ergebnisse der zweiten gesamtdeutschen Zeitungsstatistik', in *Media Perspektiven 1994*, Vol. 4, pp. 168–98.

Wulff, H. (1995) 'Rezeption im Warenhaus. Anmerkungen zur Rezeptionsästhetik des Umschaltens', in *Asthetik und Kommunikation*, yr. 24 (1995), Vol. 88 (Medien an der Epochenschwelle?), pp. 61–6.

Further reading

See under 'Further Reading' in Bibliography for Chapter 1 for previously mentioned general references.

Collins, R. (1994) *Broadcasting and Audio-Visual Policy in the European Single Market*, London: John Libbey.

Flottau, H. (1972) *Hörfunk und Fernsehen heute*, Munich/Vienna: Olzog Verlag.

Groebel, J. and Hoffmann-Riem, W. *et al.* (1994) *Bericht zur Lage des Fernsehens für den Präsidenten der Bundesrepublik Deutschland*, Bonn: Richard von Weizsäcker.

Hickethier, K. (1993) *Film- und Fernsehanalyse*, Stuttgart: J. B. Metzler.

Chapter 5 The media in Italy

References and further reading

Abruzzese, A. (1986) 'Spettacolo e società post-industriale' in Barlozzetti, G. (ed.) *Il Palinsesto*, Milan: Franco Angeli.

Ajello, N. (1976) 'Il settimanale di attualità', in Castronovo, V. and Tranfaglia, N. (eds), *La stampa italiana del neocapitalismo*, Rome-Bari: Laterza.

Ajello, N. (1985) *Lezioni di giornalismo: come è cambiata in 30 anni la stampa italiana*, Milan: Garzanti.

Albert, P. and Tudesq, A. J. (1981) *Histoire de la radio-télévision*, Paris: Presses Universitaires de France.

Bettetini, G. F. (1985) 'Un "fare" italiano nella televisione' in A.A.V.V., *Televisione: la provvisoria identità italiana*, Turin: Fondazione Agnelli.

Buonanno, M. (1975) *Naturale come sei*, Florence: Guaraldi.

Castronovo, V. (1994) 'Il sistema editoriale e l'industria dell'informazione' in Castronovo, V. and Tranfaglia, N. (eds), *La stampa italiana nell'età della tv, 1975–1994*, Rome-Bari: Laterza.

Castronovo, V. and Tranfaglia, N. (eds) (1976) *La stampa italiana del neocapitalismo*, Rome-Bari: Laterza.

Castronovo, V. and Tranfaglia, N. (eds) (1994) *La stampa italiana nell'età della tv, 1975–1994*, Rome-Bari: Laterza.

Di Dario, V. (1992) *Pippo, Mike e Raffaella: Storia della televisione italiana*, Milan: Sperling & Kupfer.

Doglio, F. (1959) *Cultura e libertà*, Rome: Bulzoni.

Doglio, V. and Richeri, G. (1980) *La radio*, Milan: Mondadori.

Eco, U. and Violi, P. (1976) 'La controinformazione' in Castronovo, V. and Tranfaglia, N. (eds), *La stampa italiana nell del neocapitalismo*, Rome-Bari: Laterza.

FIEG (Federazione Italiana Editori Giornali) (1993), *Indagine sui bilanci delle aziende editrici di giornali quotidiani 1991–92)*, Rome: FIEG.

Garante per l'editoria (1989) *Relazione al Parlamento sullo stato dell'editoria*, Rome: Poligrafico dello Stato.

Ghirelli, A. (1976) 'La stampa sportiva' in Castronovo, V. and Tranfaglia, N. (eds), *La stampa italiana del neocapitalismo*, Rome-Bari: Laterza.

Guastamacchia, L. (1976) 'I bilanci dei quotidiani nel 1975: nodi e contraddizioni della crisi' in *Problemi dell'informazione*, No. 4.

ISTAT (1953) *Annuario*, Rome: ISTAT.

Istituto Accertamento Diffusione (1972) *Relazione Annuale*, Rome: IAD.

Italmedia (1995) *Le prospettive del mercato televisivo in Italia* (researched by Augusto Preta for la Fondazione Einaudi), Rome-Chianciano: Italmedia.

Lilli, L. (1976) 'La stampa femminile' in Castronovo, V. and Tranfaglia, N. (eds). *La stampa italiana nell del neocapitalismo*, Rome-Bari: Laterza.

Megna, F. (1994) 'I conti in rosso dell'editoria giornalistica', in *L'Editore*, no. 179, February.

Menduni, E. (1994) *La radio nell'era della TV*, Bologna: Il Mulino.

Migli, P. and Protettí, C. (1995) *L'informazione elettronica verso il duemila*, Turin: Gutenberg 2000.

Monteleone, F. (1992) *Storia della radio e della televisione in Italia*, Venice: Marsilio.

Murialdi, P. (1983) 'Contributo alla storia di *Repubblica*, il quotidiano diverso' in *Problemi dell'informazione*, no. 4.

Murialdi, P. and Tranfaglia, N. (1976) 'I quotidiani dal 1960 al 1775' in Castronovo, V. and Tranfaglia, N. (eds), *La stampa italiana nell del neocapitalismo*, Rome-Bari: Laterza.

Murialdi, P. and Tranfaglia, N. (1983) 'I quotidiani negli ultimi 20 anni' in *Problemi dell informazione*, no. 4.

Murialdi, P. and Tranfaglia, N. (1994) 'I quotidiani negli ultimi 20 anni: crisi, sviluppo e concentrazioni' in Castronovo, V. and Tranfaglia, N. (eds), *La stampa italiana nell'età della tv, 1975–1994*, Rome-Bari: Laterza.

Natale, A. L. (1990) *Gli anni della radio: contributi a una storia sociale dei media in Italia*, Naples: Liguori.

Olmi, M. (1991) *Il giornalismo in Italia*, Turin: Nuova ERI.

Ortoleva, P. (1994) 'La televisione tra due crisi, 1974–1993' in Castronovo, V. and Tranfaglia, N. (eds), *La stampa italiana nell'età della tv, 1975–1994*, Rome-Bari: Laterza.

Pansa, G. P. (1977) *Comprati e venduti*, Milan: Bompiani.

Pinto, F. (1980) *Il modello televisivo: professionalità e politica da Bernabei alla terza rete*, Milan: Feltrinelli.

Presidenza del Consiglio dei Ministri (1944) *Atti relativi al decreto per la riorganizzazione del settore radiofonico*, Rome: Poligrafico dello Stato.

RAI (1995) *L'Europa degli italiani* (research RAI, Il Sole 24 ORE and Commission of the European Community; Pragma Srl), Rome: RAI.

Richeri, G. (1993) *La tv che conta*, Bologna: Baskerville.

Sartori, C. (1984) 'La nascita della televisione in Italia' in *Trent'anni della nostra storia*, Milan-Turin: Fabbri-Nuova ERI.

Sartori, C. (1989) *La grande sorella: il mondo cambiato dalla televisione*, Milan: Mondadori.

Sartori, C. (1994) *La qualità televisiva*, Milan: Bompiani.

Tasca, A. M. (1995) 'L'information Techology in Italia e in Europa' in Migli, P. and Protettí, C. (1995) *L'informazione elettronica verso il duemila*, Turin: Gutenberg 2000.

Chapter 6 The media in Spain

References

Baget, J. M. (1975) *18 años de TVE*, Barcelona: Diafora.

Baget, J. M. (1981) 'Evolució històrica de la televisió a Espanya i a Catalunya', in Pares, M. *et al*, *La Televisió a la Catalunya autònoma*, Barcelona: Edic-62.

Bustamante, E. (1982) *Los amos de la información en España*, Madrid: Akal.

Bustamante, E. (1994) 'La concentración en la comunicación y la cultura', in *Concentració i internacionalització dels Mitjans de Comunicació*, Barcelona: Centre d'Investigació de la Comunicació.

Bustamante, E. and Zallo, R. (1978) *Las industrias culturales en España*, Madrid: Akal.

Costa, P. (1986) *La crisis de la televisión pública*, Barcelona, Paidós.

Diaz Nosty, B. (1993) 'Prensa. Más que ayer menos que mañana', in *Comunicación Social 1993, Tendencias*, Madrid: Fundesco.

Diaz Nosty, B. (1994) 'Informe sobre los medios en España', in *Comunicación Social 1994, Tendencias*, Madrid: Fundesco.

Diaz Mancisidor, A. (1995) 'La radio subsidiaria', in *Tendencias, 1995*, Madrid: Fundesco.

Franquet, R. and Martí, J. M. (1985) *La radio: de la telegráfica sin hilos a los satelites (cronologia 1780–1984)*, Barcelona: Mitre.

Flichy, P. (1990) *Les industries de l'imaginaire*, Paris: Presses universitaires de Grenoble.

Gorostiaga, E. (1976) *La radiotelevisión en España*, Pamplona: Universidad de Navarra.

Mendezona, R. (1979) 'Radio España Independiente, Estación Pirenaica', in Hale, J., *La radio como arma política*, Barcelona: Gili.

Nieto, A. (1973) *La empresa periodística en España*. Pamplona: Eunsa.

Plans, M. (1981) 'Radio España independiente, "la Pirenaica" entre el mito y la propaganda', in Bassets, L. (ed.) *De los ondas rojas a los radios libres*. Barcelona: Gili.

Sánchez Tabernero, A. *et al.* (1993) *Concentración de la Comunicación en Europa*, Barcelona: Centre d'Investigació de la Comunicació y European Institute of the Media.
Timoteo Alvarez, J. *et al.* (1989) *Historia de los medios de comunicación en España*, Barcelona: Ariel.
Virseda, F. (1984) 'Las comunidades autónomas y la televisión. La ley del tercer canal', in Vilches, L. (ed.) *Jornadas de televisión autonómica*, Aragon.
Zallo, R. and Bustamante, E. (eds) (1988) *Las industrias culturales en España*, Madrid: Akal.
Williams, R. (1995) *Los medios de comunicación social*, Barcelona: Ed. 62.

Further reading
See under 'Further Reading' in Bibliography for Chapter 1 for previously mentioned general references.
Arceo Vacas, J. (1994) 'Tendencias de la Publicidad en España, in *Tendencias 1994*, Madrid: Fundesco.
Arias Ruiz, A. (1973) *50 Años de radiofusión en España*, Madrid: RTVE.
Arias Salgado, G. (1958) *Política española de la información*, Madrid: T.11.
Corominas, M. (1990) *Models de radio als paisos occidentales*, Barcelona: Centre d'Investigació de la Comunicació.
Guillaumet, J. (1990) *La circulació de la Premsa Catalunya-Espanya*, Barcelona: Centre d'Investigació de la Comunicació.
Inglesias, F. (1989) 'La transformaciones de la prensa diaria', in Timoteo Alvárez, J. *et al.* (1989), *Historia de los medios de comunicación en España*, Barcelona: Ariel.
Perez Ornia, R. (1989) 'Peculiaridades de una televisión gubberremental', in Timoteo Alvárez, J. *et al.* (1989) *Historia de los medios de comunicación en España*, Barcelona: Ariel.
Sinova, J. (1989) 'La dificíl evolución de la prensa no estatal', in Timoteo Alvárez, J. *et al.* (1989), *Historia de los medios de comunicación en España*, Barcelona: Ariel.
Vilches, L. (1993) *La Televisión: Los efectos del bien y del mal*, Barcelona: Paidos Comunicación.

Chapter 7 Conclusions

References and further reading

Axford, B. and Huggins, R. (1995) 'Media Without Boundaries: fear and loathing on the road to Eurotrash or transformation in the European cultural economy?' in *Contemporary Political Studies*, Vol. III.
Collins, R. (1994) *Broadcasting and Audio-Visual Policy in the European Single Market*, London: John Libbey.

Commission of the European Communities (1992) *Pluralism and Media Concentration in the Internal Market*, Commission Green Paper, COM 92 480 final.

Commission of the European Communities (1994) *Strategy Options to Strengthen the European Programme Industry in the Context of the Audiovisual Policy of the European Union*, COM 94 96.

Department of National Heritage (1995) *Media Ownership: The Government's Proposals*, London: HMSO.

Humphreys, P. (1995) 'The Changing Nature of the Broadcast Media in Europe: Some Key Policy Issues', in *Contemporary Political Studies*, Vol. III.

Contributors

Knut Hickethier is Professor of Media Studies in the Department of German Literature and in the Centre of Media Studies and Media Culture at the University of Hamburg, Germany.

Bernard Lamizet is Professor of Communication Science at the University of Avignon and the Vaucluse, France.

Carlo Sartori* is Professor of Theory and Techniques of Mass Communications at the University of Urbino, Italy. He is also the External Relations Advisor to the RAI.

Lorenzo Vilches is Professor of Media Studies in the Department of Journalism and Communication Science at the Autonomous University of Barcelona, Spain.

Anthony Weymouth is Principal Lecturer in the Department of Politics and European Studies at the University of Central Lancashire, England.

*Carlo Sartori wrote Chapter 5 with the assistance of Andrea Ambrogetti, an expert in communications systems and former advisor to the Ministry of Post and Telecommunications, Marco Mele, a journalist for the financial daily *Sole 24 Ore*, and Giulia Nespoli, a researcher at the University of Urbino.

Index

Main references are in bold type. Figures and tables are denoted by *fig* and *tab* following page-numbers.